THE THEOLOGY OF THE BOOK OF KINGS

1 and 2 Kings unfolds an epic narrative that concludes the long story of Israel's experience with institutional monarchy, a sequence of events that begins with the accession of Solomon and the establishment of the Jerusalem temple, moves through the partition into north and south, and leads inexorably toward the nation's destruction and the passage to exile in Babylon. Keith Bodner's *The Theology of the Book of Kings* provides a reading of the narrative attentive to its literary sophistication and theological subtleties, as the cast of characters – from the royal courts to the rural fields – are variously challenged to resist the tempting pathway of political and spiritual accommodations and instead maintain allegiance to their covenant with God. In dialogue with a range of contemporary interpreters, this study is a preliminary exploration of some theological questions that arise from the Kings narrative, while inviting contemporary communities of faith into deeper engagement with this enduring account of divine reliability amid human scheming and rapaciousness.

Keith Bodner is Stuart E. Murray Professor of Christian Studies at Crandall University in New Brunswick, Canada. A member of the editorial board of the *Journal for the Study of the Old Testament*, his recent books include *Jeroboam's Royal Drama* (2012), *The Rebellion of Absalom* (2013), *After the Invasion: A Reading of Jeremiah 40–44* (2015), and *An Ark on the Nile: The Beginning of the Book of Exodus* (2016).

OLD TESTAMENT THEOLOGY

GENERAL EDITORS

Brent A. Strawn
Professor of Old Testament
Candler School of Theology, Emory University

Stephen B. Chapman
Associate Professor of Old Testament
Duke Divinity School, Duke University

Patrick D. Miller
Charles T. Haley Professor of Old Testament Theology, Emeritus
Princeton Theological Seminary

This series aims to remedy the deficiency of available published material on the theological concerns of the Old Testament books. Here, specialists explore the theological richness of a given book at greater length than is usually possible in the introductions to commentaries or as part of other Old Testament theologies. They are also able to investigate the theological themes and issues of their chosen books without being tied to a commentary format or to a thematic structure provided from elsewhere. When complete, the series will cover all the Old Testament writings and will thus provide an attractive, and timely, range of short texts around which courses can be developed.

PUBLISHED VOLUMES

The Theology of the Book of Amos, John Barton
The Theology of the Book of Genesis, R. W. L. Moberly
The Theology of the Book of Jeremiah, Walter Brueggemann

THE THEOLOGY OF THE BOOK OF KINGS

KEITH BODNER

Crandall University

CAMBRIDGE
UNIVERSITY PRESS

University Printing House, Cambridge CB2 8BS, United Kingdom

One Liberty Plaza, 20th Floor, New York, NY 10006, USA

477 Williamstown Road, Port Melbourne, VIC 3207, Australia

314–321, 3rd Floor, Plot 3, Splendor Forum, Jasola District Centre, New Delhi – 110025, India

79 Anson Road, #06–04/06, Singapore 079906

Cambridge University Press is part of the University of Cambridge.

It furthers the University's mission by disseminating knowledge in the pursuit of education, learning, and research at the highest international levels of excellence.

www.cambridge.org
Information on this title: www.cambridge.org/9781107568709
DOI: 10.1017/9781316414910

© Keith Bodner 2019

This publication is in copyright. Subject to statutory exception and to the provisions of relevant collective licensing agreements, no reproduction of any part may take place without the written permission of Cambridge University Press.

First published 2019

Printed in the United States of America by Sheridan Books, Inc.

A catalogue record for this publication is available from the British Library.

Library of Congress Cataloging-in-Publication Data
NAMES: Bodner, Keith, 1967- author.
TITLE: The theology of the Book of Kings / Keith Bodner.
DESCRIPTION: Cambridge, United Kingdom ; New York, NY : Cambridge University Press, 2018. | Series: Old Testament theology | Includes bibliographical references and index.
IDENTIFIERS: LCCN 2018023259 | ISBN 9781107124028 (hardback : alk. paper) | ISBN 9781107568709 (paperback : alk. paper)
SUBJECTS: LCSH: Bible. Kings–Criticism, interpretation, etc. | Bible. Kings–Theology.
Classification: LCC BS1335.52 .B63 2018 | DDC 222/.506–dc23
LC record available at https://lccn.loc.gov/2018023259

ISBN 978-1-107-12402-8 Hardback
ISBN 978-1-107-56870-9 Paperback

Cambridge University Press has no responsibility for the persistence or accuracy of URLs for external or third-party internet websites referred to in this publication and does not guarantee that any content on such websites is, or will remain, accurate or appropriate.

Prayer Before Reading St. Mark's Gospel

Please attack my colonialist ego,
o lion-face, o ancient evangelist.
The carcinogenic self, gleeful
but cruel in its unhealthy glow,
needs every means of resistance,
nor do I expect your treatment to be
remotely easygoing, if any freedom
is to be won from tumor, polyp, cyst.
Don't let my withheld forgiveness
be among the glittering cargo
of my sickly little boat, battered, kissed
by fortune's surges. Let me bestow
instead regard to every fellow narcissist,
to thief and punk, humbug and arsonist.

Brett Foster (1973–2015)

Contents

General Editors' Preface	page xiii
Preface	xvii
List of Abbreviations	xxi

1   TOWARD THE THEOLOGY OF THE BOOK OF KINGS 1

Charting the Theological Plot	3
Navigating the Terrain	11
From Entry to Exile: Exploring Kings in Context	21

2   DYNASTY AND SUCCESSION 25

Aged Monarch	26
Fraternal Factions	29
Prophetic Collusion	32
The Interview	35
Some Conditions Apply?	39
Process of Elimination	43

3   PALACE AND TEMPLE 52

Foreign Alliance	53
Dispensing Wisdom	57
Administrative Moves	60

The Temple Complex	65
Dedication Ceremony	68
Gold and Horses	74

4 KINGDOM AND DIVISION 80

Disintegrations	81
Forces of Opposition	86
Fragments at Shechem	90
Golden Innovations	93
Incendiary Times	98
Rise of the Omrides	103

5 PROPHETS AND APOSTASY 109

Arrival(s) of Elijah	110
Ahab and Aram	119
Fire and Water	128
Elisha Acts	138
Royal Entanglements	145

6 UPHEAVAL AND REPRIEVE 156

Seditious Appointment	157
Circle of Treason	164
Losing Ground	169
Behind the Curtain	180
Stay of Execution	183

7 DEMOLITION AND EXILE 192

Visiting Time	193
Manasseh's Memory	199
Lost and Found	205

The Journey of Kings 213
Unchained Promise 221

8 THE THEOLOGY OF KINGS PAST AND PRESENT 227
Lasting Guarantee 228
The Two Towers 231
Other Intersections 234
The Legacy of Kings in the New Testament 237

Further Reading 243
Author Index 248
Scripture Index 251

General Editors' Preface

Some years ago, Cambridge University Press, under the editorship of James D. G. Dunn, initiated a series entitled New Testament Theology. The first volumes appeared in 1991, and the series was brought to completion in 2003. For whatever reason, a companion series that would focus on the Old Testament/Hebrew Bible was never planned or executed. The present series, Old Testament Theology, is intended to rectify this need.

The reasons for publishing Old Testament Theology are not, however, confined solely to a desire to match New Testament Theology. Instead, the reasons delineated by Dunn that justified the publication of New Testament Theology continue to hold true for Old Testament Theology. These include, among other things, the facts that (1) given faculty and curricular structures in many schools, the theological study of individual Old Testament writings is often spotty at best; (2) most exegetical approaches (and commentaries) proceed verse by verse such that theological interests are in competition with, if not completely eclipsed by, other important issues, whether historical, grammatical, or literary; and (3) commentaries often confine their discussion of a book's theology to just a few pages in the introduction. The dearth of materials focused exclusively on a particular book's theology may be seen as a result of factors like these; or, perhaps, it is the cause of such factors. Regardless, as Dunn concluded, without adequate theological resources, there is little incentive for teachers or students to engage the theology of specific books; they must be content with what are mostly general overviews. Perhaps the most serious problem resulting from all this is that students are at a disadvantage, even incapacitated, when it comes to the matter of integrating their study of the Bible with other courses in religion and theology. There is, therefore, an urgent need for a series to bridge the gap between the too-slim theological précis and the too-full commentary where theological concerns are lost among many others.

All of these factors commend the publication of Old Testament Theology now, just as they did for New Testament Theology more than two decades ago. Like its sister series, Old Testament Theology is a place where Old Testament scholars can write at greater length on the theology of individual biblical books and may do so without being tied to the linear, verse-by-verse format of the commentary genre or a thematic structure of some sort imposed on the text from outside. Each volume in the series seeks to describe the biblical book's theology as well as to engage the book theologically – that is, each volume intends to *do* theology through and with the biblical book under discussion, as well as delineate the theology contained within it. Among other things, theological engagement with the composition includes paying attention to its contribution to the canon and appraising its influence on and reception by later communities of faith. In these ways, Old Testament Theology seeks to emulate its New Testament counterpart.

In the intervening years since New Testament Theology was first conceived, however, developments have taken place in the field that provide still further reasons for the existence of Old

Testament Theology; these have impact on how the series is envisioned and implemented and also serve to distinguish it, however slightly, from its companion series. Three developments in particular are noteworthy:

1. *The present hermeneutical climate*, often identified (rightly or wrongly) as "postmodern," is rife with possibility and potential for new ways of theologizing about scripture and its constituent parts. Theologizing in this new climate will of necessity look (and be) different from how it has ever looked (or been) before.
2. *The ethos change in the study of religion, broadly, and in biblical studies in particular.* No longer are the leading scholars in the field only Christian clergy, whether Catholic priests or mainline Protestant ministers. Jewish scholars and scholars of other Christian traditions are every bit as prominent, as are scholars of non- or even anti-confessional stripe. In short, now is a time when "Old Testament Theology" must be conducted without the benefits of many of the old consensuses and certainties, even the most basic ones relating to epistemological framework and agreed-upon interpretative communities along with their respective traditions.
3. Finally, recent years have witnessed *a long-overdue rapprochement among biblical scholars, ethicists and systematic theologians.* Interdisciplinary studies between these groups are now regularly published, thus furthering and facilitating the need for books that make the theology of scripture widely available for diverse publics.

In brief, the time is ripe for a series of books that will engage the theology of specific books of the Old Testament in a new climate for a new day. The result will not be programmatic, settled, or altogether certain. Despite that – or, in some ways, *because* of that – it is hoped that Old Testament Theology will contain highly useful volumes that are ideally poised to make significant contributions on a number of fronts including the ongoing discussion of biblical theology in confessional and nonconfessional mode as well as in postmodern and canonical contexts, the theological exchange between Old Testament scholars and those working in cognate and disparate disciplines, and the always-pressing task of introducing students to the theology of the discrete canonical unit: the biblical books themselves.

Brent A. Strawn
Candler School of Theology, Emory University

Stephen B. Chapman
Duke Divinity School, Duke University

Patrick D. Miller
Princeton Theological Seminary, Emeritus

Preface

The book of Kings has an abiding relevance to the community of faith, not least because it makes a series of compelling theological claims about the durability of the Davidic promise, the role of the temple, the power of the prophetic word to undermine empires, and the consequence of exile as an opportunity for restoration and potential hope. Far from static, the divine characterization in Kings is more three-dimensional than has often been recognized, and, combined with the people of God's capacity for self-destructive political choices, presents an absorbing drama and an evocative arena for theological analysis. This book is a provisional undertaking that explores the theology of Kings within its own narrative consecution, and in his biography of Jonathan Edwards, George Marsden articulates a similar goal: "My aspiration, which I am sure has been only partially realized, is to make Edwards intelligible to widely diverse audiences by first attempting to depict him in his own time and in his own terms."[1] Of course, attending to the details of the narrative forces the interpreter to confront a text that is often disturbing, as opposed to retreating to an easier place of more comfortable abstractions. I would further

---

[1] George M. Marsden, *Jonathan Edwards: A Life* (New Haven, CT: Yale University Press, 2003), 2.

submit that literary attentiveness to the details of the narrative can open the door to a number of nuanced theological reflections, ranging from the nature of the temple and institutional kingship, to the ethics of leadership and accountability of the prophets.

In this study, I interact mainly with other biblical scholars because of space limitations and the nature of this project, but there is a rich history of interpretation, and others are encouraged to pursue such discussions. James Barr expresses an intent that parallels my own: "It was never my intention to provide in this volume a full account of the complex questions involved in the title, or to review the relevant literature in full. Nor was it possible, within the limited space available, to offer my own version of a right answer to all these questions. My plan has been rather to discuss examples that will illustrate certain contemporary discussions."[2] Some of my vigilant acquaintances in the academic guild might accuse me of eschewing the theolog*ies* of Kings in favor of an overarching meta-theology – opting for unity amid a diversity – but again, the primary interest in this study is an introductory probing of some important questions, not the final statement by any means.[3] Those scholars who maintain, for instance, a dual-redaction hypothesis of the Deuteronomistic History are welcome to compose their own books. However, I imagine that the target audience of this study are preachers and teachers in a number of traditions searching for enhanced understanding, along with students and interested parties seeking a theological reading of the

---

[2] James Barr, *History and Ideology in the Old Testament: Biblical Studies at the End of a Millennium* (Oxford: Oxford University Press, 2000), vii.

[3] See Alasdair MacIntyre, *After Virtue: A Study in Moral Theory* (London: Duckworth, 1981), 206: "Traditions, when vital, embody continuities of conflict," cited in Rowan Williams, *Arius: Heresy and Tradition*, rev. edn. (Grand Rapids, MI: Eerdmans, 2002).

story. Such an endeavor where there is no agreement on method can be formidable, and one recent writer comments on the difficulties of participating "in an enterprise – namely, biblical theology – that since the mid-1990s has often been declared difficult or impossible, and an enterprise that has been somewhat officially declared 'in crisis' since 1970. In other words, does the study of the Bible have implications for modern people seeking wisdom for modern Christian faith and practice?"[4] As a Christian reader, I am certainly interested in points of application for contemporary audiences who take the text seriously, but I hope that such forays are more indirect rather than heavy-handed, trusting that intelligent readers can take my comments in a host of directions (many of which are unforeseen to me). Unless otherwise indicated, translations of the Hebrew text are my own, and proper names are usually standardized (so, a variant between Joash and Jehoash is not always noted, but I am confident that readers can follow clearly enough).

The initial invitation from Brent Strawn and Patrick Miller to write this book was an immense privilege; Pat graciously wrote an endorsement for my book on Jeremiah (the writing of which caused a delay in this project), while Brent has been indefatigable in his support, with editorial notes that are Freedmanesque in quality and scope. I am grateful that a number of colleagues read or discussed portions of the manuscript, including Francis Landy, Jeremy Schipper, Ben Johnson, Rachelle Gilmour, Lissa Wray Beal and Mark Leuchter. The faculty and senior administration at Crandall University deserve a lengthy word of thanks for their

---

[4] Daniel L. Smith-Christopher, *A Biblical Theology of Exile* (Minneapolis, MN: Fortress, 2002), 1.

support at every turn, especially the dean of faculty development, Dr. John Stackhouse. The poem by Brett Foster originally appeared in *Books & Culture* under the editorship of John Wilson, and I am glad to honor the memory of a faithful savant of the finest literature.

Abbreviations

AB	Anchor Bible
ABD	*Anchor Bible Dictionary*
AOTC	Apollos Old Testament Commentary
AYB	Anchor Yale Bible
BDB	F. Brown, S. R. Driver and C. A. Briggs, *A Hebrew and English Lexicon of the Old Testament* (1907)
BibInt	*Biblical Interpretation*
BIS	Biblical Interpretation Series
BKAT	Biblischer Kommentar, Altes Testament
BZAW	Beihefte zur Zeitschrift für die alttestamentliche Wissenschaft
CBQ	*Catholic Biblical Quarterly*
ESHM	European Seminar in Historical Methodology
FAT	Forschungen zum Alten Testament
FCB	Feminist Companion to the Bible
FOTL	Forms of the Old Testament Literature
HAR	*Hebrew Annual Review*
HBM	Hebrew Bible Monographs
HBT	*Horizons in Biblical Theology*
HCOT	Historical Commentary on the Old Testament
HS	*Hebrew Studies*
ICC	International Critical Commentary

Int	*Interpretation*
ITC	International Theological Commentary
JBL	*Journal of Biblical Literature*
JHS	*Journal of Hebrew Scriptures*
JR	*Journal of Religion*
JSJSup	*Journal for the Study of Judaism*: Supplement
JSNT	*Journal for the Study of the New Testament*
JSNTSup	*Journal for the Study of the New Testament*: Supplement Series
JSOT	*Journal for the Study of the Old Testament*
JSOTSup	*Journal for the Study of the Old Testament*: Supplement Series
JTS	*Journal of Theological Studies*
KJV	King James Version
LHBOTS	Library of Hebrew Bible/Old Testament Studies
LNTS	Library of New Testament Studies
LXX	Septuagint (the Greek Old Testament)
MT	Masoretic Text (of the Hebrew Bible)
NCB	New Century Bible
NIBC	New International Biblical Commentary
NICNT	New International Commentary on the New Testament
NICOT	New International Commentary on the Old Testament
NIV	New International Version
NIVAC	New International Version Application Commentary
NRSV	New Revised Standard Version
OTL	Old Testament Library
OTM	Oxford Theological Monographs
OTT	Old Testament Theology

RSV	Revised Standard Version
SBLDS	Society of Biblical Literature Dissertation Series
SBLMS	Society of Biblical Literature Monograph Series
SBLSymS	Society of Biblical Literature Symposium Series
SBT	Studies in Biblical Theology
TynBul	*Tyndale Bulletin*
ÜSt	*Überlieferungsgeschichtliche Studien*
VT	*Vetus Testamentum*
VTSup	Supplements to *Vetus Testamentum*
WBC	Word Biblical Commentary
WTJ	*Westminster Theological Journal*
WUNT	Wissenschaftliche Untersuchungen zum Neuen Testament
ZAW	*Zeitschrift für die alttestamentliche Wissenschaft*

CHAPTER 1

Toward the Theology of the Book of Kings

The book of Kings begins in the palace of Jerusalem with the aged founder of Israel's greatest dynasty but ends in the palace of Babylon with the last remnant of that once-great dynasty in captivity at the mercy of a foreign potentate. In between is a vast narrative that explains how such a staggering displacement came to pass, recounting the monarchic story with its architectural highs and syncretistic lows, its prophetic oracles and attempts at reform, but also its latent compromises and ill-fated alliances that culminate in the destruction of Jerusalem and the era of the Babylonian exile. By the end of the story, which spans four centuries of historical time and contains hundreds of characters, both the Davidic monarchy and the Jerusalem temple are in ruins, inviting reflection on the provisional nature of both even as the nation contemplates its uncertain future. Despite its sprawling diversity – or perhaps because of it – Kings is a repository of theological themes and images, including temple, dynasty, kingdom, prophecy, foreign invasion and exile. Appreciating the nuances and sophistication of the story, my study presents a theological reading of Kings in its sequential unfolding. Among the key problems faced by the interpreter is how to reconcile what is referred to as "the essential beneficence of God" – manifested in ways such as the promise to the Davidic house, the election of

Zion, and the establishment of the temple – with the dismantling of those same structures and institutions in the Babylonian invasion of 2 Kings 25.[1] Building on a number of useful studies by recent scholars who deploy various methodological approaches, this book will navigate the theological complexities of Kings and present the reader with questions and interpretive options as I proceed through each major section of the text.

There are three parts to this opening chapter. The first outlines some of the central theological plot movements in the book of Kings and raises a number of the questions that will be explored in due course. George Steiner has famously said, "It is not the literal past that rules us, save, possibly, in a biological sense. It is images of the past. These are often as highly structured and selective as myths. Images and symbolic constructs of the past are imprinted, almost in the manner of genetic information, on our sensibility."[2] How are primary theological images dramatized in the book of Kings, and how might a contemporary reader access the narrative's theological tapestry? In order to chart our course for this book, a short synopsis of each chapter is provided, starting in the court of Jerusalem at the outset of 1 Kings and ending in the prison of Babylon as 2 Kings moves to a close. The second part of this introductory chapter surveys some recent attempts to explore the theology of Kings. As a point of entry, the works of three scholars are briefly canvassed in order to provide a sample of approaches and lay a foundation for my own foray. To that end, it is suggested that Choon Leong Seow,

---

[1] Gregory Mobley, "1 and 2 Kings," in *Theological Bible Commentary*, ed. Gail R. O'Day and David L. Petersen (Louisville, KY: Westminster John Knox Press, 2009), 119–43 (124).

[2] George Steiner, *In Bluebeard's Castle: Some Notes towards the Redefinition of Culture* (New Haven, CT: Yale University Press, 1971), 3.

Gregory Mobley and Lissa Wray Beal are useful interlocutors to help us access the theology of Kings and locate our study within the current scholarly milieu. The third part of the chapter addresses the position of Kings in the canon of scripture. While it is appropriate to speak of the *book* of Kings following Hebrew tradition – with the separation into two books occurring in the fourfold Greek version of Samuel–Kings called "Reigns" or "Kingdoms" – the story of Kings is surely not meant to be read in isolation.[3] As part of a larger narrative continuum, Kings assumes the material that precedes and acts as the final installment of Israel's royal history, traditionally labeled as the "Former Prophets." Since the mid-twentieth century, scholars have been probing the idea of a Deuteronomistic History, positing that Joshua, Judges, Samuel and Kings form an epic narrative informed by the teaching of Deuteronomy. Since such a concept would carry considerable theological significance, our introductory chapter concludes with a short review of scholarship on this topic and the position I assume for the remainder of this study.

CHARTING THE THEOLOGICAL PLOT

Although it continues the story of 2 Samuel, the opening section of 1 Kings also carries a sense of new beginning with a leadership transition and change in regime. Chapter 2 in this book, "Dynasty and Succession," analyzes the intricate narrative of Solomon's accession and the early consolidation of his empire. The theme

---

[3] J. A. Montgomery and H. S. Gehman, *A Critical and Exegetical Commentary on the Books of Kings*, ICC (Edinburgh: T. and T. Clark, 1951), 1–3.

of succession is foregrounded in the first scenes, as the aged David is unable to "be in heat" and therefore will sire no further contenders to the throne. Enter Adonijah, the oldest surviving son of David, who gathers allies and hosts a coronation party at En Rogel, only to have his straight path to the scepter intercepted by Nathan and Bathsheba. Due to their maneuverings, Solomon is crowned at the Gihon spring with its echoes of Eden, as suddenly David claims to have earlier sworn an oath about Solomon's future accession. In the midst of this apparent sordidness, how is a theology of succession articulated in this story, and how should the reader understand the Davidic dynasty for the remainder of the book of Kings? Even as such questions linger, David's last words to Solomon in 1 Kings 2 refer to a conditional dynasty, further complicating the matter. More practically, David also advises his successor to deal with his opponents, which happens with ruthless efficiency; the reader witnesses the death of Adonijah, the banishment of Abiathar the priest, the end of Joab, and the demise of Shimei from Benjamin. There is a seeming absence of God in this bloodshed, causing one to ask how God's involvement can be discerned in the midst of human machinations, or what Terence Fretheim refers to as the tension between "divine purpose and human intrigue."[4] This chapter includes some concluding reflections on the promise to David: How is the promise interpreted elsewhere in Kings and more broadly in biblical literature, and how might the contemporary reader make sense of this dynamic promise and its several iterations?

The material legacy of Solomon's reign can be measured by two structures: the palace of Jerusalem and, in close spatial proximity,

---

[4] Terence E. Fretheim, *First and Second Kings* (Louisville, KY: Westminster John Knox, 1999), 27.

the temple. Chapter 3, "Palace and Temple," surveys the narrative of 1 Kings 3–10 and offers an analysis of the burgeoning royal administration and the increasingly complex figure of the monarch. In 1 Kings 3, Solomon is granted the gift of wisdom, and on one level, he certainly appears to use this gift in a publicly beneficial way. But it gradually appears that Solomon's activities are at odds with Deuteronomy 17, the charter text that curtails the accumulation of wives, gold and horses (each of which Solomon has in peerless abundance). Indeed, the elaborate palace in Jerusalem is named "the House of the Forest of Lebanon," though determining whether this title is a compliment or a criticism requires some close scrutiny. The theology of the temple and its sacred space occupies significant attention in this chapter, along with a discussion of how the temple "represented a creation story written in architecture."[5] On the one hand, the construction of the temple has to be viewed as a triumph for the king, but on the other hand, even as early as the temple's prayer of dedication (1 Kings 8), there are strong hints of its eventual ruination. Moreover, the chronological notice of 1 Kgs 6:1 needs to be considered: "Four hundred and eighty years after the Israelites came out from the land of Egypt, in the month of Ziv (that is, the second month) of the fourth year of Solomon's reign, he built the house of the LORD." The conflation of two different calendars – the Canaanite agricultural month of Ziv and the Babylonian reckoning of the second month – strongly suggests that the temple is built at roughly the midpoint between the exodus from past captivity in Egypt and the future captivity in Babylon, reminding the audience that much is at stake at this juncture in the narrative. Several issues raised in this chapter will need to be

---

[5] Mobley, "1 and 2 Kings," 128.

briefly addressed later in this study: in view of the book of Kings as a whole, what theological themes are signaled about the temple early in the story, and how do such themes play out across various sectors of the book? Furthermore, although it is outside my scope here, other researchers may be interested in pursuing the question of how the various New Testament writers understand the theology of the temple, and how present-day readers might appreciate such nuances.

Solomon's empire undoubtedly glitters with a cosmopolitan court and gold in abundance, but in the end, it has all the stability of a house of cards. Chapter 4, "Kingdom and Division," turns to the division of the kingdom and its immediate aftermath in 1 Kings 11–16. Across the valley from the Jerusalem temple – atop the Mount of Olives – Solomon built installations for Molech and Chemosh, and the penalty for his divided heart is a divided kingdom in the days of his son. Rehoboam is not presented as a competent leader in 1 Kings 12, but the odds were impossibly stacked against him: "Thus the king did not listen to the people, for this twist was from the LORD, in order to establish his word that he spoke by means of Ahijah of Shiloh to Jeroboam son of Nebat" (12:15). Such a phenomenon is often referred to as *dual causality*, and numerous interpreters have delved into the relationship between divine foreknowledge and human freedom that is inscribed in the story of division. As the judgment passed on Solomon is inherited by Rehoboam, there are generous promises apportioned to the inaugural king of the northern tribes, Jeroboam. Yet even as Jeroboam is offered the chance to become a new David, there is a conditional clause attached to his reign. Consequently, Jeroboam's challenge will match that of Israel as a people, faced with "the divine demand to abandon their attempt at making their existence secure and to turn toward God in radical

Toward the Theology of the Book of Kings 7

insecurity or faith."[6] In Jeroboam's case, followed soon by most of the northern constituency and its parade of kings and transitory dynasties, the step of radical faith is not taken; instead, there are aggressive and increasingly banal attempts to attain other kinds of material security. Thus, at several moments in 1 Kings 14–15, there is a mention of divine anger, and in this chapter we consider how God's anger is represented as the story unfolds. Moreover, as the reader transitions to the next phase of the narrative – after reading the outlandish sequence in 1 Kings 16 that features the drunkenness of Elah, the incendiary self-destruction of Zimri, and the understated rise of Omri – the reader might ask how God is at work in the various political structures of north and south. Amid the instability both in this installment of the story and elsewhere in Kings, is there any theological wisdom conveyed whereby readers across the ages might sense the presence of God in a world of violence and seeming chaos?

The early days of the divided kingdom included several influential prophets, such as Ahijah of Shiloh announcing the rise and fall of Jeroboam's dynasty or Jehu son of Hanani in 1 Kings 16 proclaiming the end of Baasha's fleeting kingdom. But these characters pale in comparison to the towering figures of Elijah and his successor Elisha in the lengthy middle portion of the book of Kings, with its disproportionate interest in the northern capital city of Samaria. Chapter 5 of this study, "Prophets and Apostasy," covers a significant amount of material (1 Kings 17–2 Kings 8), and not surprisingly, an array of theological issues confronts the reader on this textual canvas. How do these prophets confront the kings

---

[6] Kevin J. Vanhoozer, *Remythologizing Theology: Divine Action, Passion, and Authorship*, Cambridge Studies in Christian Doctrine (Cambridge: Cambridge University Press, 2010), 11.

from the house of Omri? In light of the allure of Baal worship, why is so much prophetic activity centered around works of healing, providing food, engaging with every conceivable level of society, and a bevy of anonymous characters, and how is it that a single prophet cannot be apprehended, even by entire military forces? Why are there so many memorable events, ranging from mountaintop experiences of Mount Carmel and Mount Horeb to fiery chariots and rapacious she-bears? Is there a shared set of themes in the Elijah–Elisha narratives such as a resistance to tyranny, overcoming the seductiveness of state-sponsored fertility religions, and a refusal to accommodate despite myriad pressures to conform? Alongside these two dominant prophets is a startling diversity of other kinds of characters and events, and among the various episodes considered here are 1 Kings 20 – the war with Ben Hadad king of Damascus and its remarkable blend of humor and theological subtlety – and 2 Kings 5, the healing of Naaman the Syrian military commander. In light of Naaman's cleansing from leprosy, on the threshold of deeper and more extensive campaigns from foreign armies at this stage in the divided kingdom, what is the theology of "outsiders" that emerges in the narrative?[7] In these seemingly disparate prophetic episodes, can Christian readers discern any lineaments of the later gospel narratives in the New Testament that are foreshadowed?

Numerous prophets confronted and condemned the house of Omri, but it is finally terminated in 2 Kings 9 by the northern army captain Jehu son of Nimshi. Chapter 6, "Upheaval and Reprieve," analyzes the turbulent material of 2 Kings 9–19, beginning with Jehu's purge and continuing until the Assyrian invasion

---

[7] See further Frank Anthony Spina, *The Faith of the Outsider: Exclusion and Inclusion in the Biblical Story* (Grand Rapids, MI: Eerdmans, 2005).

that decimates northern Israel and nearly defeats Judah except for a miraculous stay of execution at the eleventh hour. Though successfully dethroning the Omrides, Jehu's own dynasty fares little better, lasting only four generations despite his strike at the heart of the infrastructure of northern Baal worship. Meanwhile, the southern kingdom is plagued by Athaliah – daughter of Ahab and Jezebel, and queen of Judah through intermarriage – who, upon the death of her son (also at the hands of Jehu) assumes control of the south until she is unseated in an uprising led by Jehoiada the priest in 2 Kings 11. In this episode, the Davidic dynasty hangs on by a thread – the infant Joash is hidden in the temple, only to be unveiled seven years later to a surprised Athaliah – and becomes an ominous foreshadowing of the final verses of Kings. Athaliah's reign of terror acts as a segue to a highly unstable epoch; 2 Kings 13–16 is marked by internal disruptions and frantic alliances with other nations as the Assyrian threat casts an intimidating shadow. Threat becomes reality with the destruction of the northern kingdom and its capital city of Samaria, necessitating the question: Why does God allow the Assyrian destruction of Israel? In 2 Kings 18, the Assyrian field commander is confident that Jerusalem will experience the same fate, but in response to Hezekiah's prayer, a dramatic oracle is delivered by the prophet Isaiah: "By the way that he came, by the same he shall return; he shall not come into this city, says the LORD. For I will defend this city to save it, for my own sake and for the sake of my servant David." The concluding section of this chapter includes reflection on this theology of reprieve and the efficacy of prayer, as well as the "inviolability of Zion" that will be sorely tested in the last installment of Judah's history.

The penultimate chapter of this book, "Demolition and Exile," turns to 2 Kings 20–25. After the careers of Hezekiah and

Manasseh, three other areas of the text are studied. First, Josiah's reform – anticipated even as early as 1 Kings 13 in the strange episode of the old prophet of Bethel – is given consideration, including as it does the book of the law, the eradication of high places and alternative installations, and the celebration of the Passover. However, these comprehensive reforms are not enough to offset the increasing certainty of Jerusalem's downfall. Second, the invasion of Babylon and a theology of exile is explored in this chapter, drawing together several important threads from this climactic moment in the narrative. Here, an idea of David Noel Freedman will be assayed briefly: "Babylon may have been where the dreams ended, but it is also where they could begin, and they would one day begin again. The use of the word 'Chaldeans' (Hebrew *Kasdim*), which in the Primary History is restricted to Genesis and 2 Kings (Gn 11:28, 31; 2 Kgs 24:2, 25:4 passim), reinforces the view that the opening and closing are carefully fitted together to reveal the end from the beginning, and to compel the thoughtful reader to acknowledge that the seeds were planted at the beginning and the fruits were revealed at the end."[8] Third, the end of 2 Kings 25 merits attention, as the imprisoned Jehoiachin – the last representative of the Davidic dynasty – is granted parole by the king of Babylon. Perhaps removal of his prison clothes (2 Kgs 25:29) returns us to the image of David covered "with clothes" in the opening moments of the story, but are there any other allusions in the final moments of the story that might outfit the reader with cautious optimism, even in the midst of catastrophe?

---

[8] David Noel Freedman, *The Unity of the Hebrew Bible* (Ann Arbor: University of Michigan Press, 1991), 9.

Four main areas form the basis of the concluding chapter of this study, "The Theology of Kings Past and Present." First, after considering the breadth of the narrative, how can the book of Kings be assessed as the capstone chapter of the Deuteronomistic History? In terms of 1–2 Samuel more specifically, in what ways does Kings expand or reconceptualize some of the theological trajectories in Samuel? Second, how can the book of Kings be compared with other historiographic works in the Hebrew Bible? In particular, this conclusion will briefly evaluate an interesting example from the book of Chronicles: 1 Kgs 6:1 outlines the temporal parameters for Solomon's construction of the temple, but 2 Chr 3:1 provides a different set of coordinates and spatially connects the site of the temple as Mount Moriah (see Gen 22:2). Rather than a temporal designation, Chronicles emphasizes the unique location of the temple, linking it with the actions of Abraham in Genesis. How might these two texts in Kings and Chronicles be compared, and how can differences be addressed by the interpreter at the end of this study? Third, some of the theological events in Kings are compared with other sectors of the Hebrew Bible, and this final chapter examines several relevant moments from the book of Jeremiah. Fourth, this chapter also turns to the legacy of Kings in the New Testament, and notes a passage from Luke's gospel that might serve as an encouragement for further reflections on the continuing influence of Kings and its theological import for today's world.

NAVIGATING THE TERRAIN

The book of Kings has been interpreted from a number of different perspectives. Over the past two centuries in particular, the book has been approached as a historical window into the ancient

Near Eastern world, with copious comparisons to other forms of official writings and related archival materials ranging from the Mesha Stele that provides further background to the conflict of 2 Kings 3 to the Assyrian inscriptions that shed light on Tiglath-Pileser III's campaigns in 2 Kings 15–16.[9] Furthermore, owing to its virtually Shakespearean dramatic qualities, the book has also been studied for its literary value. Scenes such as the murder of Ben-Hadad by his underling, Hazael – stealthily laying a damp cloth over his sleeping master's face and subsequently usurping the throne of Damascus in 2 Kgs 8:7–15 – have a latent theatricality that has sparked the interest of certain kinds of interpreters over the course of the book's reception history. Without eschewing such questions or approaches, our interest in this book is focused on further appreciating how Kings is configured as theological literature, and how it fits within the larger canon of scripture. Toward that end, there have been some helpful forays of late that embolden one for the task.

In a recent study, Kevin Vanhoozer pursues Paul Ricoeur's idea that "the literary forms of the Bible are forms not only of writing, but also of thinking and naming God."[10] If this is the case, the theological import of Kings is best considered within the context of its literary performance, asking questions about how God is presented and how the human characters respond to God's

---

[9] For compilations of background texts, the reader is directed to, e.g., James B. Pritchard, ed., *Ancient Near Eastern Texts Relating to the Old Testament*, 3rd edn. (Princeton, NJ: Princeton University Press, 1969); William W. Hallo and K. Lawson Younger, Jr., eds., *The Context of Scripture*, 3 vols. (Leiden: Brill, 1997–2003); Michael D. Coogan, *A Reader of Ancient Near Eastern Texts: Sources for the Study of the Old Testament* (Oxford: Oxford University Press, 2013).

[10] Vanhoozer, *Remythologizing Theology*, 11.

presence (or apparent absence) and the traditions of Israel's faith. Careful attention to the narrative dynamics and aesthetics of the book of Kings – including analysis of plot and character, motif and irony, temporal and spatial settings, wordplay and deliberate ambiguity, structure and intertextuality – is therefore a crucial step in accessing the theology of this work. Although this present study is more descriptive in nature – probing facets of the divine character that emerge from the narrative and the range of human reactions to historical vicissitudes in light of God's promises and the prophetic word – it is hoped that in analyzing these features of the text, readers will discern the relevance and applicability of the book of Kings for various communities of faith. It is fortunate that current trends in scholarship have shown a heightened awareness in balancing how a text might speak to its earliest audiences as well as to contemporary believing constituencies. As one example, Walter Brueggemann proposes that theological affirmations within the Hebrew Bible can operate in a radically countercultural manner, such as an "affirmation of *prophecy* with its imaginative power to conjure alternatives in judgement and hope is a subversive claim against the world that has stilled dissent, silenced the poets, and reduced the social processes to monologues among the privileged and powerful."[11] Altogether, these are exciting times for the theology of Kings, and there are some helpful resources to draw upon.[12] In what follows, three interpreters with different

---

[11] Walter Brueggemann, "Old Testament Theology," in *The Oxford Handbook of Biblical Studies*, ed. John W. Rogerson and Judith M. Lieu (Oxford: Oxford University Press, 2006), 675–97 (694).

[12] For an overview, see Craig Bartholomew, "Theological Interpretation," in *The Oxford Encyclopedia of Biblical Interpretation*, ed. Steven L. McKenzie (Oxford: Oxford University Press, 2013), 387–96 (387): "Paradoxically, theological interpretation is one of the newest approaches to the Bible and yet the

kinds of publications and different audiences are canvassed here by way of introduction to this present study.

"Arguably the most challenging task for the interpreter of Kings," writes Choon Leong Seow, "is to make sense of it in one's own day and age."[13] Targeted at a nonspecialist readership, Seow's commentary features the rare combination of accessible scholarship with attempts to assay the relevance of Kings at every turn, as evidenced in this general summary: "In the chaotic arena of history and amid the court intrigues, internecine warfare, and international conflicts, the story relentlessly conveys the confidence that God's will is being worked out. The story as a whole testifies to divine purposefulness in the messiness of history. Despite the impression that the affairs of the world are determined by political maneuverings and military strivings of rogues and scoundrels, it is God who will have the final say when all is said and done. History moves inexorably according to the will of

most ancient one. If we think of modern biblical interpretation as a series of turns, then the historical turn that dominated the twentieth century was followed in the 1970s by a literary turn; this was followed by the postmodern turn, which is now being followed by a theological turn. The turns do not replace the previous ones but significantly alter the landscape of biblical interpretation and raise important questions about the relationship between these different emphases. With the emergence of theological interpretation, it is as though interpretive approaches have come full circle, but a renewed theological interpretation cannot turn the clock back; it has to take account of the history of interpretation and orient itself amidst the current situation. As a relative newcomer, theological interpretation is still in its early stages, and the term covers a diversity of approaches. In essence, theological interpretation is the attempt to recover a reading of the Bible as Christian scripture for today."

[13] Choon Leong Seow, "The First and Second Books of Kings: Introduction, Commentary, and Reflections," in *The New Interpreter's Bible*, ed. Leander E. Keck et al., 12 vols. (Nashville, TN: Abingdon, 1999), 3:1–295 (6).

the sovereign God."[14] These comments are then taken a step further, for example, in Seow's analysis of Hezekiah and the Assyrian crisis, surely one of the more stressful intervals in the narrative. In 2 Kings 18, Hezekiah pays a substantial tribute to the Assyrians, who have just destroyed Samaria and northern Israel. Whether Sennacherib is dissatisfied with this payment or not, there is every indication that preparations are being made for an invasion of Jerusalem: "For all his trust in God, Hezekiah had to suffer humiliation at the hands of a foreign invader, and he even had to strip the Temple of its wealth, removing gold from the doors and doorposts of the Lord's house in order to pay off the bully (18:13–16). Trust in God will not necessarily stave off actual political threats. Trust in God may not have immediate or manifest results."[15]

Handing over treasures of the temple to the Assyrians must have been a bitter moment for Hezekiah, especially after the commendation and early victories in his reign (see 2 Kgs 18:5–8), even if this "emptying" is not the last word in this episode. But the ignominy of paying the tribute is worth pausing over, as Seow suggests, for it seems to be a necessary step before the next stage in the narrative, where the situation moves in a startlingly different direction. After the various insults from the adjutant of the king of Assyria and an intimidating letter from Sennacherib, in 2 Kgs 19:14–19, Hezekiah visits the temple to pray, having previously enlisted the help of Isaiah the prophet. Is it this humiliation – despoliation of the temple followed by the public insults and pointed rhetoric of the Assyrian field commander – that drives Hezekiah to the same (but now emptier) temple in prayer? The structure of the story implies that emptying the temple forms a preamble to the king's self-emptying that radically

---

[14] Ibid., 3.   [15] Ibid., 273.

alters the arena of war. Of course, it is tempting to immediately fast-forward to the miraculous victory narrative in the chapter's dénouement, but one might argue that the reader is first invited to suffer with Hezekiah as he is driven to desperate prayer under harrowing circumstances. Seow's comment about the absence of an instant divine intervention in 2 Kings 18 prompts us to linger over the king's adversity, not just as a prelude to the later triumph but to experience the character's situation in several different ways. This is not, after all, the last treasury crisis for Hezekiah. In 2 Kgs 20:12–21, he takes a Babylonian delegation on a tour of the temple facilities, raising the ire of the same prophet Isaiah who unfurls a scathing oracle about a forthcoming captivity. As our study proceeds, we will have further occasions to reflect on the career of Hezekiah and draw on Seow's reflections.

Gregory Mobley's succinct essay on the theology of Kings is part of a larger collection that underscores the current interest in theological reading of scripture. Among the useful points in this particular essay is the role of secondary characters in the prophetic stories of Kings, often used as foils or contrasts to the lofty figures who officially wield power in the world of the narrative: "This contrast between the clichéd formulaic texture of the accounts about the rote mendacities, petty corruptions, cruel injustices, and bungling statecraft of the big shots, and the vivid, quirky folktales about the little people – lepers, Syrian house slaves, rural juvenile delinquents, family farmers, roving bands of itinerant, undomesticated seers and the informal network of women who fed and sheltered them – may hold theological significance itself. The meek inherited and kept vital the traditional faith of Israel throughout the monarchic era."[16] To extend

[16] Mobley, "1 and 2 Kings," 123.

Toward the Theology of the Book of Kings

and apply this insight to a particularly intriguing figure, consider Obadiah in 1 Kings 18 as an instructive test case. In the third year of the drought announced by Elijah during the days of Ahab, Obadiah enters the scene at the beginning of chapter 18 with a covert identity: he is the official in charge of the king's palace (*'al-habbayit*), but is also described as one who greatly fears the LORD. This is a perilous environment, for not only has Ahab embraced Baal worship for economic and other reasons, but he also has married the fanatical Phoenician princess Jezebel, who herself is a formidable activist and promoter of the fertility cult and described as sponsoring Asherah devotees and murdering Yahwists.

Elijah comes across as a rather isolated prophetic figure when he confronts Ahab in the previous chapter, but the introduction of Obadiah – whose name means "servant of the LORD" – reveals a new perspective, for not only does Obadiah fear God, but he also has hidden one hundred prophets in caves and sustains them with food and water. Obadiah's conflict is palpable: he is a high-ranking servant of Ahab, but also is quite literally a servant of the LORD, hiding the prophets while hiding his true vocation from his royal employer. Obadiah's initial action in the story is not without irony, as he and his master are busy scouring the land and searching for the water that Baal has evidently not provided, when he encounters Elijah, who commissions him to announce his presence to Ahab. Obadiah's lengthy rejoinder to Elijah's terse imperative is revealing on several levels: in 18:9-14, he testifies to his longstanding fear of God – has he been raised by faithful parents? – and actions in hiding the prophets, but he also fears for his life and, in all likelihood, the lives of those prophets he sustains who will probably be killed when Ahab finds out his covert operations. Yet Obadiah is obedient to the prophetic summons and duly facilitates the confrontation between prophet and king before promptly disappearing from the narrative. His fate may be uncertain, but when Ahab's house is later destroyed by Jehu in 2 Kings 9 – himself empowered by a prophetic word spoken by a younger member of the sons of the prophets – the reader may recall Obadiah's task of faithfully sustaining the prophetic underground during a time of dark uncertainty. It might be argued that Obadiah is a representative character, and the preservation of his voice and deeds – with all the faith and fear – highlights Mobley's larger point about the "meek" as active agents of Yahweh during the monarchic period, and as figures who should not be overlooked as the reader pieces together the theology of the book of Kings.[17]

With a creative and carefully written earlier monograph on 2 Kings 9–11 dealing with the inimitable career of Jehu son of Nimshi, Lissa Wray Beal's commentary on the book of Kings now deals with the entire canvas.[18] A theological interest is clear from the start, with an introductory section that features particularly

---

[17] Although necessarily brief, Mobley's essay is punctuated with prescriptive urgency; it is a theologically complicated task, Mobley notes ("1 and 2 Kings," 126), "to understand the roots of antipathy in Kings for rival religions and alien symbols, *and* to resist demonizing the historians who constructed this foundation for our faith, *and* to find ways of cultivating continuities with our spiritual ancestors, *and* to boldly dissent from ancient formulations that could serve as charters for purges, crusades, and pogroms against those who do not worship as we do. Still, this might be the very task we must embrace if we hope, as the composers of the scroll of Kings did, to play our part in bearing our faith safely through a dangerous time" (emphasis original).

[18] Lissa M. Wray Beal, *The Deuteronomist's Prophet: Narrative Control of Approval and Disapproval in the Story of Jehu (2 Kings 9 and 10)*, LHBOTS 478 (New York and London: T. and T. Clark, 2007); Lissa M. Wray Beal, *1 & 2 Kings*, AOTC (Downers Grove, IL: IVP, 2014).

strong discussions of the theme of the Davidic covenant and the role of prophetic speech in Kings. We will have occasion to cite several of her insights later in this study, but since the era of Ahab and the stewardship of Obadiah were just raised, Wray Beal's remarks on 1 Kings 17 are worth considering briefly here. Of course, Ahab is not unique in opting for Baal worship during Israel's monarchic history: "Repeatedly in 1–2 Kings, kings, people and priests trade the deep reality of YHWH's presence for externals." Following in Solomon's footsteps, "Ahab makes externally advantageous foreign alliances, but through them allows Baal worship into Israel. This leads Israel to rely on Baal falsely for the externals of food, rain – and even life itself."[19] Popular beliefs about God need to be considered in this stretch of the story, and it can hardly be coincidental that the career of Elijah begins with a famine in the land.

Scholars have oft noted an absence of any meaningful introduction to Elijah, and whatever other purpose there might be for the paucity of data, the focus is squarely on the events that unfold in the first instance. The question of who sends rain – God or Baal – quickly assumes center stage: "The famine that opens Elijah's narrative shows the chapter's real concern is with covenant life. It is threatened because the people have turned to Baal and have credited him with the power of life, of rain, of crops (Hos 1:5; cf. Jer 2:7–13). It is no narrative accident that the invocation of famine follows immediately Ahab's introduction of Baal to Israel (1 Kgs 16:31–33). Famine is an expected outcome of disobedience under the covenant." Wray Beal continues, "But that YHWH moves so immediately to send his prophet to call Israel

---

[19] Wray Beal, *1 & 2 Kings*, 153.

back to covenant shows his commitment to life. Even though the covenant curses were prescribed (Dt 28), YHWH is merciful and gracious and unwilling that Israel should linger long outside covenant life. It is this that precipitates his immediate action."[20] If Baal worship is so seductive and alluring because of the assurances of satiation in season, then the abundant references to the scarcity of food and drink throughout the central section of Kings have a certain logic. While Elijah (and Elisha after him) are consistently involved in feeding the people, the kings of Israel are frustrated more often than not, as their policies lead to sterility instead of satisfaction. Indeed, the satirical accents are hard to miss when Ahab and Jezebel become food and drink for dogs in their respective deaths (1 Kgs 22:38; 2 Kgs 9:36). Combined with other studies, Wray Beal offers several useful starting points for theological appraisal of this section of the story.[21]

---

[20] Ibid., 236; cf. 232, "As proof positive that power belongs to YHWH and not Baal, the drought will last much longer than a one-yearly cycle (18:1), the agricultural period associated with Baal's ability to bring the rains once again." By "the introduction of Baal to Israel," I assume that Wray Beal is referring to a much higher state-sponsored level that any previous leader, since Baal worship was long a factor in Israelite society (e.g., Judg 2:11; 10:10; 1 Sam 7:4).

[21] E.g., Deborah A. Appler, "From Queen to Cuisine: Food Imagery in the Jezebel Narrative," *Semeia* 86 (1999): 55–71 (57): "The presence of a famine places Israel in crisis. This we discover as the narrator shifts from the announcement of Ahab's marriage to Jezebel and his subsequent promotion of Baal and Asherah to Elijah's prediction of a drought (1 Kgs 17:1). The order is ironic: this drought occurs immediately after Ahab pays homage to Baal, the Canaanite god of storms, rain, and fertility. The connection accentuates the emptiness of Baal worship; this fertility god is unable to provide food and water." See also Thomas W. Mann, "Not by Word Alone: Food in the Hebrew Bible," *Int* 67 (2013): 351–62.

FROM ENTRY TO EXILE: EXPLORING KINGS IN CONTEXT

At the beginning of Genesis 12, Abram undertakes his long journey to Canaan after setting out from Ur of the Chaldeans, as God promises that through his offspring every family on Earth would be blessed and bequeaths the land to his descendants. In 2 Kings 25, a truncated portion of Abraham's offspring make a similar journey in reverse as they are dismissed from their land because of the kind of disobedience that God repeatedly warned about. The story of this dismissal is narrated at length in the books of Joshua – Kings, predicated on the programmatic exhortation of Moses in Deuteronomy: If the people of Israel are faithful to the covenant and walk in the *tôrāh*, they will enjoy blessing in the land and be "set high above all the nations on earth" (Deut 28:1), but consistent disobedience will eventually result in expulsion as the people will be "uprooted from the land" they are entering to possess (28:63). This epic narrative begins on the other side of the river Jordan as the Israelites are camped in Moab after an eventful forty-year sojourn and finally poised to enter Canaan, but it likewise concludes on the other side of the Jordan – much further away – with Jehoiachin and the other exiles in Babylonian captivity. Because the theological challenge of Moses' last words to the Israelites echoes throughout the narrative, scholars often refer to this collection of six books as the "Deuteronomistic History."

Since the pioneering work of Martin Noth in the 1940s – with various refinements along the way – the idea of the Deuteronomistic History enjoyed something of a heyday, even if there were some differing opinions on the purpose and provenance of the work.[22]

---

[22] For excerpts from leading scholars and bibliography, see Gary N. Knoppers and J. Gordon McConville, eds., *Reconsidering Israel and Judah: Recent Studies on the Deuteronomistic History* (Winona Lake, IN: Eisenbrauns, 2000).

For instance, Noth interpreted the account as a long explanation of the reasons for divine judgment that evinces no confidence in any future restoration of the people. By contrast, Gerhard von Rad and Hans Walter Wolff accepted Noth's structural design but differed in the impetus of the work, which they interpreted as rather more hopeful or optimistic, with a discernable thread of grace to offset the unrelenting judgment stressed by Noth (although Wolff stressed that any hope rested on repentance). Furthermore, Noth envisioned an exilic compilation by a single author residing in Palestine, whereas others (especially in North America) followed Frank Moore Cross and argued for a two-stage composition: part one compiled in the era of Josiah, with an updating after the exile.[23] Notwithstanding these variations, the conception of a reasonably unified Deuteronomistic History commanded widespread assent and some of the highest levels of any consensus in the guild, even if there was disagreement in the details.

In our present-day climate, the compositional debate has become rather more vexed – like most issues in biblical studies, there are as many theories as there are towns of Judah – with varying degrees of adherence and plausibility.[24] But jettisoning the idea of a substantially coherent Deuteronomistic History may be precipitous, and while the seminal works of Noth, von Rad, Wolff and Cross are certainly subject to critique and cross-examination, the classic formulations are still valuable as a heuristic gateway into this narrative. So, even allowing for the rich

---

[23] Note the useful summary of the history of research in Thomas Römer, *The So-Called Deuteronomistic History: A Sociological, Historical and Literary Introduction* (London: T. and T. Clark, 2005), 13–43.

[24] An overview of the present state of play can be found in Brian Neil Peterson, *The Authors of the Deuteronomistic History: Locating a Tradition in Ancient Israel* (Minneapolis, MN: Fortress Press, 2014).

diversity and variations in language and style within the narrative of Joshua–Kings, the concept of a running story with an overarching theological macroplot is an optimal place to begin, and there is enough connective tissue to assume that the books are best read together.²⁵ Along these lines, there have been some promising studies of late that we will draw on during the course of our analysis. For instance, John Barton has revisited the question of how Israelite historiographic writings might function as works of theodicy, and if so, then the Deuteronomistic History might be reconsidered from this perspective.²⁶

Part of the challenge of this study, then, is to provide a theological reading of Kings as the final installment of the Deuteronomistic History, the vast and diverse narrative that aims to rebuild a broken world by restoring faith in the God who keeps promises: if Kings is written from the point of view of Jerusalem's destruction and the Babylonian exile – which it surely is, in my opinion – how are various themes from earlier books (such as the Davidic covenant, necessity of obedience, proscriptions on kingship, or centrality of worship) treated in this concluding part of the story? Martin Noth may not have been so sanguine about

---

²⁵ See Steven L. McKenzie, *Introduction to the Historical Books: Strategies for Reading* (Grand Rapids, MI: Eerdmans, 2010), 18: "I continue to assume the existence of the DtrH more or less in the guise attributed to it by Noth. That is, while fully acknowledging the use of older sources and the presence of later additions, Noth's explanation that Deuteronomy + the Former Prophets is an original unit by a single, exilic author still seems to me the most economical." McKenzie concludes, "Dtr was a true ancient historian in that he sought to offer a comprehensive, written explanation of Israel's national past that had brought about its present situation."

²⁶ John Barton, "Historiography and Theodicy in the Old Testament," in *Reflection and Refraction: Studies in Biblical Historiography in Honour of A. Graeme Auld*, ed. Robert Rezetko, Timothy H. Lim and W. Brian Aucker, VTSup 113 (Leiden: Brill, 2007), 27–33.

the hopefulness of Kings, but in this study we will argue that the narrative cultivates an optimism, but not that the monarchy will be restored or that confidence can be found in any of the typical institutions or ideological positions that failed so miserably.[27] Instead, the narrative builds a case toward a radical trust in God for a profoundly different order in the days ahead, encouraging faithful adherence to the character of God even under the shadow of empire in a vulnerable position with marginalized status. Seen in this way, the theology of Kings thus carries great relevance for contemporary readers and communities of faith.

[27] On Noth's social location, see the interesting comment of Thomas Römer and Albert de Pury, "Deuteronomistic Historiography (DH): History of Research and Debated Issues," in *Israel Constructs Its History: Deuteronomistic Historiography in Recent Research*, ed. Albert de Pury, Thomas Römer and Jean-Daniel Macchi, JSOTSup 306 (Sheffield: Sheffield Academic Press, 2000), 24–141 (52): "Noth apparently thought of Dtr as a solitary intellectual who, on the day following the catastrophe, cut off in his study, set to work to draw up an assessment of the situation. We cannot refrain from thinking that Dtr's vision of the situation reflects a little the very situation of Noth himself. In fact, Noth composed his *ÜSt* just as the war of extermination instigated by his own people was ravaging Europe and Germany. Just like his Dtr, Noth felt himself indebted to no institution, and it is tempting to think that the pessimism facing the future that he attributes to Dtr corresponded to his analysis of the contemporary situation."

CHAPTER 2

Dynasty and Succession

The opening sequence of 1 Kings narrates the eventful transition from David to Solomon and provides an early characterization of the heir and the consolidation of his kingdom. In several respects, the action of these scenes forms an overture for Kings as a whole, with a tense atmosphere in the royal court, factions and divided loyalties, prophetic activity within the corridors of power, portraits of monarchs as conflicted figures, and much less direct attribution of God's involvement than the reader might expect. The political posturing in 1 Kings 1 begins with David's courtiers procuring a young maiden, and it is not unreasonable to suspect that these courtiers are testing the king's potency and attempting to determine his fitness to rule. Adonijah likewise takes independent initiative, and his calculated bid for the throne features the gathering of allies and the hosting of a virtual coronation feast. But without any recorded speech or formal action as such, Solomon is crowned as David's successor when Nathan and Bathsheba dramatically intervene on his behalf in what must be considered rather questionable circumstances. In 1 Kings 2, the father's last words to his new replacement include an uneasy combination of injunctions from the *tôrāh* and acts of ruthlessness, operating as a segue to the early days of Solomon's reign and his violent undertakings as he strengthens his grip on the kingdom. Yet within this maelstrom of political maneuverings, there is ample fodder for theological reflection, even as the reader grapples to discern the divine purpose amid the layers of courtly scheming in the gritty world of the royal capital.

AGED MONARCH

David is the most extensively rendered human character in the historiographical literature of the Hebrew Bible. The reader variously witnesses his early life and anointing in 1 Samuel 16, followed in turn by his long fugitive period in the wilderness, his enthronement as king of all Israel in the newly conquered city of Jerusalem, the disastrous rebellion of Absalom that fractures the nation, and finally David's death in 1 Kings 2. Erich Auerbach famously remarked that in contrast to Homeric epics, biblical narrative is "fraught with background,"[1] and nowhere is this more evident than in the long and complicated story of David's reign, with its layers of irony, double-voiced discourse, strategic deployment of motifs, shades of ambiguity, multiple shifts in temporal and spatial settings, intertextuality and thematic complications that abound from start to finish. "The story of David," says Robert Alter in his study of David's complex portrait from a predominantly literary perspective, "is probably the greatest single narrative representation in antiquity of a human life evolving by slow stages through time, shaped and altered by the pressures of political life, public institutions, family, the impulses of body and spirit, the eventual sad decay of the flesh. It also provides the most unflinching insight into the cruel processes of history and into human

---

[1] Erich Auerbach, *Mimesis: The Representation of Reality in Western Literature* (Princeton, NJ: Princeton University Press, 1953), 11–12.

behavior warped by the pursuit of power."[2] But now Israel's vaunted king is a pale shadow of his former self, and by underscoring the notice of David's advanced age, the issue of succession takes on a heightened importance at the earliest point of 1 Kings. In contrast to the energetic and forceful David of earlier narratives, the aged leader is confined to his bedchamber for the remainder of his career while others act around him.

The initial scenes of 1 Kings 1 abound with collusion and intrigue: with the king seemingly on his deathbed, political factions are preparing to engage in a power struggle. David himself is the object of several competing interest groups hoping, it would appear, to fill the leadership vacuum created by the monarch's infirmity and impending death. A key point, as commentators since Leonhard Rost have discussed at length – and a main reason why party lines are forming at this point in the narrative – is that the next occupant of the throne of Israel has not yet been named.[3] David's immobility provides an opportunity for the first group of active characters, a nameless band of courtiers, to promulgate a scheme: in the absence of any named successor to the Davidic throne, they apparently initiate a test of the king's virility. "The narrative," says Walter Brueggemann, "in subtle and understated ways, lets us see the workings of aggressive power cloaked in all the niceties of royal protocol."[4] There is no reason stated, but the servants – who should be thought of as higher ranking officials in the royal administration – may want to determine if David is still capable of ruling the nation. If not, the courtiers presumably

---

[2] Robert Alter, *The David Story: A Translation with Commentary of 1 & 2 Samuel* (New York: Norton, 1999), ix.
[3] Leonhard Rost, *The Succession to the Throne of David*, trans. David M. Gunn (Sheffield: Almond Press, 1982 [1926]).
[4] Walter Brueggemann, *1 & 2 Kings* (Macon, GA: Smyth and Helwys, 2000), 11.

would need to back an alternative candidate; after all, they have a vested interest in national affairs, and their involvement is explicitly mentioned later in the story (1:9, 47).

It may be mere coincidence, but Abishag hails from the village of Shunem, in the northern tribe of Issachar (Josh 19:18) and most recently the camp for Saul's final battle (1 Sam 28:4). After the fractious civil war resulting from Absalom's seizure of his father's throne, a gesture of goodwill or an alliance with the northern tribes would not be out of order. During the latter part of David's reign, the relationship between Judah and the northern tribes has been tense (e.g., 2 Sam 19:41–43), and no obvious steps have been taken by David to repair this fissure. Of course, it is possible that by searching for a beautiful maiden, the courtiers are simply attempting to revive their aged king – whose private failings are all too real, but whose glories remain unequalled among Israel's parade of monarchs – and perhaps extend his reign as long as possible. Regardless of their motives, Richard Nelson is surely correct to point out that "Abishag was sought out to resolve a constitutional crisis, not just to comfort the shivering old king."[5] Overall, at the end of v. 4, the experiment confirms that David's potency has now evaporated, and even if it is clear that succession is soon approaching, Abishag's role in the sordid story of 1 Kings 1–2 is far from over. Hovering over the opening scene are reminders of Nathan's prophetic word in 2 Sam 7:12–13: "When your days are full and you lie down with your ancestors, I will raise up your seed after you, who will come forth from your loins, and I will

---

[5] Richard D. Nelson, *First and Second Kings* (Atlanta: John Knox Press, 1987), 16. Although Gwilym H. Jones (*The Nathan Narratives*, JSOTSup 80 [Sheffield: Sheffield Academic Press, 1990], 35–6) doubts the "originality" of these verses from a source-critical perspective, he concedes that vv. 1b-4 nonetheless "anticipate" the contention for the throne that will ensue in the narrative.

establish his kingdom. He will build a house for my name, and I will establish the throne of his kingdom forever." David may have been promised a lasting dynasty, but who will assume the throne is far from certain, nor is it yet clear how this process will unfold.

FRATERNAL FACTIONS

Conflicts among brothers occur with painful frequency in the Hebrew Bible, beginning with Cain and Abel and continuing with Ishmael and Isaac, and then most expansively with the wrestling of Esau and Jacob over the rights of primogeniture.[6] Reuben's assertion of firstborn status when he defiles his father's couch (Gen 35:22) causes a rift that is never healed, as Jacob's last words testify (Gen 49:3-4). Within David's inner circle, the violent death of the firstborn Amnon was engineered by the younger Absalom, ostensibly to avenge the rape of Tamar but quite possibly to advance his claim to the throne at the same time. In 1 Kings 1 this divisive trend continues, although initially in a more indirect way. After the deaths of Amnon and Absalom (and the disappearance of Chileab), Adonijah is David's oldest surviving son. Without any prompting from the king, Adonijah takes steps to his assert his claim, and in the absence of any other indications, the reader may conclude that he is a natural candidate. For some interpreters, Adonijah "is not actively seeking to unseat his father"

---

[6] On the question of whether Cain and Abel might be twins and if the fighting of Jacob and Esau are correspondingly foreshadowed, see R. W. L. Moberly, *The Theology of the Book of Genesis*, Old Testament Theology (Cambridge: Cambridge University Press, 2009), 92-93.

as he bursts onto the scene in 1 Kgs 1:5 with abundant royal outfitting.[7] Yet the programmatic themes of Hannah's song on the threshold of the monarchy in 1 Sam 2:1–10 about the exaltation of the lowly and the fall of the arrogant readily come to mind, and it could be argued that Adonijah's conduct in vv. 5–6 is bordering on the imperious: "Now Adonijah son of Haggith lifted himself up, saying, '*I* will be king.' He secured for himself a chariot and horses, with fifty men as runners before him. But from his earliest days his father had not restrained him, saying 'Why are you acting like this?' Also, he was very handsome in form, and he was born after Absalom."

A chariot is hardly the most practical vehicle for traversing the streets of ancient Jerusalem, and when combined with Adonijah's emphatic utterance about his intention to reign, the reader suspects that his declaration is not an inner musing. Disturbingly, Absalom also obtained a chariot and fifty runners in 2 Sam 15:1 as part of his subversive campaign to unseat his father, so the comparisons here immediately cast suspicions on Adonijah.[8] David's parenting style bore bitter fruit with Absalom, and his laxity in dispensing paternal discipline extends to Adonijah and perhaps fosters a sense of entitlement, but this does not prevent Adonijah from accumulating a host of formidable allies who rally to his cause. Most visible is Joab, the shrewd and dangerous commander of Israel's military and nephew of David, whose career has lasted ever since the fugitive days on the run from the madness of King Saul. Moreover, along with all his brothers

---

[7] See Jerome T. Walsh, *1 Kings*, Berit Olam (Collegeville, MN: Liturgical Press, 1996), 7.

[8] Cf. Marvin A. Sweeney, *I & II Kings*, OTL (Louisville, KY: Westminster John Knox Press, 2007), 54: "The narrative presents Adonijah as the self-presumed heir who acts rashly to claim his father's throne."

and the servants of the king, Adonijah also enlists the support of Abiathar the priest. Once the temple is built and Jerusalem is reaffirmed as the spiritual center of national life, priests will presumably enjoy heightened prestige and centralization, but for now Abiathar undoubtedly is a useful ally, having sided with David during Absalom's rebellion. However, Abiathar is also from the doomed house of Eli, a powerful priestly dynasty located in Shiloh but terminated because of cultic malfeasance and related crimes (1 Sam 2:27–36). As it stands, Eli's aborted dynasty is a reminder of difficulties of succession, and despite his status as the oldest son, Adonijah still faces an uphill climb: "Not even the greatest leaders in Israelite history had ever successfully passed power onto a son, not Moses or the prophet Samuel or Saul (even though he had a first-rate successor in Jonathan)."[9]

For all the support and influential backers, some names are omitted from Adonijah's guest list, and these exclusions will in fact provide a decisive twist in the plot. David's personal retinue of soldiers are not invited to Adonijah's feast, and neither is Zadok the priest, foreshadowing the later rivalry between priestly lines. Most curious, however, is the omission of "his brother Solomon," even though all the other brothers are invited. It could be argued that Solomon occupies a rather low position in the familial hierarchy, born as he was in the aftermath of David's adultery with Bathsheba and the death of the unnamed son in 2 Sam 12:24–25. Nevertheless, at the time of Solomon's birth, there are some incidents that may pique the reader's interest. Solomon's name can be translated as "his replacement," and the most immediate

---

[9] Steven Weitzman, *Solomon: The Lure of Wisdom* (New Haven, CT: Yale University Press, 2011), 33.

reflex is that he replaces the recently deceased child.¹⁰ But scribal tradition preserves a variant reading whereby Bathsheba bestows the name, inviting the inference that Bathsheba might envision her son Solomon as the replacement for David as king of Israel.¹¹ Furthermore, Solomon's name is divinely changed to Jedidah ("beloved of the LORD"), and because a name change in the Hebrew Bible often triggers a shift in destiny, Solomon's future should be closely monitored. In 1 Kgs 1:10, it is unclear whether Adonijah is merely ignoring Solomon or perceives him as an opponent – the latter seems more likely – but he soon discovers that his plan fails not because of any tactical or political reason so much as because of an act of divine will. There are ample cases where the "iron law of primogeniture" is subject to a surprising reversal, and 1 Kings 1 is about to present one more instance.¹² As the reader will be invited to conclude in this opening chapter, the stability of the Davidic house depends more on divine sovereignty than on any grasping for power or intimidating assertions of authority.

PROPHETIC COLLUSION

The highest profile absentee from Adonijah's guest list is also the most prominent prophet of David's court, and this will be the Achilles' heel of Adonijah's strategy. There is no indication why Nathan is not invited to the feast, but a glance at his backstory is

---

[10] P. Kyle McCarter, *II Samuel: A New Translation with Introduction, Notes, and Commentary*, AB 9 (Garden City, NY: Doubleday, 1984), 303.
[11] Cf. Steven L. McKenzie, *King David: A Biography* (New York: Oxford University Press, 2000), 182–83.
[12] Robert Alter, *The Art of Biblical Narrative*, rev. edn. (New York: Basic Books, 2011), 5.

revealing. After David's conquest of Jerusalem, Nathan first appears in 2 Samuel 7 where he communicates a stunning oracle to the king: although David desires to build God a house, God plans to build a house for David. In addition to an enduring dynasty, the son who succeeds him will construct the temple, and the throne of his kingdom will be established forever (7:13). Nathan next appears in 2 Samuel 12 after the king's adulterous liaison with Bathsheba, where he prompts the king to utter a self-condemnation through a story about a rich man who takes from a poor man before declaring that the sword will never depart from David's enduring house. Of significant interest is Nathan's cameo later in 2 Sam 12:25 when God sends him with the change of name for Solomon: the reader may be unsure if this name change becomes public knowledge, but it may indicate that Nathan perceives a certain destiny for Solomon. During the long rebellion of Absalom and its aftermath, Nathan is not heard from, but he resurfaces in 1 Kgs 1:11 as he stealthily converses with Bathsheba.

If it is true that political turmoil creates unlikely partnerships, then the alliance between Nathan – who was unequivocal in his condemnation of David's adultery – and Bathsheba is near the top of the list, as the latter is recruited by the prophet to question David about an alleged oath concerning Solomon's succession. As a legion of commentators has discussed, there is no record of any oath concerning Solomon in the previous narrative: perhaps it is sworn and simply not mentioned at any point, or maybe Nathan is involved in some pious subterfuge. However, he is only asking that Bathsheba pose a question to David: "Did you not, O my lord the king, swear an oath to your maid-servant, saying, 'Solomon your son will reign after me, and he will sit upon my throne'? Why then is Adonijah reigning?" Of course, it could be maintained that Adonijah is not formally reigning yet, only sponsoring a feast for his supporters. Yet Nathan's conduct will not be atypical of prophets in many sections of Kings, as sometimes they deliver authoritative oracles but at other times engage in risky and audacious backroom politicking – sometimes acting as a check on royal power and excess, and at other times ensuring that the right king is crowned.

Among the most enigmatic of the royal women in the Deuteronomistic History is Bathsheba, and her characterization in 2 Samuel 11 has generated a wealth of comment: some argue that she is a victim of kingly lechery, while others suggest that her motives may be more complex. In 1 Kgs 1:15, she wordlessly complies with Nathan's directive and enters David's crowded bedchamber, with Abishag present and certainly looking like a rival. The awkward situation is not without irony, as David asks, "What is with you" (*mah-lak*), forming a wordplay on the Hebrew verb for "reign" (*malak*) – which is exactly why Bathsheba is there. The reader is expecting Bathsheba to ask a question, as Nathan instructs, but instead she issues an emphatic statement: "My lord, you yourself swore by the Lord your God to your maidservant, 'Surely Solomon your son will reign after me and he will sit upon my throne.' But now, behold, Adonijah is reigning, and, my lord the king, you do not know!" Far from being resolved, the ambiguity surrounding the oath's existence is intensified in this transaction, not least when Nathan arrives and makes no mention of any oath, only that Adonijah is hosting a lavish party. It is not clear if David suddenly recalls a previous oath or if he is angrily reacting to Adonijah's presumption, but in his most active moment so far in the book of Kings, he proceeds to swear an oath, and within the hour Solomon is volubly proclaimed as his successor. Peter Leithart notes that "for the author of 1–2 Kings, Yahweh really does employ the timely tactics of a shrewd court prophet, the rhetorical and sexual appeal of a queen, the democratic weight of an acclamation by 'all the people' to place Solomon on the throne."[13] Within the opening chapter – the bulk of which evidently takes place on a single day – the best laid plans can be subverted by prophetic involvement that ultimately transcends even as it utilizes political power. If the Davidic house has been birthed by the prophetic word, then it will endure because of divine commitment, notwithstanding any appearances to the contrary.

THE INTERVIEW

In Genesis 27, Esau is preparing for a feast while his younger brother Jacob is simultaneously hoodwinking their aged father and usurping the firstborn prerogatives. There is a similar narrative configuration and simultaneity in 1 Kings 1, because even as Adonijah is feasting with his supporters at En-Rogel, so Nathan and Bathsheba are busy securing the crown for Solomon. En-Rogel is situated below the city of Jerusalem with a name that sounds like "Spring of the Spy."[14] This spring was a key location in

---

[13] Peter J. Leithart, *1 & 2 Kings*, Brazos Theological Commentary on the Bible (Grand Rapids, MI: Brazos, 2006), 35. Cf. Brueggemann, *1 & 2 Kings*, 20: "The beginning chapter of the books of Kings already plunges us into the most interesting and most difficult issue faced in this account of Israel's monarchy: the interplay of *raw, crude politics* and the insistence that this particular history is *an arena for God's purposes*. It is not easy to hold together in tension raw, crude politics and the sense of God's purposes, but this narrative is agile and subtle in doing just that" (emphasis original). A key theological question that emerges, in my view, revolves around the degree to which God is portrayed as willing to use human agency in order to effect the divine purpose.

[14] Adrian Curtis, *Oxford Bible Atlas*, 4th edn. (Oxford: Oxford University Press, 2007): 141–43.

the quelling of Absalom's uprising, so it is associated with failed bids for the throne (2 Sam 17:17–21). By contrast, Solomon is anointed at another spring, the Gihon, carrying echoes of the primordial river of Paradise that irrigated the garden of Eden (Gen 2:13) and the perennial source of fresh water for the city of Jerusalem (see 2 Chr 32:30).[15] Adonijah's banquet occurs at a place with murky overtones of insurgence, whereas Solomon's place of coronation relates the bestowal of Davidic kingship to the fabric of creation and endows the ceremony with the highest prelapsarian symbolism. Combined with Solomon's riding on David's own mule (in distinction to Adonijah's chariot), the sounding of the *shofar* and its memories of great battles (Joshua 6), and the horn of oil taken from the sacred tent, the overall effect is that Solomon is divinely chosen even in the midst of courtly maneuvering. For an exilic readership acquainted with the trauma of dislocation and devastation of the land, the first installment of Kings strongly suggests that Solomon – like the people of Israel – has been enthroned by providence. Indeed, akin to Jacob, Solomon is not crowned because of his own merit or any virtue he might possess: he has been given the gift of leadership, and it remains to be seen how he will use this opportunity to serve the people of God.

Solomon's coronation ritual involves a multitude of participants, and the earth is split with the sounds of the rejoicing. The first guest to hear the noise of the commotion is the ever-alert Joab, and since he is the one who sounds the *shofar* in 2 Sam 18:16 and 20:22 to signal the end of attempts to dislodge David by Absalom and Sheba son of Bicri, someone else blasting this

---

[15] Francis Landy, "Fluvial Fantasies," in *Thinking of Water in the Early Second Temple Period*, ed. Ehud Ben Zvi and Christoph Levin, BZAW 46 (Berlin: Walter de Gruyter, 2014), 437–55 (445–48).

instrument would be cause for concern. It is not without irony that Adonijah is given a detailed report of Solomon's crowning by Jonathan son of Abiathar the priest (vv. 43-48), since he too is from a rejected house that is about to be eclipsed by Zadok and his line. With the writing on the wall and his guests dispersed, Adonijah flees to the horns of the altar to seek refuge. Commentators often point to Exod 21:12-14 as the background text for this survival mechanism, presumably drawing on a broader ancient Near Eastern principle that a guilty criminal cannot be put to death in a sacred place.[16] C. L. Seow provides some perspective on Adonijah's action: "The 'horns of the altar' refers to the four horn-like protuberances at the four corners of the altar, on which sacrificial blood is smeared and atonement is symbolically effected (Exod 27:2; 29:12; 30:10; Lev 4:7; Ezek 43:20). Hence, the grasping of these horns came to signal an appeal for asylum. The prophet Amos would later threaten Israel that the horns of the altar at Bethel – one of two national sanctuaries of the northern kingdom – would be cut off (Amos 3:14), meaning that the Israelites would have no place to go when their pursuers sought their lives."[17] Interpreters have long observed the reversal of fortune, as Adonijah begins by raising himself up and announcing that he will be king, but a short while later he is brought down from the altar of asylum in obeisance before his ascendant younger brother. During this scene of the chapter (vv. 51-53), the reader encounters the previously veiled Solomon for the first time:

---

[16] Note the study of Jonathan Burnside, "Flight of the Fugitives: Rethinking the Relationship between Biblical Law (Exodus 21:12-14) and the Davidic Succession Narrative (1 Kings 1-2)," *JBL* 129 (2010): 418-31.
[17] Seow, "The First and Second Books of Kings," 22.

> It was reported to Solomon, "Behold Adonijah is afraid of King Solomon, and behold, he has seized the horns of the altar, saying, 'Let King Solomon swear an oath to me today that he will not put his servant to death with the sword.'" Solomon said, "If he will be a man of worth, then not one of his hairs will fall to the earth. But if evil is found in him, then he will die." And King Solomon sent, and they brought him down from the altar. And he came and he was prostrate before King Solomon, and Solomon said to him, "Go to your house."

There is an ironic backdraft when Adonijah asks for an oath from King Solomon: by means of some creative language with oaths, Adonijah was outmaneuvered to the throne by Nathan and Bathsheba, yet now he seeks an oath to save his life. Solomon, however, does not provide anything close to an oath of amnesty. Instead, he provides Adonijah only with a conditional utterance – an if/then scenario predicated on proper behavior – and clearly it is the king who decides whether such vague parameters have been breached. For most of this eventful opening chapter, Solomon has been concealed behind a curtain, content to let others do his bidding and voice his legitimacy. His calculating utterance will need to be revisited as the narrative continues, especially in light of the violent purge still to come. Of course, there are many examples in the Hebrew Bible of God working in the midst of venal circumstances or sleazy characters, and on this score the Davidic court with its veneer of sophistication is no different than the family squabbles in the book of Genesis. A key question in 1 Kings 1 (and beyond) is whether the reader is persuaded that God is behind Solomon's accession, as it is a challenge to separate the mysteries of providence from the lofty rhetoric of Solomon and those characters around him with the most to gain from his regime. Richard Nelson maintains that "God's involvement in the seamy world of politics seems problematic to the modern reader.

Devious political machinations, the sudden coup, the establishment of absolutist power have all too often been justified on religious grounds. We may wish to pause and ponder the dark realities of power in our world." He continues: "The good news is, however, that God is in charge even of the dark side, even of political intrigue. The political structures of this world are not running wild, outside of God's control. They too are part of God's rulership for the good of humanity (Rom 13:17; 1 Peter 2:13–14)."[18] Meanwhile, Solomon's first words to Adonijah form an apt transition to David's last words, because this is not the last time that conditional language is a prominent feature in the opening section of Kings.

SOME CONDITIONS APPLY?

There is a tradition of fathers or great leaders giving a farewell address to their son(s) or the nation of Israel, and based on the examples of Jacob, Moses and Joshua, such speeches typically include exhortations to faithfulness or forecasts of the future. David's final speech is more of a private address to his successor, and his detailed instructions to Solomon in 1 Kgs 2:2–9 have two distinct parts. The first part (vv. 2–4) is an admonishment about walking in the ways of God, and begins by invoking familiar tropes from the book of Deuteronomy; indeed, the opening lines resemble God's word to Joshua after the death of Moses,

---

[18] Nelson, *First and Second Kings*, 22. For another set of reflections that help to consider theologically this demanding narrative of Solomon's accession, see John Goldingay, "The Theology of the Hebrew Bible/Old Testament," in *The Cambridge Companion to the Hebrew Bible/Old Testament*, ed. Stephen B. Chapman and Marvin A. Sweeney (New York: Cambridge University Press, 2016), 466–82.

underscoring the relationship between success and obedience (see Josh 1:1-9). Most surprising, however, is David's remark in v. 4, where Solomon is encouraged to keep the law "in order that the LORD may establish his word which he spoke concerning me, saying, 'If your sons guard their way, to walk before me in truth with all their heart and soul, you will never lack to have a man upon the throne of Israel.'" Scholars have long discussed David's speech to his son here, because when Nathan announces the dynastic promise in 2 Sam 7:12-16, it is unconditional, yet now David equates retaining the throne with walking in the law of Moses. Bearing in mind that David is the speaker - and in light of the oath controversy in the previous chapter, human characters have varying degrees of reliability - how should the stress on a conditional kingship be interpreted? "Though God is quoted in verse 4, the prior narrative gives no indication that God has adjusted the original unconditional promise in this way. This text might reflect David's actual understanding of the promise, or it might be the way in which David chooses to put the matter to Solomon at this juncture in his life."[19] By opting to focus on the warning rather than the guarantee, perhaps David has his own struggles in view; alternatively, maybe he does not trust his successor with such an assurance or at least would prefer that Solomon act as though he held the throne on a conditional basis. To be sure, Solomon has recently informed Adonijah that his survival hinges on certain behavior, and now David tells Solomon that occupancy of the kingship has similar conditions. Since the Davidic promise is mentioned further ahead in the story and conditional language is used again, this tension will need to be revisited - certainly before the end of 2 Kings 25,

---

[19] Fretheim, *First and Second Kings*, 28.

where the city of Jerusalem is in ruins and the last king of Judah hangs by a slender thread.

The second part of David's speech to Solomon in vv. 5–9 is comparatively easier to interpret but is not easy to stomach: David has just counseled Solomon to walk in the divine statutes and ordinances, but he then unleashes a torrent of vitriol and directs his son to dispatch the gray heads of his adversaries to Sheol. For Marvin Sweeney, "David's testament to Solomon presents a warped understanding of Torah observance insofar as David instructs his son to eliminate his opponents on questionable grounds."[20] The first target is Joab, David's nephew and steadfastly loyal military leader, whose often dubious acts were unquestionably beneficial for David, but as we saw earlier in 1 Kgs 1:7, Joab has backed Adonijah's candidacy. The grounds for Joab's termination – the deaths of Abner and Amasa at various points in David's career – are not altogether convincing, and the reader intuits that Joab is simply too hazardous for Solomon to keep around.[21] A second target is Shimei of Benjamin, who vehemently cursed David during his ignominious flight from Jerusalem (2 Sam 16:5–13), but subsequently brought one thousand other Benjaminites to apologize and restore the king to Jerusalem after Absalom's rebellion ended (2 Sam 19:16–23). Unlike Joab, however, Shimei was not a supporter of Absalom, so why is Solomon told to use his wisdom and circumvent David's oath to Shimei? As Steven Weitzman theorizes, "Shimei's very existence reminded the people that David was a

---

[20] Sweeney, *I & II Kings*, 60. In the context of the larger narrative, Sweeney (p. 61) further comments: "David's testament to Solomon indicates that the dynasty was corrupt at its very foundation."
[21] Cf. Alter, *The David Story*, 375–76.

usurper, and that there were alternatives to whom they might turn, which is why, in his last words to Solomon, David urges his son to send Shimei to his grave – not just as payback for a public insult but as a preemptive effort to snuff out any potential revival of Saul's dynasty after his death."[22] To reiterate, David's specious reasoning is difficult to reconcile with his injunction that Solomon abide by the *tôrāh* and walk in obedience. Furthermore, Solomon is encouraged to act according to his wisdom (*ḥokmah*) in dealing with Joab and Shimei, a rather vicious introduction to an important theme in this stretch of Kings.[23]

Bracketed between the virtual execution orders for the two adversaries is a notice concerning the sons of Barzillai, as David directs Solomon to reward them because of loyalty shown during the tense period of Absalom's uprising (2 Sam 17:27). More specifically, they are to eat at the king's table, continuing an earlier motif from the careers of Saul and David (e.g., 1 Sam 20:29; 2 Sam 9:7) and one that appears later in the narrative as well (see 1 Kgs 18:19 for Jezebel's sponsorship of her prophets). Solomon's table will certainly be noted for its sumptuous fare and bevy of attendees (1 Kgs 4:47; cf. the Queen of Sheba's testimony in 10:5), but Iain Provan warns of an inversion of such largesse toward the end of the story, "where the eventual end of Davidic rule over Judah/Israel, the obverse of Solomonic splendour, is given pathetic illustration by the fact that king Jehoiachin sits at the table of the king of Babylon (2 Kgs 25:29). The nations no longer flock to

---

[22] Weitzman, *Solomon: The Lure of Wisdom*, 44.
[23] On the larger theme, see Walsh, *1 Kings*, 44: "As the term recurs over and over again in the remaining chapters of the Solomon story, Solomon's wisdom is a divine gift, admirable in its exercise and positive in its results. But here, at its origin, the theme is shadowed by the violence of the advice to which David attaches it."

supply David with food. David is instead to be found as a dependent upon *them*."²⁴ It is curious that David clearly directs his son to dispense favoritism to his allies, but given the pressing north/south problem – indeed, favoritism toward Judah will cause substantial misery – the reader may wonder why it is ignored here. A larger question raised by David's last words surrounds the manner by which the kingdom is secured: by fidelity to the *tôrāh* or by a brutal political expediency?²⁵ Does David believe the two can be held together, or is there a bifurcation in his thinking? Since the rest of this chapter is famous for the ruthless violence that is undertaken by Solomon, it might be argued that David bequeaths a divided consciousness to his son, after whose death the kingdom divides irreparably.

PROCESS OF ELIMINATION

When advising Solomon about dispatching opponents, David made no mention of Adonijah son of Haggith, the most obvious

---

24 Iain W. Provan, "Why Barzillai of Gilead (1 Kings 2:7)? Narrative Art and the Hermeneutics of Suspicion in 1 Kings 1-2," *TynBul* 46 (1995), 115.

25 Compare the longer reflection of Seow, "The First and Second Books of Kings," 34–35: "From a moral viewpoint, the passage is difficult to appropriate. Herein one finds attitudes and actions that are utterly deplorable. We see examples of human cunning, vindictiveness, pettiness, insecurity, and sheer dishonesty. David and Solomon, God's anointed ones, are just as guilty of questionable ethics as are the others – if not more so. They are no role models for righteous conduct, except in negative ways. One might attempt a defense of their conduct in the light of ancient Near Eastern cultures, arguing that their actions sprang from culturally specific and antiquated attitudes about the power of curses, the abiding consequences of blood guilt, and the like. Still, the text remains morally problematic in the light of the totality of Scripture's teachings about right relationships among human beings." Contemporary readers are invited to inquire: how different are matters today?

rival for the throne. But after David's death, in 1 Kgs 2:13–25 Solomon evidently needs no advice on how to deal with his older brother, who brashly requests Abishag for a wife. Based on earlier precedence, such a request could be construed as less of a romantic gesture and more of an attempt to lay claim on the throne; the most graphic situation in recent memory is Absalom's raping of David's concubines in 2 Sam 16:21–22, since taking royal women is tantamount to seizing the kingship (cf. 2 Sam 3:6–7; 12:8, 11). Whether Adonijah has ulterior motives is almost immaterial, since his request could quite easily be interpreted as sedition, and in light of Solomon's calculated warning is surely unwise. For the second time, Bathsheba is recruited to make a risky approach to the king. Yet here Adonijah may have committed his biggest blunder, since Bathsheba has her own throne beside her son (see v. 19) and presumably has no interest in surrendering it to Haggith. Adonijah's speech to Bathsheba is intriguing, and while the sincerity is hard to gauge, he admits that the turn of events that resulted in Solomon's coronation is the divine will. Adonijah's acknowledgment fits with the larger narrative, but the fact that he uses it as a preface to his request – as though he at least deserves Abishag as a kind of silver medal after his loss – is more problematic. At the very least, it forms an apt introduction to an episode where speeches can hardly be taken at face value, and religious language is frequently coopted into various political agendas.

Bathsheba duly delivers Adonijah's request to Solomon, stating that she has a "small" (*qeṭannah*) request to make (the same Hebrew root as "younger," a tacit reminder of Solomon's status). At the end of the previous chapter, Adonijah asked Solomon for an oath and did not get one; now, in vv. 23–24, Solomon swears a double oath about Adonijah's death. So, for a second time,

Adonijah underestimates Solomon, but he will not make that mistake again, because Benaiah is sent to dispatch him to the grave. A vocal (and now violent) supporter of Solomon's regime – note his pious exclamation in 1 Kgs 1:36 – Benaiah has much to gain from the demise of Adonijah and his faction, which is probably why he unquestioningly goes about his business. With a striking absence of any conditional language, Solomon rationalizes Adonijah's death by appealing to his own enthronement. Walter Dietrich rightly notes: "To our consternation, Solomon refers to the Davidic covenant as justification: was it meant to be invoked in this way?"[26] For Solomon and those after him, a persistent temptation will be to justify ruthlessness in the name of a divine promise. Still, it could be argued that Adonijah is asking for trouble, and as Frank Moore Cross has quipped, "He deserved to be executed – for stupidity!"[27] But within the wider narrative canvas, Adonijah's death dovetails with Nathan's prophetic indictment of David in 2 Sam 12:6, when David inadvertently invokes a self-curse and proclaims that the guilty rich man should make a fourfold restitution for his crime. Adonijah is now the fourth son of David to experience a violent death, which, despite the murky circumstances of the Solomonic court, creates the impression of a more powerful hand at work.[28]

---

[26] Walter Dietrich, "1 & 2 Kings," in *The Oxford Bible Commentary*, ed. John Barton and John Muddiman (Oxford: Oxford University Press, 2001), 235.

[27] Frank Moore Cross, *Canaanite Myth and Hebrew Epic: Essays in the History of the Religion of Israel* (Cambridge, MA: Harvard University Press, 1973), 237, cited by Wray Beal, *1 & 2 Kings*, 76.

[28] The LXX records a *sevenfold* punishment, with interesting implications for the larger narrative as noted by Jeremy Schipper, "Hezekiah, Manasseh, and Dynastic or Transgenerational Punishment," in *Soundings in Kings: Perspectives and Methods in Contemporary Scholarship*, ed. Mark Leuchter and Klaus-Peter Adam (Minneapolis, MN: Fortress, 2010), 82: "Dtr repeatedly

Another figure not formally appearing on David's hit list is Abiathar, the priest from the house of Eli who backed Adonijah and who is mentioned by Solomon in v. 22 as a member of the faction. Reading between the lines of David's advice, Solomon's treatment of Abiathar suggests that he is eliminating every avenue of potential threat. But in this case, Benaiah's services are not called upon, as Abiathar is sentenced to reside in the town of Anathoth: even though the priest is worthy of death, Solomon asserts, owing to his loyalty to David he will be spared. Since Abiathar is still officially listed as a priest in Solomon's cabinet in 1 Kgs 4:4, it would indicate a political banishment away from Jerusalem (where in short order silver will be of no value; see 10:21). Yet again there is a connection with an antecedent prophetic word, though unlike Adonijah, it is explicitly marked in v. 27, "So Solomon drove out Abiathar from being a priest of the LORD, in order to fulfill the word of the LORD that he spoke concerning the house of Eli at Shiloh." As discussed earlier, an anonymous man of God denounces the Elides in 1 Sam 2:27–36, and Abiathar's exile decades later is the culmination of this prophetic word. Solomon may be acting out of his own self-serving motives, but the event happens to intersect with a more powerful movement and reminds the reader "of the greater story, of which Solomon's kingdom is just a part, the saga of Yahweh's dealings with Israel from exodus to exile."[29] In retrospect, the reader may note that the exile of Abiathar – from a chastened dynastic house, and hoping for a morsel of bread – bears a striking resemblance to

uses various sevenfold formulas to depict dynastic punishment (seven sons, seventy sons, the seventh king) when it narrates the loss of power by Saul, David, and Ahab's descendants."

[29] Nelson, *First and Second Kings*, 27.

the fate of Solomon's descendent Jehoiachin in 2 Kgs 25:27–30, and so despite the king's triumphant rhetoric, there is an implicit warning at this early point in the narrative.

It is unlikely that Joab appreciates any theological nuances in Abiathar's banishment when he hears the report and rightly deduces his vulnerable position: with shades of Adonijah, Joab seeks asylum at the horns of the altar, an increasingly popular site in Solomon's nascent kingdom. The intense scenes in vv. 28–35 provide a telling perspective on the management of the Solomonic regime, starting with Joab's daring invitation to Benaiah – who previously served under Joab, but now has been commissioned to eliminate him – to enter the sanctuary and shed blood, at which the assassin balks. Maximizing the irony, it needs to be said that Joab's legacy has been forged on murders that David did not officially sanction, as dangerous figures such as Abner (2 Sam 3:27) and Amasa (2 Sam 20:10) were executed by Joab without direct authorization by the king. Yet Solomon takes the opposite approach: whereas David may resemble a modern president who makes a career out of plausible deniability or has crucial information not disclosed in order to be shielded from incrimination, Solomon personally equips the hesitant Benaiah with a necessary justification to murder Joab in the sanctuary. Predictably by now, the king loquaciously informs Benaiah that Joab is worthy of death because Abner and Amasa were covertly killed with the sword, and therefore Joab should bear the guilt while "for David and his seed, his house and his throne, there will be peace forever from the LORD." Benaiah evidently is equipped with sufficient legal persuasion, because he strikes Joab down in accordance with the king's words; Joab is then buried at his home in the indeterminate location of "the wilderness," a suitable location for the interment of Solomonic nonconformists. Benaiah's conscience may have been assuaged, but the reader might wonder about the blatant disregard of *tôrāh* or invoking categories like "bloodguilt" to merely advance the royal agenda. The opening segment of 1 Kings highlights the important role of the use of language by royal figures; Solomon makes numerous speeches in his career – he probably deserves the title of the most long-winded monarch in Israel's history – and so the manner in which he speaks will need to be carefully monitored as we proceed.

Just as Zadok is promoted in the wake of Abiathar's exile, so Benaiah is rewarded with Joab's position, and it would appear that upward mobility in the Solomonic economy is earned through acts of allegiance or relational proximity to the king (see 4:11, 15). But before any further promotions, there is still one more demotion in 1 Kings 2, as the final scenes of the chapter turn to the last name on David's list of targets, Shimei of Benjamin. After the slaying of Joab beside the altar, Benaiah's killing of Shimei is comparatively more straightforward, although it occurs a few years later in the story. Indeed, Solomon is rather patient here, probably because the case is tricky: David had sworn an oath to Shimei in 2 Sam 19:23, and it takes time for Solomon to devise a way to circumvent it. Given strict orders not to leave Jerusalem, Shimei agrees to a form of house arrest: "The action is likely a part of monitoring the continuing threat from the north," says Walter Brueggemann, "but the restriction does not hold. Shimei violates parole."[30] When the king learns that Shimei had temporarily left Jerusalem in order to retrieve his runaway slaves from Achish king of Gath in Philistine territory – conjuring memories of David on the run from the manic Saul – Solomon is furnished with his

---

[30] Brueggemann, *1 & 2 Kings*, 36.

necessary excuse, and Shimei is executed by the erstwhile Benaiah. Notably, Solomon accuses Shimei of breaking a sworn oath in v. 42, even though there is no record of any oath sworn by Shimei in the Hebrew text, only an assent to the king's terms. Jerome Walsh also points out that Solomon makes God responsible for the death of Shimei, but "the king's pious invocation of the divine will would be more credible if he had not already decided the issue by royal decree."[31] After he is informed that God has returned evil upon his own head, the last words that Shimei hears ("But King Solomon shall be blessed, and the throne of David shall be established before the LORD forever") are consonant with Solomon's earlier claims after ordering the deaths of Adonijah and Joab. By way of analogy, it may be submitted that Solomon uses words like the (rejected) house of Eli uses implements. Back in 1 Sam 2:13, Eli's sons design an innovative three-pronged fork to increase their share of the offerings; this is the only time that such an instrument is mentioned in the Hebrew Bible, and it becomes a central pillar in their indictment (1 Sam 2:29).[32] Eli's dynasty suffers greatly because they abuse their position of leadership among God's people and commandeer the privileges granted by God for ignoble purposes, inviting a further question of what will happen to David's sons should they be found guilty of equivalent offenses.

---

[31] Walsh, *1 Kings*, 64.
[32] See Keith Bodner, *1 Samuel: A Narrative Commentary*, HBM 19 (Sheffield: Sheffield Phoenix Press, 2008), 31: "It has been noted that the implement 'the hook of three teeth' is not otherwise attested in the Hebrew Bible. Walter Brueggemann [*First and Second Samuel* (Louisville, KY: John Knox Press, 1990), 28] refers to the fork as 'bigger-than-regulation.' Perhaps, then, the fork is an Elide innovation aimed at increasing the priestly portion, and as such, personifies their flippancy."

Following the abrupt termination of Shimei's career, the final sentence of the chapter in v. 46 ("the kingdom was established in the hand of Solomon") may in fact serve to undermine much of Solomon's rhetoric and actions in the chapter because it stands in an uneasy tension with v. 12, "Solomon sat on the throne of David his father, and his kingdom was firmly established." On the one hand, Solomon's actions in 1 Kings 2 are a harbinger of later actions, since ruthless purges are not uncommon in the Israelite monarchy (e.g., 1 Kgs 16:11; 2 Kgs 10:11). On the other hand, the notion that Solomon's kingdom is firmly established prior to any of the executions strongly suggests that the security of his reign was never in question: "He is predestined to succeed by the God who is 'sovereign over the kingdoms of men and gives them to anyone he wishes' (Dan 4:25), 'who sets up kings and deposes them' (Dan 2:21). That is the ultimate reality, no matter what the human players in the drama may think."[33] The reader is thus invited to reflect that Solomon's vicious consolidation of the throne is at odds with his unlikely election as king, a divine choice that is subtly communicated as early as 2 Sam 12:25 through Nathan's delivery of the name Jedidiah ("beloved of the LORD") – strongly suggesting that Solomon's brutality was misguided and unnecessary. Solomon's birth occurs after the darkest failure and arguably the lowest point of David's life, but the announcement of a new name signals a new dynamic in the narrative, illustrating that God has the capacity to redeem or transform even the most egregious of failures. Like the exile itself, even the lowest moment is not outside the aegis of God's redemptive possibility, and despite the sordid events in these opening chapters – replete with self-interested politics and violent efforts to consolidate a throne

---

[33] Iain W. Provan, *1 and 2 Kings*, NIBC 7 (Peabody, MA: Hendrickson, 1995), 37.

that was already established – an audience carrying the scar tissue of exile might nonetheless be able to perceive new contours of divine sovereignty amid wicked human machinations. At the end of 1 Kings 1–2, those readers who may have thought that Babylon (or even Persia or Greece) is the main enemy of God's people might revise their thinking, for this narrative is a sober reminder of other internal forces of disaster. Glancing ahead to what comes next in the story, the most substantial threat to Solomon's kingship will not be opponents such as Joab, siblings such as Adonijah, or even the Egyptian pharaoh; the greatest threat to Solomon's kingship will be Solomon himself.

CHAPTER 3

Palace and Temple

Once Solomon has strengthened his grip on the throne, the next phase of the story moves in some new directions as his kingdom takes on a much more cosmopolitan flavor than at any previous point in Israelite history. Among the issues that surface in 1 Kings 3–10, the key areas for our study include the character of the king and the expansion of the regime's infrastructure. In the first category, examples include Solomon's marriage to Pharaoh's daughter, his dream at Gibeon, the gift of wisdom, and the accumulation of gold and horses – each of which merits some analysis. If, for instance, there was a sense of divine commitment despite moral unworthiness in the opening chapters of 1 Kings, how will this continue as Solomon's career reaches its apogee? As far as the second category, in this chapter the reorganization of the kingdom into more advantageous tax districts and the construction of Solomon's exceptionally ornate palace certainly need to be considered. Moreover, the most dominant architectural project in 1 Kings is the Jerusalem temple, and various questions surface in this section of the story – perhaps most pressingly, how is the building of the temple configured in the text, and how should the temple be theologically interpreted in the wider scope of the narrative?

Palace and Temple 53

FOREIGN ALLIANCE

As has already been noted, the form of the story is significant and needs to be taken into account when studying the text for its theology. Concerning the Christian Bible, Kavin Rowe and Richard Hays remark: "Even given the indisputable and inseparable role of doctrine in the canonical process, the church did not simply draw up lists of crucial beliefs but actually canonized particular texts with particular shapes. The implication would seem to be that the particular form of the writings is constitutive of, rather than incidental to, the theological construal of the whole."[1] The challenge of experiencing the theological import even within the narrative texture of the story continues in the next major installment, for the opening line of 1 Kings 3 is not without controversy: "Then Solomon became a son-in-law to Pharaoh king of Egypt, and he took the daughter of Pharaoh and brought her to the city of David until he finished building his house, the house of the LORD, and the wall surrounding Jerusalem." Placing this event immediately after the internal purge of his opponents indicates Solomon's ongoing concern with security: once he consolidates his kingdom on the inside, his attention shifts to external matters. Becoming a son-in-law to

---

[1] C. Kavin Rowe and Richard B. Hays, "What Is a Theological Commentary?" *Pro Ecclesia* 16 (2007): 31. They also note (p. 32), "Theologians have often complained that commentaries written by biblical scholars have been mere repositories of historical information that fail to illuminate the theological message of the text... the church's great theological commentators – Chrysostom, Augustine, Luther, Calvin, Barth – did not write histories of interpretation. Instead they employed the history of scriptural interpretation in the context of a primary engagement with the biblical texts; their chief aim was not to collect significant statements from the past but to hear the word of God in the text and to articulate it freshly for their own time."

Pharaoh has nothing to do with romance and everything to do with a strategic partnership. David's practice was similar; for instance, in 2 Sam 3:3, he marries the daughter of Talmai king of Geshur, a small kingdom to the northeast of Israel. But Solomon's marriage alliance with Pharaoh is in a completely different league: historians are unsure of the exact identity of this particular pharaoh, but there is general agreement that the Egyptian royal family was not quick to give its daughters away.[2] Consequently, this marriage represents a public relations triumph for Solomon and marks his arrival as a player on the international stage. Later references to Pharaoh's daughter in 7:8 and 9:24 indicate a special residence, implying that Solomon regards her as a trophy wife, so to speak. Still, questions might be raised about the level of influence that Egypt will have in Solomon's kingdom. In 1 Kgs 9:16, it turns out that Pharaoh bequeaths the Israelite city of Gezer as a wedding gift after he conquers it, with the biting irony that Solomon receives his own land from a foreign king.[3] Furthermore, it should be noted that in Deut 7:1–6, intermarriage is presented as far from ideal, with stringent warnings that such relationships invariably bring on apostasy, thus clouding this moment of royal triumph. Steven Weitzman notes that the marriage is less about glamor and more of an ominous portent that surrounds Solomon's reign:

> For ancient Israelites, however, the memory of Egyptian rule was colored by the story of the Exodus, in which the Pharaoh emerges as the arch-villain, and in this context the parallel

---

[2] J. Gray, *I & II Kings*, 2nd edn., OTL (London: SCM, 1970), 118–19.
[3] See Sweeney, *I & II Kings*, 79: "This is a stunning role reversal in the DtrH – that is, an Israelite king who depends upon the Egyptian pharaoh to complete the conquest of the land of Israel."

between Solomon and Pharaoh takes on a very specific significance, casting Solomon in the worst possible light. Solomon's reign was supposed to be the culmination of the Exodus. The Israelites had reached Canaan many generations earlier, but it was only now, thanks to Solomon's success in securing the borders of Israel and building a house for God, that it can feel fully settled in the land, fully at home in the Promised Land. By aligning himself with Egypt, however – marrying the daughter of a pharaoh, trading in Egyptian horses, behaving like a pharaoh himself – Solomon not only spoils the redemptive ending of the Exodus story, he reverses it, forcing his people to relive its bondage in Egypt.[4]

Building on this comment, Solomon may not be guilty of causing the people of Israel to return to Egypt, but a case could be made that he is certainly on course to bring Egypt to them. For the moment, though, interpreters have puzzled over this initial section of chapter 3 because not only is there no overt narrative condemnation for Solomon's marriage, but also the announcement is followed in vv. 2–3 by a seeming commendation that Solomon loved God, which is immediately qualified: "However, the people were sacrificing on the high places because the house for the name of the LORD had not been built to that point. And Solomon loved the LORD, walking in the prescribed tasks of David his father; however, on the high places he was sacrificing and burning incense." It would be a challenge to find a section of Kings with more caveats than this short passage, and it underscores something important about the king: he walks in the statutes, but also sacrifices at the high places. At this particular moment in time, the high places may

---

[4] Weitzman, *Solomon: The Lure of Wisdom*, 96.

not be overtly negative, but as the story progresses they become increasingly ambivalent.⁵ The same might be applied to Solomon himself: at this particular juncture he has not abandoned the faith, but syncretism will increasingly move to the fore. One might further argue that the trajectory of Solomon's own life will be mirrored in the people: "Solomon's own life sets the pattern for what happens in the life of Judah later in the narrative. He begins by sitting lightly to God's law, tolerating worship of the LORD at the high places (3:2; cf. 1 Kgs 22:43; 2 Kgs 12:3; 14:4; 15:4, 35), and he ends up being drawn into full-blown apostasy at them (11:7–8; cf. 2 Kgs 18:4; 21:3–9)."⁶ At the outset of 1 Kings 3, it nonetheless appears that matters remain open-ended, and despite a conflicted start to his career and the problematic optics of the alliance with Egypt, it is not too late. He is several years into his reign, but Solomon still will be given every chance to succeed – nowhere is this more evident than in the dream sequence at Gibeon.

---

⁵ For assessment of a "high place" (*bāmāh*) as a public shrine constructed on a promontory having some continuity with Canaanite religious traditions, see William G. Dever, "Archaeology and the Question of Sources in Kings," in *The Books of Kings: Sources, Composition, Historiography and Reception*, ed. Baruch Halpern, André Lemaire and Matthew J. Adams, VTSup 129 (Leiden: Brill, 2010), 517–38 (535–36).

⁶ Provan, *1 and 2 Kings*, 48. With the forthcoming storyline in mind, Provan (p. 46) summarizes: "First Kings 3:1–3 presents us, then, with a Solomon who loves God – who does share his father David's basic commitment to God (3:3) – but who right at the beginning of his reign also carries with him the seeds of his own destruction. His lack of wholeheartedness, already outlined here, will eventually become fully evident (11:4), and in the end his lack of personal unity or integrity will be the catalyst, not only for his own apostasy but also for the fracturing of Israelite unity that we shall read about in chapters 11–12."

Palace and Temple 57

DISPENSING WISDOM

The remainder of 1 Kings 3 unfolds two episodes where wisdom and testing are prominent. First, vv. 4-15 present the famous event at Gibeon, where God invites Solomon to ask for whatever he wants. Eschewing the obvious choices of riches or long life – surely the route most kings would opt for – Solomon instead asks for "a listening heart," or, in an alternative rendering, "an obedient mind" (*lēb shōmēaʾ*). Bearing in mind the recent executions and his marriage to Pharaoh's daughter, this is quite a request for Solomon to make: "The prayer for 'a listening heart' is not simply that he should be made clever or discerning, but that he be attuned to Yahweh's guidance and purpose for justice. Thus the new king wants to have the sensitivity and wisdom to order Israel's life by the will of Yahweh."[7] Under the circumstances, this has to be considered the right choice: in the most explicit declaration of divine feeling to this point in the book, v. 10 records that Solomon's response is upright in the eyes of God, an inversion of the chaotic final sentence in the book of Judges (21:25) and a strong marker that Solomon's reign has an unprecedented opportunity to flourish. Because the king has not asked for wealth or the death of his enemies – although there are not many of those left internally, so external enemies must be in view – God grants his request and more: Solomon will have not only unequalled wisdom and discernment, but also honor, riches and long life, although the latter is predicated on walking in God's ways. Solomon then awakens from the dream and returns to Jerusalem and stands before the ark of the covenant (1 Kgs 3:15), on the threshold of great possibility.

---

[7] Brueggemann, *1 & 2 Kings*, 48-49.

As recently as 1 Sam 28:6, dreams are mentioned as a mode of divine revelation. In Saul's case, God chooses not to answer by dreams or any other mechanism, but Solomon does receive the favor of an unmediated word from God in 1 Kings 3. To be sure, this is not the last time he will hear directly from God, but it is certainly the most positive instance, since God's words in 6:11–3 and 9:2–9 are fraught with warning. But in 1 Kings 3, the situation is more optimistic, and commentators are often impressed with Solomon's request for a listening heart: whether the king is tacitly acknowledging that it was unwise to marry Pharaoh's daughter is uncertain, but his expressed desire to judge God's people with equity and differentiate between good and evil is surely laudable. But as Terence Fretheim explains, there may be a catch: "In effect, Solomon himself sets the standards by which his own rule will be judged, finally in negative terms. His rule is a good illustration of the disjunction between intention and action (see Rom 7:15–23)."[8] Regardless of the final verdict, this episode illustrates that Solomon undoubtedly knows the right thing to do and that God is pleased with his request, even amid all the murkiness in his reign so far. Even with the divine pleasure, there is still a measure of testing in God's lengthy response surrounding the length of days allotted to the king: "But it is precisely those days that are shadowed. Unlike the other gifts God grants Solomon, 'length of days' is conditional. 'If you walk in my ways,' says the Lord, 'then I will lengthen your days.' This 'if' sounds a cautionary note in an otherwise unrestrained celebration of divine bounty."[9] In other words, Solomon has rightly responded to God's invitation and asked for a listening heart, but he will need to continue listening if he is to live a long and faithful life as Israel's king. He has been

---

[8] Fretheim, *First and Second Kings*, 31. [9] Walsh, *1 Kings*, 76.

given incomparable gifts, but can he maintain fidelity for the duration of his reign? Solomon's wisdom, as promised, will be vast – he even has the wisdom to sift out a lying prostitute – but will he also apply this wisdom in examining his own heart? The second event in 1 Kgs 3:16–28 furthers the theme of wisdom in this section of the story and showcases the wisdom of Solomon in action through a situation involving two prostitutes. The case is difficult, for in the absence of any witnesses, the king needs to discern who is lying. Calling for a sword – indeed, the first use of the sword that does not involve dispatching an enemy so far in the story – should probably be interpreted as the king's strategy for finding the true mother: "Solomon's proposed solution successfully arouses the compassion of the mother of the living child. Her compassion is a deeply felt emotion (the same phrase appears in Gen 43:30; Hos 11:8). Here the phrase is particularly appropriate, for 'compassion' (*raḥămîm*) shares the same root as 'womb' (*reḥem*), thus emphasizing her compassion arises out of her mother-love."[10] In the final line of the chapter, the people hear the report and fear the king, realizing he has been given divine wisdom "to enact justice." Herein lies Solomon's task: he has made a remarkable judicial ruling, and now his challenge is to transact justice in the land. An intriguing trend in recent commentary on 1 Kgs 3:16–28 is to view the harlots in symbolic fashion. Arguing for a series of links between this episode and the later secession of Israel and Judah in 1 Kings 12, Matthew Michael contends: "Within this reading, in a concealed way, the voices/speeches of the prostitutes arguing over the living child appear to foreshadow the rift and conflict between the northern

---

[10] Wray Beal, *1 & 2 Kings*, 88; cf. Dietrich, "1 & 2 Kings," 236.

and southern kingdoms."[11] If this is plausible, then it stands to reason that one of Solomon's central tests will be equity between Judah and northern Israel, avoiding the kind of partiality that will create an irreparable breach: he has the wisdom to discern between two harlots, so fairness between north and south should be within his repertoire. It is probably not coincidental that the narrative is structured so that right after this judicial episode is a catalogue of Solomon's organization of the kingdom, decidedly imbalanced and tilted toward the south.

ADMINISTRATIVE MOVES

When the theatrics and dialogue with the prostitutes draw to a close, there is an apparent shift in genre as 1 Kgs 4:1–19 carefully delineates various lists of royal officials distributed throughout the land. Yet in spite of the archival feel and seeming lack of any plotline, there are several details that should not be overlooked in this section, since it reveals potential cracks in the foundation of the Solomonic edifice. By way of example, there are some familiar and expected names on the cabinet roster in vv. 1–6, such as Benaiah (who replaced Joab after the latter's demise) and Zadok (whose ascendancy is complete after the banishment of Abiathar,

---

[11] Matthew Michael, "The Two Prostitutes or the Two Kingdoms? A Critical Reading of King Solomon's Wise Ruling (1 Kgs 3:16–28)," *HBT* 37 (2015): 79. Cf. Daniel J. Hays, "Has the Narrator Come to Praise Solomon or to Bury Him? Narrative Subtlety in 1 Kings 1–11," *JSOT* 28 (2003): 164–65: "Is the child symbolic? Are the prostitutes symbolic? It may be significant to note that the majority of usages of the term prostitute (*zōnah*) in the Hebrew Bible are figurative references to apostasy, specifically the phenomenon of Israel chasing after foreign gods. In the context of the upcoming civil war between Judah and Israel, the struggle for the throne, and the immediate lapse into foreign idolatry, this story is rather suggestive."

Palace and Temple   61

who remains on the official register, though not in the court). But the last name on this list is a point of concern: Adoniram, in charge of forced labor. First mentioned as one of David's appointees back in 2 Sam 20:24, Adoniram has an enormously long career in the service of three different monarchs. Forebodingly, the term for "forced labor" (*mas*) is used for Israelite slavery in Exodus 1; in light of the heavy construction to come under Solomon's leadership, it raises the question of whether the king will conscript foreign labor or resemble an Egyptian tyrant by forcing Israelites to build royal projects.[12] Such enterprises will be expensive, and this may help explain why the kingdom is reorganized in vv. 7-19, where scholars point out that Solomon modifies Israel's traditional tribal arrangement into more favorable taxation districts.[13] Several governors of these districts have a rather close relationship to Solomon, again suggesting that proximity to the king carries certain privileges. Furthermore, the reader would have to search very hard for any reference to Judah among these districts, causing some to infer that Judah is exempt from the same taxation scheme applied to the rest of Israel.[14] If Solomon is cavalier with Israel's boundaries and

---

[12] See Christoph Berner, "The Egyptian Bondage and Solomon's Forced Labor: Literary Connections between Exodus 1-15 and 1 Kings 1-12?" in *Pentateuch, Hexateuch, or Enneateuch: Identifying Literary Works in Genesis through Kings*, ed. Thomas B. Dozeman, Thomas Römer and Konrad Schmid (Atlanta, GA: Society of Biblical Literature, 2011), 211-40.

[13] E.g., Mordechai Cogan, *I Kings: A New Translation with Introduction and Commentary*, AB 10 (New York: Doubleday, 2001), 205-11. Cf. Seow, "The First and Second Books of Kings," 55: "He seems to undermine traditional sociopolitical structures in order to ensure his influence throughout his domain, now reorganized into fiscal regions to support the prodigious expenses of his palace and his military machinery."

[14] Cf. Walsh, *1 Kings*, 87.

showing partiality to his own tribe of Judah, both of these issues will be of grave concern to his successor.

Those interpreters desiring a positive portrayal of Solomon may well turn to the second half of 1 Kings 4 for support, as vv. 20–28 repeatedly stress the stability of the kingdom and vv. 29–34 describe the amazing scope of Solomon's knowledge. Although there are reasons to congratulate Solomon in this section, there are also caution signs woven into the text. The reader does not have to be cynical or overly subtle to discern these signs, for it could be argued that the story is deliberately composed so as to provide a more veiled critique of the monarch, and it may require wisdom to hear the unfolding theology. It could be suggested, for example, that the territorial holdings stretching from the Egyptian border to the Euphrates River redound to the king's credit, but the geographical specifications suggest it is God's doing in accordance with past promises (e.g., Gen 15:18) rather than Solomon's individual achievement. Furthermore, the king's table certainly would impress leaders from the surrounding nations and is duly supplied with heaping amounts of food by the district governors. But in 1 Kgs 5:13, Solomon will conscript a labor force of thirty thousand Israelites, and although the matter is qualified in 9:22 where it is maintained that no Israelites were made slaves, the northern tribes are deeply aggrieved in 1 Kgs 12:1–7.[15] Meanwhile, an immense retinue of horses and chariots helps to ensure the security of the kingdom, but as we will discuss later, such a cavalry is deeply at odds with Deut 17:16–17. As 1 Kings 4 ends, the knowledge of Solomon is without rival and draws visitors from many nations. Of course, this breadth of mind is an

---

[15] Nelson, *First and Second Kings*, 43.

outworking of the gift of God, and his speeches on plant life and the animal world are reminiscent of Adam in Eden. In fact, scholars have recently suggested that there are evocative parallels between Solomon and Adam, and John Davies summarizes as follows:

> A fruitful way of doing justice to the complex data the book of Kings provides on Solomon is to see him as an Adam figure who on the one hand typifies a fulfillment of aspirations for a restored Eden, while on the other hand being responsible, through his disobedience, for a second expulsion from the sanctuary-land and the end of the monarchy – that is, the loss of Yahweh's visible rule and protection, and of Israel's dignity among the nations. Through such a portrayal, the writer keeps alive the prospect of a new Adam in a new creation beyond the covenant failure presided over by Solomon.[16]

In this same vein, there are intriguing points of correspondence between the imagery of the Garden of Eden and the Jerusalem temple, and 1 Kings 5 formally begins the story of the temple by narrating Solomon's extensive negotiations with Hiram of Tyre to secure the building materials.[17] Scant information was provided when Solomon becomes a son-in-law to Pharaoh at the outset of chapter 3, but there is an array of detail with Hiram, as all of chapter 5 is devoted to the correspondence between the two kings leading up to the deal and the aftermath of the transaction. For the purposes of this study, several points need to be emphasized. As we note, 1 Kings 5 is the first time Solomon himself directly mentions the temple, and it is in dialogue with a foreign monarch. Hiram had earlier sent materials for David's house (2 Sam 5:11), so

---

[16] John A. Davies, "Discerning between Good and Evil: Solomon as a New Adam in 1 Kings," *WTJ* 73 (2011): 40.
[17] Weitzman, *Solomon: The Lure of Wisdom*, 85.

he probably senses another opportunity with David's successor. But Solomon's explanation to Hiram about why David did not build the temple is inconsistent with 2 Samuel 7, and instead of articulating that the God of Israel is beyond the need of any physical dwelling place, he boasts about his own peaceful borders and absence of any opposition.[18] It is clear that Solomon is keen to secure the famed cedars of Lebanon – no doubt wanting the best possible material for the house of God's name – but not mentioned here is the fact that Solomon also will build his own house, which as it turns out takes nearly twice as long to build as the temple (7:1) and eventually is named "the house of the Forest of Lebanon" (e.g., 7:2, 10:21). Under the banner of temple building, it would seem that the king has numerous projects in mind and is willing to pay the steep price of supplying Hiram's royal table with food every year. Adoniram ensures that the forced labor crews meet the quota requirements, as Hiram and Solomon cement their alliance. For at least the second time, Solomon enters into a pact with a foreign king. He has inched toward becoming like Pharaoh, and now the influence of Tyre might creep even into the heart of Israelite worship. There is no outright condemnation of Solomon here, but the reader may pause: "Moreover, the 'cedars of Lebanon' are named in v. 13 as an emblem of pride and arrogance. More extensively, Isaiah 23 and Ezekiel 26–28 view Tyre, later on, as a trading operation modelling autonomy, arrogance, self-indulgence, and indifference to any moral, covenantal dimension of reality. Solomon's engagement with Hiram, in the

---

[18] Cf. Hays, "Has the Narrator Come to Praise Solomon or to Bury Him?" 166: "Solomon refers back to Yahweh's covenant with David in 2 Samuel 7 as part of his rationale for building the temple. However, Solomon seriously misquotes the situation and the words of Yahweh as recorded in 2 Samuel 7."

context of prophetic faith, is to be viewed with deep alarm, as sure to distort the community."[19]

THE TEMPLE COMPLEX

Chapter 5 describes the preparation for building the temple, but 1 Kings 6–7 provide the story of its construction in elaborate detail, along with a brief digression to narrate the schematics of the royal palace. The point of view in much of this stretch of the text is configured as a ground-level tour of the Jerusalem temple, as though personally conducted by the king with a wealth of luxurious specificity. Such a tour is not surprising given the status of the temple in Israel's cultural memory: if we imagine an audience in exile hearing these details of the temple, perhaps there is a wistful sense of paradise lost, as they once possessed this Eden-like sanctuary, but it was forfeited due to collective malfeasance. The term "paradise" is not an overstatement, since the temple is replete with cosmic symbolism that ranges from the standing pillars of stability named Jachin ("he establishes") and Boaz ("strength"), to the twelve oxen and sculpted cherubim, precious metals and floral imagery from creation that highlight God's fecundity, to the molten sea that points to the control of chaos: "In some basic sense the temple is viewed as a world in

---

[19] Brueggemann, *1 & 2 Kings*, 78; see also Seow, "The First and Second Books of Kings," 58: "Despite the allusion to Solomon's wisdom (vv. 7, 12), the alliance foreshadows the problems the kingdom will soon face. Solomon notes that God has given him peace and that he has neither adversaries nor misfortunes. Yet, because of his alliances with outsiders, his kingdom will soon be threatened by one adversary after another (11:14, 23)." Cf. Dietrich, "1 & 2 Kings," 237: "The core of the reports is surely correct, given that (unpaid!) forced labour is later the cause of the kingdom's partition (I Kings 12)."

microcosm, well-ordered and secure, in which the God who dwells in the cosmos becomes intensely present for Israel. In the temple and its worship, a world is re-created in the midst of the chaos of Israel's larger experience."[20] It is of great consequence that the timing of this project is highlighted at the outset in the opening sentence of 1 Kings 6: "Four hundred and eighty years after the Israelites came out from the land of Egypt, in the month of Ziv (that is, the second month) of the fourth year of Solomon's reign, he built the house of the LORD." This chronological reckoning thus locates the temple at roughly the midpoint of Israel's history between rescue from Egyptian slavery and the forthcoming Babylonian captivity.[21] Moreover, two different calendars are conflated in this verse, with the traditional Canaanite agricultural calendar (Ziv) combined with Babylonian nomenclature (the second month): it is as if one calendar remembers the oppression of Egypt, while the other calendar anticipates the Babylonian exile. In all likelihood, there was some silent opposition or resistance to the idea of a fixed temple among various constituencies within Israel, but in the context of the book of Kings, its construction at the halfway point functions as a kind of midterm evaluation. For all the compromises so far in Israel's history and Solomon's career, could it be that the future is open-ended from God's perspective and the people are free to worship and be defined by the symbols of the temple and its appurtenances instead of by the ideologies of the surrounding nations?

[20] Fretheim, *First and Second Kings*, 41. Note also Jon D. Levenson, "The Temple and the World," *JR* 64 (1984): 297: "The world which the Temple incarnates in a tangible way is not the world of history but the world of creation, the world not as it is but as it was meant to be and as it was on the first Sabbath."
[21] Nelson, *First and Second Kings*, 47–48.

The tour of the temple is interrupted, however, by a sobering divine word in 1 Kgs 6:11-13 as God speaks to Solomon without mediation: "This house which you are building: if you walk in my statutes, exercise my judgments, and guard all my commandments by walking in them, then I will establish my word with you, that I spoke to David your father. I will dwell in the midst of the Israelites, and I will not abandon my people Israel." Various Israelites and foreign dignitaries may be impressed by the grandeur of the temple, but God makes no comment on the effort or the expense involved in its construction. Instead, there is a clear condition attached to any divine presence in the building: if the king is faithful, God's word will be established. This incomparable structure certainly provides no guarantee for Solomon: "The presence of the Temple will not ensure the dynasty's stability, nor will it bring about God's presence in Israel's midst. Only obedience will."[22] When he awoke after the dream at Gibeon, Solomon's response was to offer sacrifices in the presence of the ark in Jerusalem. Here in 1 Kings 6, by contrast, Solomon has no recorded response at all to the divine word. Solomon has already shown himself rather loquacious, but his silence – whether out of humility or seeming indifference is not stated – is disconcerting. The "tour" of the temple duly continues, as though somewhat oblivious to the gravity of the divine communiqué, but there is another digression at the beginning of chapter 7. On this occasion, it is not a divine word of interruption but rather a description of the palace of which the temple seems to be a part. The organization of the narrative is striking: "Almost by chance, we learn that the temple is integrated into a larger complex of government buildings. Going by the construction period and

---

[22] Seow, "The First and Second Books of Kings," 62.

its measurements, the temple can hardly have been more than a palace chapel."[23] While it might be possible to accuse Solomon of subsuming the temple with the larger network of palace buildings, v. 8 certainly underscores the separate house for Pharaoh's daughter. Commenting that the preferable translation of the underlying Hebrew text would be "Solomon *was* also *to make* a house like this hall for Pharaoh's daughter," Jerome Walsh emphasizes the importance of the syntax: "This interruption within an interruption points to a motif that runs through the entire Solomon story: his entanglements with foreign women and the disaster they eventually bring upon him."[24] Altogether, the tour of the temple is punctuated with various kinds of warning signs and red flags, and such warnings do not abate in the next section of the story; in fact, many of them will be voiced by Solomon himself.

DEDICATION CEREMONY

In Gen 2:1–2, the work of creation is "finished" (*kālāh*), and by analogy the work of the temple is likewise finished (*kālāh*) in 1 Kings 6–7 using the same verb. With the task complete, Solomon concludes the enterprise by depositing all the valuables accumulated by David into the treasuries of God's house (7:51). There is

---

[23] Dietrich, "1 & 2 Kings," 238. Cf. Hays, "Has the Narrator Come to Praise Solomon or to Bury Him?" 169: "The location and centrality of the temple in Solomon's new camp is quite different than the role and centrality that the tabernacle played in Moses' camp."

[24] Walsh, *1 Kings*, 106. Note also Seow, "The First and Second Books of Kings," 68: "If only in an implicit way, the text raises some questions about Solomon's worldly ambition (7:1–12). It was not for purely altruistic and pious reasons that the Temple was built so gloriously. It is a reflection of the vanity of Solomon and the dangerously compromising character of his reign."

an atmosphere of triumph here, yet in a very short time – barely five years after Solomon's death – Shishak king of Egypt will pilfer the same treasuries and humiliate the son of Solomon, despite the high-profile marriage alliance sealed earlier between the two nations. Prior to any Egyptian despoliation, however, Solomon presides over a lengthy liturgical sequence in 1 Kings 8, starting with the installation of the ark of the covenant in the heart of the most holy place. The timing of the ark's procession is notable, taking place nearly a year after the temple's completion during the Feast of Booths, when a sizeable crowd in Jerusalem could safely be assured.[25] Apart from Solomon's motives for choosing this date, the crowd is treated to an uncommon spectacle, as divine glory fills the house with echoes of the tabernacle of old in Exodus 40. There may have been some controversy and dubious moments so far in Solomon's reign, but the divine presence in the temple indicates that God is willing to provide every opportunity for the temple to be a success.

Solomon has not only assembled the elders of Israel, but he also gathers the heads of Israel's tribes (rather than tax districts) for this unprecedented occasion. There are also ample priests on hand, but it is the king who dominates the proceedings. While Solomon might be criticized for exercising such authority in this sacral setting, it undoubtedly allows him to frontload his particular agenda during these festivities. As it turns out, the king is the only speaker here, and this chapter features the highest concentration of direct speech by any figure of Israelite royalty in the Deuteronomistic History. In vv. 15–21, the king's oration reiterates

---

[25] Robert Alter, *Ancient Israel: The Former Prophets: Joshua, Judges, Samuel, and Kings: A Translation with Commentary* (New York: W. W. Norton, 2013), 634.

the impetus and background for building the temple that started with David and is now completed by his successor, under the aegis of the covenant set in motion through the events of the exodus. But the longest narrated event within the ceremony is Solomon's sweeping prayer in vv. 23–53 – the most comprehensive prayer in the entire book of Kings – mainly structured in the form of "seven petitions that reflect the language of blessing and curse in Deuteronomy 28–30."[26] There is a wide stream of scholarly debate on this exceptionally long prayer, with scholars often postulating a composite text that reflects a theological debate spanning multiple generations.[27] While worthy of an independent and meticulous analysis, for this study there are several intriguing points that emerge from Solomon's prayer. In the first instance, the prayer is important within the king's overall characterization. Nowhere are his rhetorical skills on greater display than in this grand synthesis that weaves together various aspects of Israelite tradition in a way that is applicable to different segments of the community across time periods and circumstances of God's people. In more personal terms, Solomon does note the conditionality that his father David raises in 1 Kgs 2:4, so these words do carry an acute sense of warning (see 8:25–26). In the larger context of the Deuteronomistic History, it is important that it is a king who is praying here, and praying in this way, acknowledging conditions: like the temple, institutional kingship is ultimately provisional, and the exiles will depend on the abiding theological truths of this prayer as they seek to navigate a return to the land and begin to rebuild their broken world.

---

[26] Sweeney, *I & II Kings*, 133.
[27] E.g., Montgomery and Gehman, *Kings*, 185–88.

As far as the spatial capacity of the temple, Solomon acknowledges that it cannot "contain" God, as even the highest heavens are inadequate. At the outset of his speeches in vv. 12–13, Solomon states, "The LORD has said that he would dwell in the thick cloud. I have indeed built you an exalted house, a place for you to dwell in forever." Lest this be misunderstood by his immediate audience, God's dwelling is qualified in the prayer so as to dispel the notion that God is limited to a single locale. In other words, Solomon's characterization of God in this prayer is worth attending to, for he tacitly admits that the temple is only a partial approximation. Much more dynamic and unrestricted, God's freedom cannot be curtailed; if those in exile have a deficient view of God, then elements of this prayer provide a necessary corrective and outline a more expansive view of God's mobility and transcendence. Furthermore, Solomon's prayer reminds the people that failure is not the end of the story, and the possibility of restoration after collective disobedience that results in being led away as captives to a foreign land is clearly emphasized. For an exilic audience, this would carry a certain poignancy, and even after destruction there is a message of hope. The king's prayer concludes, and the festivities draw to a close with a dismissal in vv. 62–66 as all the Israelites return to their tents: "This picture of a happy, unified kingdom stretching from Egypt to the Euphrates very much corresponds to the picture in chapter 4. It will not be very long now, however, before Israelites will be found going 'to their tents' for a very different reason and in a very different mood."[28] Dedicating the temple has been an impressive performance that might even be inspiring, but its

---

[28] Provan, *1 and 2 Kings*, 82–83.

force is rather blunted by a divine word and a series of disclosures in the next segment of the story.

The general reaction to Solomon's performance in chapter 8 is reported to be gladness and joy, as one would expect in a tightly controlled regime where there is no expressed dissent among the populace. However, in 1 Kgs 9:1–9, another divine word again comes to Solomon without mediation: in the previous chapter, the king spoke voluminously about the temple, but now God appears to Solomon and addresses the same subject along with a searching declaration for the monarch. In addition to the dream at Gibeon, we recall that God also spoke to Solomon in 1 Kgs 6:11–13 just as temple construction began, with a warning threaded amid words of promise. Now with the temple completed at the outset of chapter 9, there is another oracle, albeit a longer and more structured one with three interwoven movements. First, God provides an assurance in v. 3 that Solomon's prayer has been heard and that God's "eyes and heart" will always remain committed. In light of the tension between divine mobility and the fixity of the temple, such unwavering commitment is remarkable. Second, vv. 4–5 are a personal challenge to the king: if he walks before God as David did, then his throne will be established like David. On the one hand, this is a conditional and sobering pledge: "Just because Yahweh swears devotion to the temple does not mean the same unconditional commitment of Yahweh applies to Solomon or to the dynasty."[29] On the other hand, maintaining integrity and faithfully executing God's statutes do not sound overly burdensome in this context and are surely achievable. God makes a clarion call to responsibility – indirectly reminding Solomon of the position of trust held by the

---

[29] Brueggemann, *1 & 2 Kings*, 121.

king – but it is a startling offer nonetheless, for he can enjoy a standing that approximates that of his father.

Third, vv. 6–9 unfold a multilayered caveat that outlines the implications for either Solomon or his sons spurning this offer and turning aside from the commandments. If they follow after other gods, not only can they expect to be cut off from the land, but also the recently sanctified temple will become a pile of rubble and Israel will become a "proverb" among the nations: "This threat against land and temple strikes at the very center of Israel's existence. The threat echoes ironically the good news of verse 3 by reversing its promise ('my eyes will be there') into a threat ('I will cast out of my sight,' v. 7; literally, 'send away from my face')."[30] Recalling that Solomon's prayer made special provision for the foreigner in 8:41–43, it is not without irony that in God's remark, a central voice is that of the foreigner who articulates the central question of theodicy ("Why did the LORD do this to this land and this temple?") only to provide an answer to the question and explain why such evil has befallen them: they abandoned the God of the exodus, and thus there is a causal connection between exile and suffering. In terms of the narrative organization, therefore, moments after the temple is completed in all its glorious and detailed array, a strong warning is voiced by God about the possibility of its destruction. Forming a counterpoint to the divine

---

[30] Nelson, *First and Second Kings*, 61; note his further summary: "Both the conditionalized promise of verses 4–5 and the frightful threat of verses 6–9 are sobering reminders that fidelity and obedience do not become optional for those who live under God's gracious promise (v. 3). The New Testament too insists that God's grace is not a license to sin (Rom 6:12). Life under promise is instead the context for 'faith working through love' (Gal. 5:6). Lest this text become an occasion for proclaiming moralism and legalistic coercion, however, the reader must remember that God's gracious promises always come first (3:11–14; 8:15–16, 20)" (ibid., 62).

word in chapter 3 – where Solomon is given incomparable gifts and also a test – this communiqué in chapter 9 forebodingly sketches the consequences of seeking other gods and the ensuing national disaster in the form of a ruined temple and the people becoming a byword. Despite three separate divine addresses to Solomon distributed at successive points in the narrative with ample opportunity for amendment, the reader senses that time might be running out for David's heir.

GOLD AND HORSES

There is no response from Solomon to the latest divine word after the dedication of the temple. It is possible that the king takes the message seriously, but on the basis of the remainder of chapter 9, such an inference is difficult to sustain. In 1 Kgs 9:10–28, transactions with foreign kings and related royal business are featured, and the combined effect of the data creates a "sense of irony that amounts to an understated but clear critique of the monarchy."[31] On the basis of chapter 8 and the exhaustive dedication ceremony, it might be expected that the temple would dominate the rest of the Solomon narrative. But other than some oblique references – mainly in a summary of the king's practices of sacrifice – there is little mention of the temple in 1 Kings 9, and it is overshadowed by the palace and international initiatives. Considerably more attention, for example, is devoted to a real estate deal with Hiram of Tyre, who previously supplied the king with building materials for the temple. Among other payments, Hiram is given twenty cities in the northern Galilee region, though he seems perturbed about their quality. Whether the cities are inferior is beside the

---

[31] Brueggemann, *1 & 2 Kings*, 121.

point, because Solomon's concession of land to a foreign king is a dangerous precedent by any measure: "What does Solomon do about the inheritance or property rights of the inhabitants of these cities? In a story that is hurtling downward toward the complete exile of the people from the land, Solomon's casual release of 20 cities is ominous."[32] Later in 1 Kgs 9:26–28, Solomon and Hiram cooperate in a seafaring enterprise, a lucrative venture that yields upward of 420 talents of gold. Given the characteristic Israelite aversion to the sea or shipbuilding endeavors, overcoming such antipathy to partner with Hiram underlines Solomon's commitment to procuring such cargo.[33] Of course, God promises Solomon uncommon wealth (*'āšer*) earlier in 3:13, and so the various acquisitions listed in 2 Kings 9–10 point to the fulfillment of the promise. But the vast amount of gold raises another issue, because Deut 17:16–17 – the passage that adumbrates the duties of the king – specifically warns about the accumulation of gold: "The king, moreover, must not acquire great numbers of horses for himself or make the people return to Egypt to get more of them, for the LORD has told you, 'You are not to go back that way again.' He must not take many wives, or his heart will be led astray. He must not accumulate large amounts of silver and gold." Copious quantities of gold are mentioned in chapter 9, and there is even more to come in the second half of chapter 10, so we will return to this matter after briefly considering a unique visit from a mysterious head of state.

---

[32] Hays, "Has the Narrator Come to Praise Solomon or to Bury Him?" 171.
[33] Jill Middlemas, "Ships and Other Seafaring Vessels in the Old Testament," in *Let Us Go Up to Zion: Essays in Honour of H. G. M. Williamson on the Occasion of his Sixty-Fifth Birthday*, ed. Iain Provan and Mark J. Boda, VTSup 153 (Leiden: Brill, 2012), 407–21.

Numerous royal dignitaries have paid a visit to Solomon's kingdom – e.g., 1 Kgs 4:34, "people of all nations came to hear the wisdom of Solomon, and from all the kings of the earth, who had heard of his wisdom" – but the most famous and enchanting has to be the Queen of Sheba, who arrives from an elusive locale with caravans of gold and finery in order to probe Israel's king with hard questions. The extra-biblical fame of the queen is hardly equaled – she has generated a plethora of speculation, usually of the more amorous variety – and she is mentioned in the New Testament as an earnest seeker who is a foil to the hard-hearted: "The Queen of the South will rise up with the men of this generation at the judgment and condemn them, because she came from the ends of the earth to hear the wisdom of Solomon; and behold, something greater than Solomon is here" (Luke 11:31; cf. Matt 12:42). It could also be argued that the queen is a foil to Solomon himself on several levels in 1 Kings 10, not least in the fact that she is impressed with the glittering externals and takes for granted – perhaps like the reader – that Solomon's heart is equally faithful: "Perhaps, then, the author of 1 Kings gives more attention to the queen than to any other of Solomon's visitors because he knows that we will recognize ourselves in her; her mind wants to know the secret of things but does so in the limited way our minds do, without the illumination of divine wisdom, confined to the realm of observable experience."[34] Her theological appraisal in 10:9 includes the assumption that Solomon is executing righteousness and justice throughout the realm, but it sounds faintly ironic in light of the forced labor referred to in 9:15 and the

---

[34] Weitzman, *Solomon: The Lure of Wisdom*, 138. Note also Susanne Gillmayr-Bucher, "'She Came to Test Him with Hard Questions': Foreign Women and Their View on Israel," *BibInt* 15 (2007): 135–50.

accompanying references to Pharaoh and his daughter. The queen's speech has some similarities with Hiram's courtly rhetoric in 5:7, except that he had much more to gain economically from an alliance with Solomon, whereas the queen gives abundant commodities along with 120 talents of gold as her visit draws to a close. Even so, her lavish gift pales in comparison to Solomon's annual income as disclosed in the rest of 1 Kings 10 (vv. 14–15; 28–29):

> Now the weight of gold that came to Solomon in one year was six hundred and sixty-six talents of gold, besides what came from the merchants, goods from the traders, from all the kings of Arabia and governors of the land... Horses were acquired for Solomon from Egypt and Kue, and the king's traders procured them from Kue for a price. A chariot was exported from Egypt for six hundred shekels of silver, and a horse for one hundred and fifty. By means of the king's traders they sold them to all the Hittite and Aramean kings.

The revenue streams and opulence of Solomon's domain are without equal in the book of Kings, and 1 Kgs 10:14–29 delineates a wealth of detail and innovative uses for the income that range from the acquisition of exotic pets and decorating of the ivory throne to accoutrements such as drinking vessels and a fleet of Tarshish ships. There is little doubt about the creative and innovative ideas for these products, but a larger concern exists with how the prosperity is directed: "We read about his accumulation of wealth for himself and his acquisition of horses. Indeed, Solomon had become a king just like those of the other nations, thus contrary to the deuteronomic ideal of the faithful king (Deut 17:14–20; 1 Sam 8:1–18)."[35] Because of the gold that is foreshadowed

---

[35] Seow, "The First and Second Books of Kings," 87. Cf. Nelson, *First and Second Kings*, 67: "When read as a whole against the contextual background of Deuteronomy, this text develops into a critique of national pride, high

in the first part of the chapter, Solomon is able to afford the horses that occupy the closing section, even to the point where he can pay in silver owing to his vast reserves. But not only is Deut 17:16 clear that the king should not multiply horses, equally clear is the admonition that the king not import them from Egypt – yet this is exactly what Solomon does. Elsewhere in the Hebrew Bible, the horse is used as a symbol of aggression and pride (e.g., Exod 15:1; Ps 147:10; Job 39:19–25), and it could be submitted that in Solomon's kingdom, horses and chariots typify military hubris. Such hubris is extended to the export trade as well, surely taking advantage of Israel's relative geographical centrality in the Levant to control the movement of horses from Egypt to the neo-Hittite domain. For all his wisdom, it is rather astonishing that Solomon becomes an arms dealer who imprudently outfits his opponents with the weapons of war.[36] The king is acting in contravention to Deuteronomy and simultaneously undermining the future security of the kingdom: "Hittites are mentioned in 9:20 as descendants of Canaanites that Israel failed to destroy. Solomon provides horses for Canaanites and apparently contributes to making the Hittites a regional power (2 Kgs 7:6). Even worse, Solomon exports arms to the Arameans, and during the following century Aram emerges as a constant threat to Israel (1 Kgs 11:23–25; 20; 22; 2 Kgs 5; 7). Solomon, the wisest man in the world, funds

---

standards of living, and cultural ingenuity. As gifts of God used in faith, such things have the potential for good (3:9; 10:8–9). But human beings more readily follow Solomon in letting wisdom and prosperity grow into forces for injustice, into objects of concern which ultimately prove corrosive to faith (Mt 6:24–33; Lk 12:13–21)."

[36] Brueggemann, *1 & 2 Kings*, 137.

his enemies."³⁷ The potent combination of wisdom abuse and *tôrāh* neglect prepares the reader for the implosive events that are revealed in the next chapter. After the completion of the temple, God's word in 9:1–9 presages its destruction, and now after a survey of the wealth of Solomon's empire, it too is appearing increasingly fragile and not nearly as secure as it seems. In 1 Kgs 3:9, Solomon asked God for an "understanding mind" to distinguish between good and evil, yet his eschewing of the law and his manifest disregard for heeding the divine voice have set the king on a precipitous course for collapse.

---

37   Leithart, *1 & 2 Kings*, 81. In arguing for the figure of Solomon as an Adam figure who experiences a "fall" despite the divine presence, see Davies, "Discerning between Good and Evil: Solomon as a New Adam in 1 Kings," 56: "But if Solomon is the new Adam, then he has followed the primal man in his failure to live as those invited to share God's space must live. He has set his own appetites and his autonomous wisdom above God's revealed purposes for him and his people."

CHAPTER 4

Kingdom and Division

When confronted with Nathan's tale of a rich man who exploited the poor owner of a ewe-lamb in 2 Sam 12:5–6, David's reaction is harsh and unequivocal: "As the LORD lives, surely the man who did this is a son of death!" After Nathan's unmasking, it quickly becomes apparent that David has passed a sentence on himself and has uttered what scholars label a "self-condemnation," along the same lines as Ahab in 1 Kgs 20:39–42.[1] There is a similar situation with Solomon, who, like his father, arguably utters a self-condemnation in 1 Kgs 8:61, except that in this case it is not a prophetic voice that calls him to account. At the end of his very long address to the nation during the dedication ceremony, Solomon's climactic words are an exhortation to unwavering loyalty: "May your heart be completely aligned (*shālēm*) with the LORD our God, walking in his statutes and keeping his commandments, just like today." As it turns out, these are Solomon's last recorded words in the narrative, and they ironically rebound to become his self-condemnation as 1 Kgs 11:4 lifts the curtain to reveal that his heart was not completely aligned (*shālēm*) with God. For all the glitter of the cosmopolitan Solomonic

---

[1] For an alternative, see Jeremy Schipper, *Parables and Conflict in the Hebrew Bible* (New York: Cambridge University Press, 2007), 113.

empire and for all the lengthy narration, it crashes rather quickly: ten chapters are devoted to describing its expansion, but the next two chapters chronicle a chain reaction that leaves the empire irreparably fractured, with a number of theological questions emerging from the rubble in 1 Kings 11–16. Is it Rehoboam's fault that the north secedes, or is it because of the father's malfeasance rather than the son's incompetence? Why is Jeroboam given such a promising start, and why does his reign likewise implode? How can the turbulence and chaos of these chapters in 1 Kings be explained, and how is the divine anger configured in the text? Finally, how is the reader prepared for the arrival of the fiery prophetic figures Elijah and Elisha in the next phase of the story?

DISINTEGRATIONS

No monarch in Israelite history surpasses Solomon in the material realm, but it cannot be coincidental that after a detailed inventory of Solomon's horde of gold and stables full of horses, there is a decisive shift in tone in 1 Kgs 11:1–13. In terms of the narrative design, there has been a subtle critique in the first ten chapters that generally hovers below the surface, and even while reporting Solomon's wealth and achievements, there are warnings both implicit and explicit. Daniel Hays contends that the allusions to Deuteronomy 17 in chapter 10 bring the critical appraisal to a crescendo, and thus "there is strong evidence to support the view that the narrator is not schizophrenic, praising Solomon for ten chapters and then suddenly condemning him. Rather the narrator develops a fascinating but negative critique of Solomon throughout the Solomonic narratives. His critique is subtle, employing irony, word associations and implicit rather than explicit references to Deuteronomy, 1–2 Samuel and the rest of 1–2 Kings."[2] After a lengthy delay that must be owing to God's forbearance, judgment now unfolds, and Solomon's infidelities have implications for the entire nation. For those readers who have been mesmerized by the urbane sophistication and seduced by the international delights of the new regime, Solomon may not be the only one unmasked in the next section of the narrative.

Along with the gold and horses that Deut 17:17 outlaws the king from accumulating, there is also the admonition that the king must not multiply wives, and thus the opening line of chapter 11 belatedly unloads the most controversial announcement yet: not only has Solomon married women from a host of different nations, but the total is seven hundred wives and three hundred concubines. It may have been supposed that Pharaoh's daughter was the first – and the only directly mentioned – wife, and a "cipher for Solomon's blemished rule" and capacity for excess.[3] But it turns out that the Egyptian princess is merely at the head of a very large class. For many contemporary readers, such an astronomical figure is mind-boggling, but as noted in the case of Pharaoh's daughter, such relationships are about political and trade alliances rather than romance: "Insofar as relations between nations were generally cemented by marriage between royal families of each nation, the enumeration of the nationalities of Solomon's wives and the large numbers of wives and concubines noted in v. 3 portray his power and status as a major ruler among the nations."[4] The verb "hold fast" (*dābaq*) is elsewhere

---

[2] Hays, "Has the Narrator Come to Praise Solomon or to Bury Him?" 173–74.
[3] Wray Beal, *1 & 2 Kings*, 170.
[4] Sweeney, *I & II Kings*, 155. Again it should be noted that David also multiplies wives (see 1 Sam 25:42–44; 2 Sam 3:2–5, 5:13; cf. 2 Sam 12:11), likewise in tension with Deut 17:17 and related passages.

used in the context of loyalty, as in Deut 11:22 where Israel is exhorted to hold fast to God in order that the land may be fully possessed. Not only do Solomon's wives represent his sprawling network of alliances with other nations, but his love for them also stands in contrast to his reported love for God earlier in the narrative:

> The narrative turns from Solomon's love for the Lord (3:3; see Deut 6:5), as God had loved him (2 Sam. 12:24), to his love for foreign wives (vv. 1–2); these two references bracket the reign of Solomon. This is a love story gone awry. God's continuing love does not overwhelm Solomon's decision to turn his love toward that which is not God, to violate his own call for complete devotion to God (8:61).[5]

Solomon's apostasy is cemented through a wordplay on his name. In 8:61, he implores the nation to be completely aligned (*shālēm*) with God, but now Solomon (*shelōmōh*) is guilty of not living up to his own exhortation: "In turning away after other gods, Solomon leaves behind not only the example of David but his own deepest identity as well."[6] David is guilty of many things in the Deuteronomistic History, but turning aside to other gods is not one of them.[7]

The pantheon of deities in 1 Kgs 11:5–8 – an inventory that rivals Solomon's cache of gold and horses – is as jarring as the king's algorithm of foreign wives.[8] For Walter Brueggemann, it is

---

[5] Fretheim, *First and Second Kings*, 62.   [6] Walsh, *1 Kings*, 135.
[7] Cf. Provan, *1 and 2 Kings*, 91. Leithart (*1 & 2 Kings*, 83) has a slightly different appraisal: "When David 'did evil' in seizing a married woman (2 Sam 11–12), the kingdom was temporarily divided by the rebellion of Absalom. Solomon does evil in taking many women, and the result is a longer-lasting breach in Israel."
[8] For possible reasons why the reader is informed of the wives and foreign deities in retrospect, see Yong Ho Jeon, "The Retroactive Re-evaluation

likely that this listing of deities "gathers together representative names of gods as typical of the betrayal of Solomon. In the judgment of many scholars Astarte (Asherah) was a goddess who in some forms of heterodox Yahwism was considered Yahweh's consort, a claim firmly rejected in Deuteronomic theology. The gods Milcom and Chemosh were known to be the gods of neighboring peoples, and Molech is perhaps a confusion with and derivation from Milcom. The point of the passage does not depend upon any clear identification of the deities."[9] Although the foreign women are implicated for turning the aged Solomon's heart, surely it is not their fault that he imports horses from Egypt or retains Adoniram as the head of forced labor. The text is either engaging in some ironic overstatement, or else stressing the inevitable consequences of eschewing the law: if marrying foreign women leads the heart astray, then the reader should not be surprised at the scale of Solomon's apostasy. The concrete manifestations are the alternative installations constructed for these deities, as Solomon evidently uses his skill and experience in building the temple to sponsor these rival sanctuaries. The spatial setting is "the mountain across from (or east of) Jerusalem," and assumed by most scholars to be an implicit reference to the Mount of Olives (cf. 2 Kgs 23:13). If so, it is notable that David has a powerful experience at this same location in 2 Sam 15:30–31 at arguably the lowest moment in his life: he is forced to flee from Jerusalem because of his son Absalom, and as he climbs the Mount of Olives, he is informed of Ahithophel's treachery. Yet as David arrives at the place "where God was

---

Technique with Pharaoh's Daughter and the Nature of Solomon's Corruption in 1 Kings 1–12," *TynBul* 62 (2011): 15–40.

[9] Brueggemann, *1 & 2 Kings*, 142.

worshipped," he prays that Ahithophel's counsel be turned to foolishness, and moments later Hushai the Archite arrives – seemingly as the immediate answer to David's prayer – marking the turning point of David's fortunes. The same place where God was worshipped is now utterly defiled by Solomon and renovated into an Israelite acropolis for foreign deities, with the Jerusalem temple in clear view across the Kidron Valley. Readers of the later gospel narratives will recognize a familiar landscape in Luke 22:39–48, where a Davidic descendant is similarly betrayed by a member of his inner circle en route to a redemptive act of sacrifice.

Prior to the advent of any gospel narratives, however, there is divine anger directed at Solomon for such iniquity, and in vv. 11–13 God speaks directly to the king once more: after Solomon's death, the kingdom will be ripped away and given to one of his servants. "It comes as no surprise to readers of Kings to find God becoming angry with Solomon because of his apostasy (v. 9) or announcing that the kingdom is going to be torn from him. That is what 2:4, 8:25, and 9:4–5 have led us to expect."[10] There is a partial mitigation of this penalty because of the Davidic covenant, so we are led to infer, because God adds that one tribe will remain under the control of Solomon's son "for the sake of David my servant and for the sake of Jerusalem that I have chosen." The penalty for Solomon's divided heart, as it were, is a divided kingdom, a fissure that will be abruptly exposed after Solomon's death. The fact that a "servant" will inherit a substantial portion of the kingdom has shades of the Saul-David conflict in the book of 1 Samuel, complete with the verb "tear" (see 1 Sam 15:27–28), which makes Solomon a new Saul figure in the narrative. There are several other

---

[10] Provan, *1 and 2 Kings*, 92.

connections with the Saul narrative that will be mentioned below, but it should be pointed out that God speaks to Solomon for the last time here. Furthermore, this is one of the final occasions where God speaks directly to any king: "From this point on, God will speak through the prophets."[11] And, as we will see, in the last section of 1 Kings 11, a prophet indeed arrives on the scene with a further message about the longer term implications of Solomon's apostasy.

FORCES OF OPPOSITION

During his correspondence with Hiram in 1 Kgs 5:4, Solomon boasted to his colleague that there was no "opponent" (*sāṭān*) or dangerous threat in his realm. Unfortunately for Israel's wealthy monarch, this assertion is not quite true, because 11:14–25 features two opponents – introduced by way of flashback – who are active "all the days of Solomon" (v. 25). "These adversaries are rival warlords, Hadad in Edom and Rezon in Syria, whom the Solomonic government was unable to pacify and who bedeviled the united kingdom on its northeastern and southeastern borders throughout Solomon's reign."[12] In fact, the land of Egypt is deeply problematic, since Hadad is also invited to marry into the Egyptian royal family. Since this is quite conceivably the same pharaoh allied with Solomon (or at least his immediate successor), it rather deflates the king's pretensions and strongly suggests that Egypt is an untrustworthy ally (see 1 Kgs 14:25–26). As an interesting aside, Hadad only departs from Egypt after he learns that Joab is dead, and therefore after Solomon's execution order is carried out by

---

[11] Fretheim, *First and Second Kings*, 64. Cf., however, 2 Kgs 10:30.
[12] Mobley, "1 and 2 Kings," 129.

Benaiah. So David's advice that Solomon follows now appears in a more dubious light, and it is not the last time that David's previous actions cause mischief for his successor.[13] Furthermore, the very presence of Hadad and Rezon as longtime adversaries serves to undermine Solomon's rhetoric – how seriously does the reader now take Solomon's other speeches? – and also reveals that God is willing to use foreign leaders to buffet the David house, foreshadowing the rise of Assyria and Babylon as instruments of chastisement.[14] Of more pressing concern for Solomon personally, though, is a different kind of challenger: Hadad and Rezon are foreigners, but the next opponent hails from much closer to home.

Ever since Nathan secured the coronation of Solomon, prophets have not been noticeably active in the political life of Israel. But in 1 Kgs 11:26, Ahijah of Shiloh emerges from the shadows and accosts Jeroboam while the two are alone in the field. Ahijah's Shilonite provenance is notable because in 1 Samuel 1–4, the priestly house of Eli exercises stewardship over the sanctuary, but their dynastic leadership is terminated on account of cultic transgressions. It is consequential, therefore, that Ahijah hails from a city that is acquainted with dynastic judgment and

---

[13] Note the summary of Simon J. DeVries, *1 Kings*, 2nd edn., WBC 12 (Nashville, TN: Thomas Nelson, 2003), 151: "David had indeed been a man of blood. His harshness toward Syria and Edom created implacable enemies even while Solomon (whose name means 'peace') enjoyed the wealth and power created by that harshness. A few generations hence, Syria would become a threat to Israel's very existence. A few centuries hence, Edom would possess the desolate wastes of Judah (cf. Ob 11–14; Ez 35:10–15). Josephites pressed into hard service for Solomon's works of grandeur would rise in revolt against his son. One day only a single 'lamp' would remain to David in Jerusalem.... Thus does Yahweh raise up adversaries to those who rule falsely in his name."

[14] Cf. Leithart, *1 & 2 Kings*, 86.

surely destroyed because of consistent malfeasance (see Jer 7:12–14; 26:4–6). Moreover, Ahijah's furtiveness suggests that prophets are not overly welcome in the Solomonic empire, especially those intending to anoint non-Davidic secessionists. To be sure, he accosts Jeroboam in order to offer him a startling appointment. Of Ephraimite lineage and promoted to a high position within the Solomonic labor machine, Jeroboam has no father to lobby for him (cf. the district governors who are connected to the king in 4:7–19), and therefore his advancement is due to his own merits. Most poignantly, Jeroboam is labeled as a servant (*'ebed*) of Solomon, prompting the reader to recall that in 11:11, God informs Solomon that the kingdom will be torn from him and given to his servant (*'ebed*), cloaking Jeroboam in great expectations.

According to the NRSV rendering of vv. 29–30, Ahijah is wearing a new robe for this occasion: "Ahijah had clothed himself with a new garment. The two of them were alone in the open country when Ahijah laid hold of the new garment he was wearing and tore it into twelve pieces." There is a syntactic ambiguity, but the Hebrew text can certainly be read with Jeroboam as the cloak (*śalmāh*) wearer.[15] As a descendant of Joseph – who sported a famous coat – Jeroboam is perhaps the more natural candidate for the cloak, and in light of his promotion by the king, it is not unreasonable that he would be so attired. Moreover, the connection with Joseph might also imply that Jeroboam is serving under the aegis of an Israelite pharaoh whose forced labor (Ex 1:11; 1 Kgs 9:15) and storage cities (Ex 1:11; 1 Kgs 9:19) have led the nation into its own house of bondage.

---

[15] See S. Min Chun, "Whose Cloak Did Ahijah Seize and Tear? A Note on 1 Kings XI 29–30," *VT* 56 (2006): 268–74.

No specific reasons are given as to why Jeroboam is chosen, but the encounter with Ahijah carries reminders of the Samuel/Saul account in 1 Sam 15:28, where a garment is prominent in a prophetic illustration. When Saul rips Samuel's robe, it symbolizes – according to the prophet's riposte – the ripping of the kingdom away from him; when Ahijah rips the new cloak (*śalmāh*), it represents the kingdom being ripped from Solomon and given to Jeroboam, sealed with a wordplay on Solomon's name (*shelōmōh*) as his kingdom is dismantled. Not so long ago, Solomon gave cities to Hiram king of Tyre (1 Kgs 9:11–14), and now the ten northern tribes are handed to Jeroboam, one for each fragment of the robe torn by Ahijah. Even so, one tribe will remain because of David, but during the days of Solomon's son this tearing can be expected. In v. 33, the entire community seems to be implicated – note the switch to plural verb forms – and evidently Solomon's example has been widely followed. But though the future appears bleak for Solomon's successor, the opposite is the case for Jeroboam as Ahijah's oracle continues in vv. 37–39. The kingdom will be radically reconfigured, and Jeroboam is invested with considerable promise: according to Ahijah, if Jeroboam listens (*shāma'*) and walks in God's ways, then God will build him an enduring house just like David. Solomon had earlier asked for a listening (*shāma'*) heart, and now Jeroboam is adjured to listen in order that he might be given a lasting (*ne'emān*) dynasty, conditioned on his obedience. Consequently, Jeroboam's forthcoming reign is now infused with high hopes, for if he maintains fidelity, he can be a new David for the northern tribes.[16] This is an important theological moment in the book of Kings, and raises the question relevant to any interested reader: how will Jeroboam respond

---

[16] Note Mark Leuchter, "Jeroboam the Ephratite," *JBL* 125 (2006): 51–72.

to the opportunity and gifts that God has given him? It can be inferred that Jeroboam has had occasion to see first-hand where Solomon went wrong, and presumably he has Ahijah the prophet for support. But at the end of Ahijah's oracle, there is no recorded response from Jeroboam, in contrast to David's voluble prayer in 2 Sam 7:18–29 when God promises him a lasting (*ne'emān*) house. Jeroboam's first words, in fact, are delayed until 1 Kgs 12:26–27 and will be an internal deliberation where seeds of doubt (rather than faith and confidence in the prophetic words) are at the forefront of his mind.

FRAGMENTS AT SHECHEM

Even though Ahijah and Jeroboam are alone in the field during the secret investiture, somehow Solomon finds out – like Absalom and David, maybe he also has an underground surveillance network (see 2 Sam 17:17–20) – and seeks to kill his northern labor supervisor. Like Saul trying to destroy David on account of the prophetic word spoken about him, Solomon tries to eliminate his new rival. But like other adversaries such as Hadad, Jeroboam finds safe harbor in Egypt, making it again appear to be a dubious ally. Solomon's lengthy career ends, therefore, on this note of relative failure: the king does not succeed in apprehending Jeroboam, and vv. 41–43 provide a brief obituary that recounts his wisdom but is otherwise silent on his spiritual bankruptcy. For the first time, Solomon's successor Rehoboam is mentioned – for all of his wives, Solomon has only one recorded son – but even prior to any introduction, we are aware that he has been bequeathed a fractured kingdom. As matters unfold, it does not take long for the fracture to manifest itself in the fateful 1 Kings 12. The spatial setting of Shechem is mentioned a number of times over the course of Israel's history, but most recently is the sordid site where Abimelech is crowned king in Judges 9. Whether this event has any bearing on the present meeting – are the northerners threatening Rehoboam with the prospect of becoming a rogue state? – is uncertain, but Rehoboam journeys to Shechem to hear the northern demands: if Rehoboam lightens their workload, they are willing to serve him. Despite being overworked by Solomon, they are still prepared to acknowledge Solomon's successor as their king, and as the elders counsel, this is as good a deal as Rehoboam could have expected. It does not redound to Rehoboam's credit when he rejects the elders' counsel and opts to follow the advice of cronies (whose crudeness is exceeded only by their contempt, it must be said, especially when they encourage the king to say "my little one is thicker than my father's waist") and refuses to grant the northerners' request. Not surprisingly, the northerners do not respond favorably to this harsh language, and the division of the kingdom proceeds as forecast in 1 Kgs 11:11–13 and reaffirmed in Ahijah's oracle.

Several theological points surface during this disastrous episode, starting with the character of Rehoboam. Unquestionably, he emerges as reckless and immature, starting with his refusal to countenance the elders' advice about servant leadership and ending with Adoniram – the chief of forced labor, and surely a central object of northern wrath – being sent out to pacify the mob. The latter decision is a nearly fatal lapse in judgment, and if Rehoboam had not hastily mounted his chariot, he would have likewise been stoned by the rabid crowd that pelted Adoniram to death. Rehoboam's folly is therefore hardly in dispute, but the reader may still ask about how much mentoring he received or how Solomon equipped him for the difficult task of succession. Although deeply conflicted, at least Solomon gets some paternal attention from David and a "deathbed" speech; Rehoboam is not recorded as receiving either, and this must be yet another indictment of Solomon, who fails to exercise any wisdom in this critical area. Nevertheless, the reality that the kingdom is ordained to split is underscored in v. 15 by a narrative interruption that scholars often label as *dual causality*, usually defined as an explicit notice of divine intervention into the normal plane of human events (cf. Judg 9:23–24; 2 Sam 17:14) and frequently in the context of retribution for corrupt leadership.[17] Rehoboam's incompetence is thus overshadowed by Solomon's transgressions. Jeroboam is also present in 1 Kings 12, and he would be wise to heed these various factors: "The continuance of Jeroboam's dynasty is wholly dependent on Jeroboam's obedience. Conversely, while David's house could be disciplined for its disobedience (as the present prophetic word reveals) its surety is not dependent upon obedience."[18] Finally, just before stoning Adoniram, the northerners lift their voices with a rallying cry in v. 16, and it is actually a recycled variation of an earlier rebel yell from the days of Sheba son of Bicri in 2 Sam 20:1. Sheba's revolt took advantage of the fractiousness in the aftermath of Absalom's bitter rebellion, itself arguably brought about by David's misdeeds in 2 Samuel 11–12. The schism at Shechem, consequently, is the aggregate of numerous compromises over several generations, and in this regard prefigures the Babylonian exile at the end of the book of Kings (an event that likewise takes place because of many transgressions over multiple generations).

---

[17] E.g., Christopher T. Paris, *Narrative Obtrusion in the Hebrew Bible* (Minneapolis, MN: Fortress, 2014), 117–18.
[18] Wray Beal, *1 & 2 Kings*, 174.

GOLDEN INNOVATIONS

From 1 Kgs 12:19–20 onward, there are two nations, Israel and Judah: Solomon's violations result in a loss of land, and so the very existence of a northern kingdom epitomizes what happens when kings drift off course. Nonetheless, from the perspective of the larger Deuteronomistic History, there is no reason why this experiment with two kingdoms should not work. It must be considered hasty when, in response to Jeroboam's crowning, Rehoboam seeks to recapture his squandered territory through military aggression. The massive host of 180,000 soldiers that gathers to Rehoboam may indicate a sudden surge in his leadership aptitude, but this group is much more likely to get a better deal from the Davidic house than from any northern monarch. Yet civil war is averted through the prophetic word of Shemaiah (*shemay'āh*), a figure who is neither introduced nor mentioned again. The gathered southerners "listen" (*shāmaʿ*) to the prophetic utterance, and although 14:30 indicates that conflict between Rehoboam and Jeroboam was ongoing, in this instance a calamitous event is avoided because the people are obedient, and thus the present episode is a positive harbinger of "listening." Consequently, Rehoboam survives in what could be haltingly described as the finest hour of his otherwise inept seventeen-year reign. But the rest of his woeful biography will not be resumed until 14:21, as attention switches to the north in v. 25, beginning a narrative pattern of alternating between Israel and Judah variously followed until the Assyrian invasion in 2 Kings 17. In the present context, therefore, Judah's submission to the prophetic word represents a challenge as the narrative focus shifts to Jeroboam: will he listen as Ahijah adjured and thus be granted an enduring house, or will he be tempted to follow in the path of Solomon?

Jeroboam's first initiative in 12:25 is to fortify the strategically located cities of Penuel and Shechem, probably because he is anticipating further hostilities with his southern counterpart. His energetic building program is soon followed with a reflective moment and a turning point in the story: an internal deliberation that provides a window into Jeroboam's mind that uncovers a deep insecurity regarding defection. Although recently crowned by the northerners who almost stoned Rehoboam to death, Jeroboam nonetheless is afraid that his constituents will repledge their loyalty to the Davidic house if they venture to Jerusalem for worship. Within the pages of the Deuteronomistic History, 1 Kgs 12:26–27 is a stunning revelation, as the reader is privy to an inside view of Jeroboam's calculations to eschew theological obedience in favor of political expedience. To minimize the risk of pilgrimages to Jerusalem evoking any southern sentiments, the new northern king embarks on another building program: a pair of golden calves.[19] Ahijah encouraged him to walk in the statutes, but this enterprise reveals how quickly he has departed: Solomon accumulated gold, and Jeroboam invests gold in cultic objects – installed at Bethel and Dan for maximum geographical effectiveness, in a rebooted version of Exodus 32 where a golden calf is likewise borne out of anxiety and fear of the crowd. Whether Jeroboam intends the calves to be interpreted as pedestals for the deity and symbolic markers of a decisive break with Solomon's Pharaonic tyranny or as a cynical ploy to control his constituents and avoid a revolt is up for debate, but given the preponderance of bull imagery in Canaanite religion (e.g., Judg 6:25), it was an

---

[19] See further August H. Konkel, *1 & 2 Kings*, NIVAC (Grand Rapids, MI: Zondervan, 2006), 249–50; W. I. Toews, *Monarchy and Religious Institution in Israel under Jeroboam I* (Atlanta, GA: Scholars Press, 1993).

extremely risky strategy. As matters proceed, the calves are just the tip of an iceberg worth of innovations – ranging from the enfranchisement of a nonlevitical priesthood to a changed religious calendar – as Jeroboam implements almost as many cultic aberrations as Solomon had wives and installations for foreign deities. It could be argued that Jeroboam strays from the statutes even as Solomon breaks the covenant (11:11), defined by Walter Brueggemann as follows: "*Covenant* with its stipulations and requirements is a subversive claim against a world of autonomy in which relationships are sustained only by convenience, and not fidelity, in which duty and responsibility are overridden in self-indulgence that devours self, neighbor, and environment."[20] Solomon was given ten chapters before judgment catches up with him, but for Jeroboam it will arrive much sooner, and instead of moving toward an enduring house, he lurches toward a more sordid legacy: "the sins of Jeroboam" will be a leadership paradigm and an enduring moniker that plagues the northern kings until the dissolution of the country at the hands of foreign invaders.

To be sure, the dissolution of the northern kingdom is forecast much sooner than might be expected, as the enigmatic 1 Kings 13 presents a pair of related episodes that variously envelope the north in a cloud of divine judgment. After a lengthy absence of prophets during the reign of Solomon, Ahijah and Shemaiah show up in rapid succession, shortly followed by an anonymous man of God from Judah who arrives uninvited to the dedication ceremony of Jeroboam's new altar in Bethel. The arresting scenes of 13:1–10 begin with Jeroboam presiding over the ceremony like Solomon in 8:22, except that rather than the Jerusalem temple,

---

[20] Brueggemann, "Old Testament Theology," 694.

one of the golden calves is in view.[21] Addressing the altar itself using the comparatively rare category of prophetic apostrophe, the man of God makes an even more rare predictive prophecy about the arrival of a Davidic scion named Josiah nearly three centuries in advance.[22] Under the circumstances, this must be considered a most unsettling utterance for Jeroboam: he is already feeling vulnerable about a reversion of his constituency to the south, yet now he hears about a future southern king who will sacrifice illegitimate priests on the very altar he has built in order to prevent such defection in the first place. Ten fragments of the kingdom were ripped from the hand of Solomon and given into the hand of Jeroboam, but when he sends forth his hand ordering the apprehension of the man of God, his hand "dries up," inadvertently portending the sterility of his own kingdom. Reversing the arrest order and asking the man of God for prayer indicate Jeroboam's lack of confidence in his own priesthood, and further reveal that his religious projects have a brazenly political rationale. For his part, the man of God is willing to pray for the king, but when God responds to his entreaty – extending the pusillanimous Jeroboam a chance for repentance – the man refuses to accept a reward from the king. He states that he has been ordered not to eat or drink "in this place," but this prohibition is put to the test in the next episode as the reader discovers that prophets are indeed held to the same standard of obedience as kings. In fact, the next scenes in 1 Kings 13 illustrate the complexity of the prophetic office, for just as monarchs need to resist the temptation to expedience, prophets can likewise lose their way. The man

---

[21] Provan, *1 and 2 Kings*, 113.
[22] On prophetic apostrophe as the addressing of an inanimate object, see Walsh, *1 Kings*, 177.

Kingdom and Division 97

of God from Judah does well to reject Jeroboam's gift, but he will fall short because of a false oracle in the next episode, foreshadowing the false oracles of comfort – rather than the harder path of obedience – that are a stumbling block for later kings in the narrative.

There are some bizarre episodes in the Deuteronomistic History, but 1 Kgs 13:11–34 in particular has long perplexed interpreters because of the wildly unpredictable sequence of events: an old prophet of Bethel deceives the man of God from Judah with food and drink, resulting in the man's death from a lion, only to have the old prophet request a burial in the same tomb, stating, "For the word that he proclaimed by the word of the LORD will certainly come to pass against the altar at Bethel and against all the high places in the cities of Samaria" (v. 32).[23] Within the parameters of our study, several intriguing points emerge here. In terms of characterization, the man of God has more in common with Jeroboam than one may suppose: both are raised up to counter corruption, and both depart from the way (although the man of God at least has the excuse that he was deceived). Without any deception, Jeroboam willfully departs from the prophetic word and, like the man of God, can expect to face the ravenous consequences. Furthermore, the lion is a figure of judgment in the story, as in Judg 14:8–9 and later in 1 Kgs 20:36 and 2 Kgs 17:25–26. The lion not only exacts judgment here, but also foreshadows the lions of Assyria and Babylon that are divinely sent to chastise both Israel and Judah in the days to come. At the end of

---

[23] Among modern systematic theologians, Karl Barth has a lengthy discussion in *Church Dogmatics* II.2, 393–409; on Barth's view that this interaction foreshadows interactions between north and south, see David Bosworth, "Revisiting Karl Barth's Exegesis of 1 Kings 13," *BibInt* 10 (2002): 360–83.

the episode, the old prophet's predictive prophecy about Samaria – the future capital city of the northern kingdom purchased by Omri in 16:24 – is similar to the long-term prophecy about Josiah in 13:3, and therefore the destruction of Samaria is anticipated even before its founding. In light of the dramatic signs of Jeroboam's healed hand and the exploded altar, the reader may have expected some sustained repentance on his part, but vv. 33–34 emphasize that he persists in his evil ways, installing deviant priests to operate his liturgical machinery and doing nothing to alter his course for disaster. The various prophets in recent episodes are precursors to the underground network called "the sons of the prophets" prominent during the Omride regime headquartered in Samaria. Presaging the arrival of Elijah and Elisha, the prophetic word has the capacity to terminate powerful dynasties, as demonstrated by Ahijah in the next sequence of 1 Kings 14.

INCENDIARY TIMES

Ahijah is the prophet of Jeroboam's investiture, but he has not been heard from since then, and so presumably the king has scant interest in receiving further counsel from him. But Ahijah returns to center stage in the first part of 1 Kings 14, and, as it turns out, he is a unique prophet whose word rips apart both southern and northern dynasties. The exigency of his son's illness prompts Jeroboam to send his wife with a modest gift to seek an oracle from Ahijah in Shiloh, although the fact that she is sent in disguise raises the question of whether Jeroboam is trying to fool his constituents or the prophet.[24] If the former, it implies that he

---

[24] For the motif of *disguise* in Israel's royal history, see R. Coggins, "On Kings and Disguises," *JSOT* 50 (1991): 55–62.

doubts the efficacy of his own religious establishments, but if the latter, the charade suggests that he thinks he can manipulate the prophet despite his clear departure from "the way" outlined by Ahijah himself and his inability to placate the man of God from Judah in 13:7. Regardless, in the context of the story, it must be that the physical illness of Jeroboam's son is a reminder of spiritual sickness that plagues his realm.

Jeroboam's efforts to disguise his wife are ultimately an ineffective ruse. Ahijah is blind, and so the costume is an act of desperate futility; moreover, God reveals in advance that Jeroboam's wife is en route. Ahijah's verbal welcome to the queen is unremitting. In his long oracle of vv. 6–16, the prophet's piercing word provides a gloomy projection: instead of an enduring dynasty, Jeroboam can only expect the dismemberment of his family. Other northerners are likewise affected, and the national consequences are mapped in geographical terms, as the population will inevitably be dispersed beyond the river: "The people who came through the sea of reeds will be shaken like a reed in the water; the people whom God planted as his vine and as his oak will be uprooted and scattered; and the people who long ago left Gentile Egypt, the land of the Nile, to settle in the promised land will one day return to another Gentile nation, beyond the River Euphrates (1 Kgs 14:15)."[25] Ahijah fades from view after unfurling this bold and occasionally crude utterance, but his declaration that the son will die finds fulfillment in the episode's dénouement in vv. 17–20. Jeroboam's hand is healed in the previous chapter, but his son dies as soon as the disguised mother crosses the threshold of the (soon to be empty) palace. As recently as 1 Kings 11, there were high hopes and great expectations for Jeroboam's future,

---

[25] Leithart, *1 & 2 Kings*, 106.

but only three chapters later, his other son Nadab inherits a throne under a death sentence.

The dismal fate of Jeroboam's line is temporarily held in abeyance as the narrative focus moves south to resume the Rehoboam strand in 1 Kgs 14:21; although his succession is not threatened like Jeroboam's, it is not because of any merit. Rather, as the text makes clear, the southern throne is stable only because of unmerited divine commitment, even in the midst of high places and various cultic accoutrements outlined in vv. 22-24. Still, there are immediate repercussions in the form of an Egyptian incursion, as Shishak attacks Jerusalem and loots the treasury. Shishak is the same potentate who harbors Jeroboam in 11:40, emphasizing the imprudence of Solomon's alliance with Egypt just as Rehoboam's bronze replacement shields underscore the economic losses. Moreover, 1 Kgs 14:21 (see v. 31) belatedly reveals Rehoboam's Ammonite mother: combined with his age of forty-one, there is reason to suspect that David arranged Solomon's marriage with the Ammonites, reinforcing the precarious nature of such diplomatic protocols.[26] When Abijam (or Abijah) takes over the kingdom, the reader may not be sanguine based on past precedence. But even though "his heart was not wholly aligned" with God, he retains the kingdom because of God's pledge to the Davidic line. God preserves a "lamp" in Jerusalem (see 11:36), a luminous theological symbol that represents a human descendant while stressing that the flame of promise will not be extinguished despite the most tempestuous winds. Based on the regnal formula of his son Asa in 15:9, there is a chance that Abijam marries his

---

[26] For the ongoing influence of Solomon's foreign marriages, see Jesse C. Long, *1 & 2 Kings*, College Press NIV Commentary (Joplin, MO: College Press, 2002), 188.

mother. Irrespective of this incestuous possibility, Asa is commended for his whole-hearted commitment even though he forges an agreement with the king of Aram to offset the advances of northern Israel.[27] A late blemish on Asa's career is diseased feet, a malady that Jeremy Schipper argues is a euphemism for some kind of genital ailment and an intimate retribution for the king's transgression of Deut 24:5.[28] Asa imposes burdensome labor on all of Judah and thus infringes upon the law that exempts newly married men from any kind of state projects so they can share happiness with their wives, and therefore Asa agonizingly discovers that curtailing the deuteronomic injunctions is costly. But Asa's successor, Jehoshaphat, will have even more painful issues than diseased feet to deal with, for he injudiciously enters into a marriage alliance with northern Israel in due course.

Jehoshaphat's northern alliance will not be transacted with the house of Jeroboam, however, because 15:25–32 narrates its much-anticipated demise at the hands of the otherwise nondescript Baasha. As the narrative focus shifts back to the north, the fulfillment of Ahijah's word unleashes several violent overthrows in a relatively short textual span. So far the royal characters – David, Solomon, Rehoboam and Jeroboam – have been highly individuated, but Nadab is the flattest character to this point, symptomatic of his hopeless predicament. Other than doing evil and walking in the ways of his father, the only action ascribed to Nadab is a fight against Gibbethon – a levitical city (Josh 19:44) located on the Danite tribal border – trying to wrest it from

---

[27] See Linda S. Schearing, "Maacah," *Anchor Bible Dictionary*, 6 vols. (New York: Doubleday, 1992), 4:429–30.

[28] Jeremy Schipper, "Deuteronomy 24:5 and King Asa's Foot Disease in 1 Kings 15:23b," *JBL* 128 (2009): 643–48.

Philistine control. While occupied with this siege, Baasha executes his conspiracy – the first of many such overthrows in the north – and proceeds to liquidate the house of Jeroboam and inaugurate his own twenty-four-year reign. It might be assumed that Baasha is a military figure, but there is no mention of his position or status; more ominously, Baasha receives no prophetic investiture or announcement of any divine promise. But in short order, there is a prophetic word about his downfall delivered by the prophet Jehu: Baasha has been raised up from the dust presumably to eliminate the house of Jeroboam because of its iniquity, but will himself be dismissed for the same reasons and in a similar manner. Yet any hopes Baasha may entertain for a northern dynasty quickly evaporate, for alongside other crimes, he is guilty of kindling the divine anger (16:2). Solomon, Jeroboam, Nadab and Baasha have all aroused God's wrath, which is poised to reach an even higher plane during the Omride era, as will be noted in the next phases of this study.[29]

With scant attempt to whitewash or exculpate the divine character from such emotions such as anger or jealousy, the tradents of Israel finally responsible for the book of Kings appear content with a more complex view of God's character. For those in exile experiencing times of spiritual crisis, such contours of the divine personality are much more three-dimensional than might be supposed: far from a detached deity, Israel's God is passionately involved with the people even during this chaotic stage in the narrative. But as Richard Nelson remarks, contemporary readers may likewise be

---

[29] On the anger of the Moabite god Chemosh as an analogy (cf. 2 Kgs 3), see Reinhard G. Kratz, "Chemosh's Wrath and Yahweh's No: Ideas of God's Wrath in Moab and Israel," in *Divine Wrath and Divine Mercy in the World of Antiquity*, ed. Reinhard G. Kratz and Hermann Spieckermann, FAT II/33 (Tübingen: Mohr Siebeck, 2008), 92–121.

challenged: "The text reveals to the modern reader a God different from the sterile, tame, predictable god of public religion. The God of this text manipulates political events to divine ends. This God evaluates persons and nations on the basis of whole-hearted fidelity to divine commandment. This God's concern is not personal ethics, at least in this text, but idolatry or improper worship at improper places by improper priests (vv. 9, 15; 13:33)." While God is exceptionally patient, Nelson further adds that it is unwise to continually test such patience: "This God reacts harshly to faithlessness and rebellion, experiences anger, uses coarse language, and brings death to individuals, families, and nations. This God tears, burns, cuts off, shakes, uproots, scatters. This is not a God with whom it is easy to feel comfortable but who must be taken seriously."[30] Part of the relevance of Kings for communities of faith in our present day, one could submit, is to remedy rather anemic notions of the divine character, who in 1 Kings 11–16 appears less interested in popularity and more passionate about justice and accountability. And yet, while neither indulgent nor remote, the God revealed in the book of Kings thus far remains active and even accessible in the midst of political turbulence, and does not quickly abandon even those who have left the path of faith.

RISE OF THE OMRIDES

The fleeting dynasty of Baasha is terminated by Zimri's conspiracy, just as Baasha conspired against and destroyed the house of

---

[30] Nelson, *First and Second Kings*, 96. Cf. Fretheim, *First and Second Kings*, 93: "God cares deeply about this relationship with Israel, and *because of that,* cares about what Israel does with its allegiances. The divine jealousy is a sign that God is not unmoved by Israel's unfaithfulness. Jealousy is a complex emotion, entailing (at least) pain, sorrow, disappointment, and anger."

Jeroboam. However, the circumstances surrounding the conspiracies are pathetically different: Nadab is at least battling against the Philistines (15:27), but Baasha's successor Elah is getting drunk at an associate's house when Zimri – commander of half of the king's chariots, implying that Deut 17:16 continues to be eschewed – strikes him down and reigns in his place. Without any tribal provenance or related data, Zimri's introduction portrays a figure whose military position allows for the necessary access to Arza's house to take advantage of Elah's drunken stupor. It has been suggested that Arza may be a co-conspirator in this regicide, but Zimri proceeds to liquidate even the "friends" of Elah, so it is unclear if Arza survives.[31] In the midst of Zimri's predatory carnage stands the reminder, sobering as it is, of Jehu's prophetic word about the dynasty of Baasha that is terminated after just two years of Elah's reign: Nadab likewise reigned for only two years before Jeroboam's house was decimated, and this chronological similarity reinforces the ideological conformity of these two northern houses. Earlier scholars such as Gerhard von Rad and Helga Wieppert were keen to underline the pattern of prophecy and fulfillment woven into the theological fabric of the Deuteronomistic History.[32] More dynamic and creative than some later interpreters have appreciated, however, it seems that the outworking of an authentic prophetic word, while inevitable, can be

---

[31] See Wray Beal, *1 & 2 Kings*, 222.
[32] E.g., Gerhard von Rad, *Old Testament Theology*, vol. 1: *The Theology of Israel's Historical Traditions*, OTL (Louisville, KY: Westminster John Knox, 2001 [1962]), 340; Helga Wieppert, "'Histories' and 'History': Promise and Fulfillment in the Deuteronomistic Historical Work," in *Reconsidering Israel and Judah: Recent Studies on the Deuteronomistic History*, ed. Gary N. Knoppers and J. Gordon McConville (Winona Lake, IN: Eisenbrauns 2000 [1991]), 47–61.

Kingdom and Division 105

fulfilled in unexpected ways and unusual time frames. Elah's demise therefore was never in doubt, but at least Baasha had a successor, however briefly; Zimri, by contrast, has no heir, and in a record for ridiculousness has only a seven-day reign. The instability of the period is epitomized in a rapid sequence of events, as the report of Zimri's conspiracy causes Omri – commander of the army – to be proclaimed as king over Israel while occupied with the siege of Gibbethon. Setting his sights immediately on Tirzah, Omri redirects the army from a foreign conflict to a domestic target, resulting in the career of Zimri being torched after one week: "Now when Zimri saw that that the city was captured, he entered the stronghold of the palace, then burned the royal palace over him with fire, and died" (v. 18). Within his seven-day reign, Zimri still manages to walk in the sins of Jeroboam – and so he dies because of his evil – even if there were strategic errors as well: indeed, Elah blunders by getting drunk, while Zimri probably makes the tactical mistake of carrying out his regicide "without the support of the army, which proved to be his downfall."[33] Elah evidently preferred inebriation in Tirzah to accompanying his troops to battle against the Philistines at Gibbethon, the site of Nadab's assassination two decades earlier (15:27). When Omri abandons the siege of Gibbethon to attack Tirzah, this geographical shift becomes a subtle point of condemnation within the wider narrative:

> Twenty-four years of siege warfare ends with Israel walking away from the battle, and they never return. Gibbethon is never again mentioned in Kings or in the rest of the Old Testament, and the text leaves us with the distinct impression that Gibbethon

---

[33] Rod R. Hutton, "Zimri," *Anchor Bible Dictionary*, 6 vols. (New York: Doubleday, 1992), 6:1095.

remains forever in the hands of the Philistines. Twenty-four years of supplies, death, blood – all wasted. From the Philistine perspective, Gibbethon is saved because there are many princes in Israel. It happened before: while Saul chases David around the country, the Philistines seize the opportunity to make inroads into Israel, unprotected by its distracted king (1 Sm 23). When the people of God battle among themselves, Gentiles recover territory. Israel's experience shows, as Henry shrewdly comments, that "Philistines are sure to gain when Israelites quarrel."[34]

From the smoldering ruins of Zimri's self-destruction, a civil conflict ensues that gives rise – after an enigmatic leader named Tibni dies in 16:22 – to the most dominant northern dynasty in the kingdom's history: the house of Omri.[35] Only a short section of text is devoted to Omri himself, but there are some striking similarities with the life of David: both have a high-ranking military background, enjoy popular support, end up victorious in a protracted civil war with a rival group, purchase real estate with silver, and establish a new capital city.[36] Like Jeroboam, we infer, Omri might be considered a new David on account of these parallels, but ideologically they could not be more different, as

---

[34] Leithart, *1 & 2 Kings*, 118 (citing the eighteenth-century commentator Matthew Henry).
[35] For reference to the house of Omri in Moabite and Assyrian sources, see Lester L. Grabbe, "The Kingdom of Israel from Omri to the Fall of Samaria: If We Had Only the Bible...," in *Ahab Agonistes: The Rise and Fall of the Omri Dynasty*, ed. Lester L. Grabbe, LHBOTS 421/ESHM 6 (New York and London: T. and T. Clark, 2007), 54–99.
[36] E.g., Niels Peter Lemche, "Is It Still Possible to Write a History of Ancient Israel?" in *Israel's Past in Present Research: Essays on Ancient Israelite Historiography*, ed. V. Philips Long, Sources for Biblical and Theological Study 7 (Winona Lake, IN: Eisenbrauns, 1999), 391–414; Peter J. Leithart, "Counterfeit Davids: Davidic Restoration and the Architecture of 1–2 Kings," *TynBul* 56 (2005): 19–35.

Omri exceeds in wickedness all who precede him. The reader may suppose that a prophet will arrive and unveil a word of condemnation because of such iniquity, but with the house of Omri – foreshadowing the next major stretch of narrative – matters are invariably more creative: the city of Samaria is established in 16:24, but its ideological obliteration has already been announced by the old prophet of Bethel in 13:32. Consequently, in spite of the malignancy that is discharged from this Omride epicenter of idolatry, Samaria is doomed to fail even before its inception.

A further similarity between David and Omri is the prominence of their respective successors, Solomon and Ahab. Both are given a vast amount of coverage in the narrative, and both are skilled at building deviant installations: Solomon's high places east of Jerusalem honor a constellation of deities in accordance with his many wives, and Ahab erects a Baal temple (for the Canaanite storm god and his female consort, Asherah) in Samaria. Solomon secures a coveted alliance with Pharaoh's daughter, but Ahab – as though it is trivial to walk in the sins of Jeroboam – marries the Sidonian princess Jezebel. Solomon may have seven hundred wives, but Jezebel is among the fiercest figures of either gender in the Hebrew Bible, virtually embodying many of the characteristics of the goddess Anat (who is by turns seductive, violent and deceptive).[37] The reader should be alert to the shades of satire in

---

[37] For detailed comparisons between Anat and Jezebel, see Michael S. Moore, "Jehu's Coronation and the Purge of Israel," *VT* 53 (2003): 97–114. Note also Neal H. Walls, *The Goddess Anat in Ugaritic Myth* (Atlanta, GA: Scholars Press, 1992); Arvid S. Kapelrud, *The Violent Goddess, Anat in the Ras Shamra Texts* (Oslo: Universitetsforlaget, 1969); Steve A. Wiggins, *A Reassessment of Asherah, with further Considerations of the Goddess*, Gorgias Ugaritic Studies 2 (Piscataway NJ: Gorgias Press, 2007).

Jezebel's presentation in the book of Kings, since from the outset her name (reflecting her Phoenician origins and meaning "Where is the prince") is intentionally distorted: "The Masoretic texts polemically revocalize the name of the Phoenician god Zebul as zebel, 'dung.'"[38] Before any satirical undermining of Jezebel, though, the Omride dynasty is firmly ensconced and Ahab does more to "provoke" the LORD to anger than any of the previous kings. Building on our above discussion of divine anger, Terence Fretheim adds: "It is important to note that God is not imaged as a wrathful God, as if anger were a divine attribute. God is *provoked* to anger. Anger is a divine response to a specific human situation."[39] In Ahab's case, his deliberate defiance raises God's ire (see 21:22), and like many Israelites in this phase of the story, the king has a vacillating and conflicted attitude toward the covenantal traditions of Israel's faith. The first sign of collateral damage under Ahab's regime involves Hiel of Bethel, and it is not incidental that the final lines of Ahab's introduction refer to Joshua 6:26 and the ancient curse on the rebuilding of Jericho that falls on Hiel and his sons (1 Kgs 16:34).[40] Alluding to the conquest of Canaan directs the reader toward the heightening conflict of royal decree versus prophetic resistance, and suggests the land will need to be "reconquered" in light of Ahab's strategies of Canaanization. The state-sponsored fertility religion under Ahab and Jezebel evokes the strongest prophetic response, starting with Elijah's abrupt arrival in the next sequence of the story.

---

[38] Alter, *Ancient Israel*, 686. [39] Fretheim, *First and Second Kings*, 93.
[40] For Wray Beal (*1 & 2 Kings*, 225), 16:34 invokes the era of Joshua as a proleptic comment on Ahab's policies: "The context of Joshua's prophecy includes one man (Achan) whose non-covenantal actions threatened the ongoing covenant life of Israel (Josh 6–7). Similarly, Ahab's non-covenantal actions will threaten the covenant life of the whole nation."

CHAPTER 5

Prophets and Apostasy

After the division of the kingdom in 1 Kings 12, there is a basic narrative rhythm of alternating between north and south, because notwithstanding the sociopolitical realities of the schism, the story continues to be about "one people under the direction of one God."[1] But the alternating rhythm is placed in a holding pattern for the majority of 1 Kings 17 through 2 Kings 8, and although there are a few southern cameos, most of the narrative attention is squarely focused on the Omride dynasty in the north. What are the major reasons for this disproportionate attention? Of course, Ahab and Jezebel are imposing figures who are memorably sketched, and in a unique collaboration they aggressively promote "a virulent form of Canaanite religion that threatened the very

---

[1] Nelson, *First and Second Kings*, 99. In terms of the larger narrative, Nelson further emphasizes that the narrative is a call for faithfulness to the God who is revealed herein: "In the same way as the exilic readers, we face choices of fidelity to the God of the Bible. The dangers are no longer foreign gods, but other, more contemporary idolatries. This text reorients us toward a wholehearted keeping of faith with the real God it has unmasked for us. It evokes fidelity towards the God who punishes infidelity, whose gracious choices are mysterious, and whose arena of action remains the real world of the political, the economic, the historical" (97).

future of Yahwism."[2] Moreover, the Omride dynasty is given inordinate focus in the book of Kings because as its tentacles extend, it engulfs the southern kingdom and the Davidic line is nearly consumed: "Though never stated explicitly, the Omride programme seems to have been to reunite the northern and southern kingdoms under a new dynasty and around a new cult."[3] But the Omride ambitions are not uncontested, and from this lengthy stretch of text emerge the most imposing prophetic figures in the book of Kings. Thus, our analysis will pay attention to the representation of Elijah and Elisha along with some remarkable facets of the divine character that feature in these confrontational episodes.

ARRIVAL(S) OF ELIJAH

Originating from the outback of Gilead on the eastern side of the Jordan and far from the corridors of power in Samaria, 1 Kings 17 begins with the word of Elijah ("and he said," *wayyō'mer*) as he announces a forthcoming drought to Ahab. Elijah declares that God, rather than Baal, is the source of life and orchestrator of rain, and his assault on the regnant power structures is reminiscent of earlier ideological battles: "The conflict between Baal and Yahweh takes on historical and bodily form in the figures of Ahab

---

[2] Bruce C. Birch, Walter Brueggemann, Terence E. Fretheim and David L. Petersen, *A Theological Introduction to the Old Testament*, 2nd edn. (Nashville, TN: Abingdon, 2005), 258. As far as the larger society, the authors further reflect: "The reasoning may well have gone like this: Why not revere Yahweh while at the same time honoring the god responsible for the fertility of the land and the life cycles? Such a syncretistic theology and associated idolatrous worship practices became increasingly common and deeply compromised Israel's commitment to Yahweh" (259).

[3] Leithart, "Counterfeit Davids," 25.

(and Jezebel) and Elijah, a newly configured embodiment of the conflict between Pharaoh and Moses."[4] As abruptly as he appears before Ahab, the divine word straightaway prompts Elijah to hide himself at the Wadi Kerith (17:2–6), a dry riverbed that Jerome Walsh renders as "Cut Off Creek" to capture a wordplay at work.[5] The verbal root *kārat* (from which root the name *Kerith* is related) is not insignificant in the story, since God is about to cut off the supply of rain and the reader later discovers that Jezebel is "cutting off" the prophets during this period (18:4). Elijah is sustained, however, by ravens who deliver provisions morning and evening, with echoes of the Israelites' nourishment in the desert when they relied on God for bread and meat in harsh conditions (Exod 16:8). Ravens are listed as unclean birds in Lev 11:15, and because birds of prey could hardly be expected to provide such largesse unless by divine intervention, it anticipates the next scenes in 17:7–16 where noteworthy divine feeding takes place in "unclean" territory.[6]

Elijah is able to drink from Cut Off Creek, but when the water supply dries up, he is instructed to hide in Sidon, deep within Jezebel's territory. It is not without irony that Jezebel's own country is evidently afflicted with famine (see Lk 4:25–26), yet here it will be the God of Israel – rather than Baal and his consort – who has the power to give life. Although Elijah is informed that a Sidonian widow has been commanded to feed him, it seems rather improbable as she is despairingly gathering sticks so she and her son can partake of a final supper. However, when the vulnerable widow responds to the prophet, she is blessed with a miraculous fund of flour and oil reserves, for not even

---

[4] Fretheim, *First and Second Kings*, 95. [5] Walsh, *1 Kings*, 228.
[6] Seow, "The First and Second Books of Kings," 126.

"exile" in a foreign land can negate the efficacy of God's word. Lest the reader become overly confident, the last scenes of the chapter (17:17–24) complicate matters, as the widow's son stops breathing and is apparently dead. The Sidonian widow accosts her guest and talks about sin and guilt, but Elijah does not verbally respond: earlier in v. 13, he issued the prophetic imperative "do not be afraid," but here he prays to God in the upper chamber and stretches himself out on the child, who lives. Scholars often discuss the polemical thrust of this miracle directed toward principal deities within the Canaanite worldview: "In Canaanite religion it was Baal who had authority over the rain. Its absence meant the absence of Baal, who must periodically submit to the god Mot (death), only to be revived at a later date and once again water the earth. It is this polytheistic view of reality that Elijah now challenges."[7] Just as importantly, this episode illustrates Elijah's role as an intercessor, a role that takes on national significance in the next chapter. It also could be argued that the boy's resurrection points to a larger theme in the narrative, because the story of Kings is about Israel's death but also its (anticipated) resurrection by the power of the prophetic word and action, and here the theme is communicated by means of an anonymous outsider who is not even an Israelite.[8] Furthermore, the concluding utterance of the widow ("the word of the LORD in your mouth is truth") intersects with Elijah's earlier declaration to

---

[7] Provan, *1 and 2 Kings*, 132; Sweeney, *I & II Kings*, 214: "As the god of rain and fertility, Baal is ultimately responsible for the life or death of the land; it is presumed that all life is the result of Baal's capacity to bring rain. Indeed, the mythologies of Canaan and the larger Mesopotamian world indicate that that restoration of life plays an important role in ancient theology concerning the fertility deity."

[8] Cf. Leithart, "Counterfeit Davids," 29–33.

Ahab ("there will be no dew or rain in these years except by my word"). In 1 Kings 17, God's word through Elijah is effective even in the most unlikely of places – this notion of God's international sovereignty would be of relevance to any exilic audience – and the woman's testimony is a foil to Ahab's syncretism, embrace of alterative deities, and, as we will see below, his antipathy to Elijah.

The most common chronological reckoning in the book of Kings is the regnal formula, as time is measured primarily in the "royal years" of the king's reign. Such a measurement is interrupted at the beginning of the next chapter, however, and replaced with a reference to the third year of the drought announced by Elijah, a signal that Ahab will be thwarted in the extraordinary events of 1 Kings 18. But the build-up to the confrontation is both serious and mildly comical, and there is a new character in vv. 2–16 whose speech and actions contribute to the overall plot. Obadiah ("servant of the LORD") is strategically positioned in Ahab's administration, but he is secretly a devout Yahwist and somewhat comparable to Daniel in the era of the exile. Obadiah has been hiding prophets in caves and feeding them – using the same language as Elijah's being fed by the ravens – even as Jezebel is cutting off (*kārat*) the prophets. Obadiah's vocational conflict is palpable, and as he and Ahab search for pasture, the king appears more ridiculous than regal: he cannot find Elijah and he cannot find grass for his mules, a fruitless quest that foreshadows his ultimately failed career. When Elijah commandeers Obadiah to summon his master, Obadiah objects and in his own defense recounts a litany of biographical facts that are informative on multiple levels: he has feared God from his youth (though he seems to fear Ahab as well), and Elijah has a penchant for being taken away on a divine whim.⁹ Despite his protests, Obadiah obediently facilitates the meeting between Elijah and Ahab but is not heard from again, and it is uncertain if his fears are ever realized. Ahab's accusation ("troubler") is an allusion to Josh 7:25, but Elijah responds that the members of the house of Omri have been the "new Achans" of Israel, preparing the way for the duel on Carmel:

> By making explicit the connection between the drought and apostasy (v. 18), Elijah transforms the conflict between Ahab and Elijah into a contest on a higher level. Ahab is accused of following the local baals. Whether the contest to follow is with the Canaanite high god Baal (Hadad), the local baal of Carmel, or the foreign god imported by Jezebel (Melqart or Baal Shamem) is totally immaterial in this context. Apostasy is apostasy no matter what the details. Indeed, the narrative's refusal to be precise is itself testimony to the worthlessness of all other gods. They are lumped together and dismissed. To specify precisely which Baal failed at Carmel would dilute the sweeping condemnation of them all. Israel is gathered to witness the contest (vv. 19–20), for it is their exclusive loyalty to Yahweh that is at stake (v. 21).¹⁰

Long a staple of homileticians and Bible teachers, the contest at Mount Carmel between Elijah and the hundreds of Baal prophets is famous for victory procured against the odds, dramatic fire from heaven, and Elijah's parting advice to Ahab about hitching up his chariot lest it get stuck in the mud from the eagerly awaited rainfall that ends the drought and brings Elijah's original

---

[9] For commonalities between Obadiah and the Sidonian widow, see Wray Beal, *1 & 2 Kings*, 242: "Both charge Elijah with visiting their sin upon them and bringing death (17:18; 18:9); both initially resist Elijah's command (17:12; 18:9–14); both invoke the oath 'As YHWH your God lives' as part of their reluctance (17:12; 18:10); both receive Elijah's assurance (17:13–14; 18:15)."

[10] Nelson, *First and Second Kings*, 116.

prophecy in 17:1 to a storming fulfillment. On its own, this lengthy episode of 18:17–40 deserves a more sustained analysis – for instance, the pointed ideological polemics at work, the rituals of self-mutilation within fertility religions along with frantic prophesying, and the absence of any long-term Yahwistic revitalization in the aftermath of Baal's public failure are all interesting – but for our purposes, several other issues need to be discussed. Elijah's riposte of the Israelite crowd as he asks how long they will "limp around on two crutches" indicates that Ahab is not the only one guilty of compromise. The example of Obadiah illustrates that it is possible to be faithful even in the midst of widespread corruption, and when the crowd assents to Elijah's test of divine supremacy in v. 24, it implicitly reveals that they are wavering in their commitment to God. Moreover, the Israelite crowd is not the only object of Elijah's ire, as the Baal prophets themselves are mocked with a variety of inquiries (such as the euphemism that Baal is "occupied") before Elijah prepares his own contribution to the sacrificial duel.[11]

Repairing the altar and dousing his own sacrifice with twelve barrels of water – confirming that the Mount Carmel contest has implications for all of God's people despite the schism – Elijah's prayer in vv. 36–37 includes a request for hearts and minds to be "turned around." On the one hand, the prayer is surely answered with the spectacular divine fire that consumes the sacrifices and elicits the corporate assent from the people, "The LORD, he is God!" But on the other hand, glancing ahead in the storyline, there is not the kind of lasting repentance that Elijah asks for, perhaps throwing the prophet into the tailspin that is narrated in the next chapter. Consequently, some interpreters caution that

---

[11] For further details on Elijah's taunt, see Cogan, *1 Kings*, 441.

this episode in 1 Kings 18 should not be used to suggest that God cannot lose in any contest: "To be consistent, such a perspective would have to claim that there was no loss for God in the apostasies of Jeroboam or Ahab or anyone else in the spiraling downfall of Israel. The alternative is for apostasy to be considered the will of God. And, if that is so, God has no business being angry at what happens. The apostasy we encounter in these texts means that the will of God is resistable. And if resisted, that is a loss for God and the occasion of divine grief (Ps 78:40; Eph 4:30)."[12] Elijah may have been commissioned to dismantle the Omride dynasty, but it will take longer than he might expect and requires others to be enlisted in the battle, as is evident in the next chapters of the story. Furthermore, Elijah slaughters the prophets of Baal in the Kishon Valley, but they are quickly replaced (see 22:6), and so his violence is not an effective solution.[13] The contest at Mount Carmel formally concludes, therefore, in the Kishon Valley with echoes of Deborah and Barak's victory over the iron chariots of Sisera and the Canaanite king Jabin. Ahab and Jezebel's policies of Canaanization pose just as dire a threat, if not more of one, than Jabin and Sisera's iron chariots in Judges 4, and despite the high-voltage sacrifice in 1 Kings 18, much more darkness has yet to be endured.

---

[12] Birch et al., *A Theological Introduction to the Old Testament*, 278–79.

[13] "Although some decry Elijah's violent act," notes Marvin Sweeney (*I & II Kings*, 229), "it demonstrates the prophet's actions to remove a threat to his life, the lives of the prophets of YHWH, and the integrity of the nation of Israel. The reference to the Wadi Kishon reinforces this perspective insofar as it recalls the victory by Deborah and Barak over the forces of Jabin and Sisera (Jgs 4:7; 5:21; Ps 83:9)," citing Montgomery and Gehman, *Kings*, 406, and Volkmar Fritz, *1 & 2 Kings*, Continental Commentary (Minneapolis, MN: Fortress, 2003), 194.

To this point Jezebel has only been indirectly mentioned within the storyline, but at the outset of 1 Kings 19, she formally enters the stage and issues a menacing polytheistic death threat to Elijah when Ahab reports on the events at Mount Carmel: "May the gods do to me and more also, if I do not make your life as the life of one of them by this time tomorrow." Even though he has just confronted a sizeable group of Israelites (along with the king) and slaughtered a host of Baal prophets, Elijah's response is unexpected, as he apparently runs for his life in the direction of another mountain – eventually revealed to be Horeb/Sinai – where he repeatedly tenders his prophetic resignation. In these scenes where he variously is kept alive with divine provisions, has a powerful theophany on the mountain, and is further tasked with prophetic deeds, there are several points that should be highlighted. First, Elijah's plea of "take my life" indicates intense despair, and perhaps even prophetic depression. But his corollary remark that he is the only one left strikes the reader as odd, since Obadiah has already informed him that at least one hundred other prophets are hidden in caves (18:13). John the Baptist quite conceivably has a similar experience in the gospel narratives (see Mt 11:3–4; Lk 7:18–19), so it seems that prophetic leaders can feel isolated and be in need of periodic renewal. Nonetheless, Elijah has asked God to "take his life," which will occur in ways that neither he nor the reader is prepared for when his life quite literally is taken in 2 Kings 2 by a fiery chariot. Second, the sound of sheer silence (cf. the Common English Bible rendering, "After the fire, there was a sound. Thin. Quiet.") and the revelation of God's character in the cave on Mount Horeb is replete with larger echoes of Israel's own wilderness wanderings, ranging from the divine provisions of food to the mountaintop theophany.[14] In this chapter, Elijah emerges as a kind of new Moses figure who is tasked with leading the nation toward its promised land, but who is also given a prophetic successor, a new Joshua who continues to lead the people's (re)conquest of the land after Ahab and Jezebel's return to the Canaanite fertility religion. Third, Elijah's successor is Elisha son of Shaphat, and he is mentioned in the context of several individuals God instructs Elijah to appoint: an internal usurper (Jehu) and external menace (Hazael of Damascus), who along with Elisha will assist in subduing the Omride empire in the days ahead.

The appointments of Hazael and Jehu do not occur for quite some time (2 Kings 8–9), but the last scenes of the chapter in 1 Kgs 19:19–21 introduce an important character who in fact appoints those leaders and occupies more textual space than any other prophetic figure – Elijah included – in the book of Kings. Elijah's origins are obscure, but Elisha is firmly rooted in the land, and he is introduced while plowing. The twelve pairs of oxen have signaled to some interpreters that Elisha is from a wealthy family, but a symbolic element should not be quickly dismissed. If there are allusions to Moses in the Elijah episodes above, then Elisha's plowing with twelve pairs of oxen is reminiscent of Joshua's twelve stones, and implies that he will continue Elijah's work and himself become a lasting monument or testimony.[15] As Elijah throws his mantle toward Elisha, he does not elaborate on the

---

[14] On the possibility that the text invites a comparison between the cleft of rock with Moses in Exodus 33:21–23 and *the* cave of Elijah here, see Brent A. Strawn, "Elijah, Narcissism, and (Especially) Me," *Journal for Preachers* 38 (2014): 32–35.

[15] On the Joshua stones, see Thomas B. Dozeman, *Joshua 1–12: A New Translation with Introduction and Commentary*, AYB 6a (New Haven, CT: Yale University Press, 2014), 290–91.

prophetic vocation or provide any further details, but Elisha seems to quickly grasp the consequences of the action: sacrificing the oxen suggests that he will not return to his former occupation, and feeding the people anticipates the lineaments of his forthcoming career as he follows in Elijah's footsteps and encourages Israel to respond to the prophetic word.

AHAB AND ARAM

Instead of Elijah and Elisha being prominently featured in 1 Kings 20, there are a number of other anonymous prophetic figures who engage with Ahab in the course of this chapter, which begins with the aggression of the Aramean king Ben-Hadad. The preliminary deliberations showcase a different side of Ahab's personality as he grows frustrated and eventually responds with caustic wit to Ben-Hadad's increasing demands, leading some critics to refer to Ahab as a "sinister clown" in the Shakespearean sense.[16] As for Ben-Hadad, his confidence is undaunted by Ahab's quip (only four words in Hebrew, loosely translated: "One who puts on armor should not brag like one who takes it off"), and he dispatches the order to attack while getting drunk with his thirty-two allied kings. In Judg 9:26–41, the inebriated challenge of Gaal ben Ebed ("Loathsome, son of Slave") does not end well when he is routed by Abimelech, so Ben-Hadad's apparent celebration before the battle might be premature.[17] Elah's drunkenness in 1 Kings 16:9, similarly, was a prelude to his murder. Although drunk, the

---

[16] Northrop Frye, *The Great Code: The Bible and Literature* (New York: Harcourt Brace Jovanovich, 1982), 40.

[17] For Gaal's name, see Robert G. Boling, *Judges*, AB 6A (New York: Doubleday, 1975), 30.

king of Aram is nonetheless commanding a vast army, yet in 20:13-22 a prophet announces to Ahab that God will give the army into his hand "so you will know that I am the LORD." Not only is Ahab's military strength inferior to Ben-Hadad's, but the prophet further informs him that Ahab himself will lead an unlikely group into the fray. Despite the New International Version's translation of the group as "the junior officers under the provincial commanders," a preferable rendering is "the young men of the rulers of the provinces" (*na'ărê sārê hammedînôt*) – a theologically important nuance, as any victory would be even more difficult because of the involvement of regional administrators rather than trained soldiers. The victory in unlikely circumstances (vv. 20-21) must be designed to once more provide Ahab with unambiguous evidence of God's authority, but when the prophet returns to him and warns that hostilities will resume the next spring with another attack from Ben-Hadad, the reader might infer that Ahab has not adequately internalized the message.

When Aramean aggression duly resumes in 1 Kgs 20:23-34, a telling shift in logistical strategy occurs based on theological reasoning by the Aramean officers: because "Israel's gods are gods of the mountains," the arena of battle needs to be on the plains so that Aram can prevail. Ben-Hadad also listens to their advice and replaces the drunken kings with military captains, and his gathered host dwarfs the Israelite army that is figuratively described as two little flocks of goats. As in the previous section, a "man of God" arrives to forecast Israel's improbable victory – a startling success, as even the wall of Aphek joins in by crushing an additional 27,000 Aramean troops – although the dénouement in vv. 35-43 provides a condemnation of Ahab for sparing his captive Ben-Hadad and cutting a covenant (*berît*) for a renewed economic partnership. There is an irony in the words of Ben-Hadad's servants, who state that the kings of the house of Israel have a reputation for mercy, but in reality it is God who has extended considerable mercy toward the northern kingdom. Ben-Hadad is penitent toward Ahab and wears rope and sackcloth, but Ahab is not penitent before God, nor does he subjugate Aram for the security of Israel, leading to a prophetic condemnation. Scholars have grappled with the reason(s) for the prophetic sentencing in vv. 35–43, but a clue can be found in the collapse of Aphek's wall with its allusions to Jericho and the "holy war" (*ḥērem*) motifs in Joshua 6.[18] A central text outlining holy war conduct is Deut 20:16-18, and although it applies to Canaanite cities, the incursion of Ben-Hadad into Israelite territory – coupled with God's declaration in v. 13 that "I will deliver them into your hand today" – is sufficient warrant for its relevance in this battle with Aram.[19] The manner of Ahab's indictment, however, comes in the form of a juridical parable whereby the king is entrapped by his own words.

---

[18] Nelson, *First and Second Kings*, 137: "For exilic readers living in an environment in which accommodation to the surrounding culture was a fact of life, this narrative was a call to re-examine their behavior in light of God's law. What on the surface might seem an acceptable and even enlightened action, could on deeper reflection turn out to be a fatal betrayal of their religious identity." Nelson moves toward a contemporary application by conceding that holy war bans are not within the purview of readers today, but there is a deeper challenge in this episode: "What betrayals and violations of God's will are hidden in the everyday morality of our modern lives?"

[19] Cf. Schipper, *Parables and Conflict in the Hebrew Bible*, 87: "The elders advised Ahab to resist Ben-Hadad rather than accommodate his wishes. In v. 22, the prophet tells Ahab to consider the situation with Ben-Hadad carefully. Yet, whereas the elders of the land encourage resistance to Ben-Hadad, ultimately Ahab opts for accommodation when he makes a treaty with Ben-Hadad and sends him home in vv. 31-34."

Far from being straightforward, the concluding scenes of 1 Kings 20 have some strange twists, and before Ahab is formally indicted, an unnamed member of the "sons of the prophets" is also on the wrong side of judgment. There are some parallels here with 1 Kings 13, such as unusual prophetic behavior and the arrival of a lion who kills a colleague for not obeying a command, and in both episodes the kings (Jeroboam and Ahab) have been given multiple opportunities to turn away from their disastrous course. It is unclear exactly how Ahab recognizes the prophet when he lowers the bandage from his eyes in v. 41, but it does imply much more interaction between the king and various prophets, a point that is picked up again in 1 Kgs 22:13 and suggest that Ahab has been approached by prophets numerous times in his career. Furthermore, in v. 42 the anonymous prophet announces Ahab's penalty of death ("your life for his life, your people for his people"), so it is not without irony that Ahab is wounded and eventually dies courtesy of an Aramean arrow in battle in 22:34–35. The prophetic sentence includes more than Ahab, for the people will suffer as well, confirming Elijah's earlier retort that Ahab has become a troubler of the land, like Achan who also violates the rules of holy war.[20] The brooding reaction of Ahab ("vexed and sullen") might be caused by reflecting on his punishment, or perhaps he is angry after being hoodwinked by the prophet, but his emotional vicissitudes continue in the next chapter, where other violations of Israel's traditions loom large.

Jezebel is last heard breathing out murderous threats against Elijah, and it is an apt introduction to her role in the sordid episode involving Naboth of Jezreel and his vineyard in 1 Kings 21. Ahab is labeled *king of Samaria*, an oblique reminder that

---

[20] Seow, "The First and Second Books of Kings," 153.

Samaria was purchased by Omri in 16:24 for two talents of silver, and now Ahab offers silver (or a comparable trade) to Naboth. Behind this attempted real estate transaction, commentators note that vineyard imagery is often used for Israel (e.g., Isa 5:1–7; Jer 12:10), while *vegetable garden* only otherwise occurs in Deuteronomy 11:10, where it is a synecdoche for Egyptian abundance: "Symbolically, Ahab's intention is to turn the vineyard of Israel into an Egyptian vegetable patch, and this is consistent with his entire policy of 're-Canaanitization' of Israel."[21] The grounds of Naboth's refusal are best understood in terms of *tôrāh*, as his oath reflects traditions such as Lev 25:23, "The land will not be sold permanently, for the land is mine; with me you are but aliens and tenants." In the previous chapter, Ahab was "sullen and vexed" after the prophetic confrontation and has the same reaction to Naboth's insistence that he will not barter with the inheritance of his ancestors. The king descends to a new level of immaturity by sulking and refusing to eat, paving the way for Jezebel to assume control: David once crafted a deadly letter that resulted in the murder of Uriah the Hittite, and now Jezebel writes in the king's name and orders the nobility to create a pretext for Naboth's execution during a "fast" (*ṣôm*). Rather cynically, she cleverly exploits the blasphemy law of Exodus 22:28 ("You shall not revile God, or curse a leader of your people") in order to annex Naboth's land, using the *tôrāh* against itself. It is unclear if the elders comply because of fear or narrow self-interest, but Naboth is duly executed, and Jehu later asserts (2 Kgs 9:26) that Naboth's sons are also put to death, allowing the king to take possession of the vineyard without hindrance. In 1 Sam 8:14, the nation was warned that kings would take

---

[21] Leithart, *1 & 2 Kings*, 154.

vineyards, and now Naboth and his sons have their inheritance taken away by Jezebel's cunning artifice. En route to taking possession of Naboth's vineyard, Ahab is (again) confronted by a reactivated Elijah: God sends the prophet with a terse message of doom, and the scope is expanded by Elijah to include the utter eradication of Ahab's house and Jezebel's evisceration by dogs.[22] The punishment outlined by Elijah is tailored to the crime, and as Ahab and Jezebel are guilty of violently taking a life, so their lives will be violently terminated with no hope for any dynastic inheritance (like Jeroboam and Baasha before them). Instead of his customary "sullen and vexed" response, Ahab walks around "meekly" clothed in sackcloth. Considering the narrator's excoriation of Ahab in vv. 25–26 as the worst of the wicked, the reader might be skeptical about Ahab's sackcloth, especially because Ben-Hadad was likewise attired for purely political and survival reasons (20:31–32). Moreover, Naboth is framed by means of a fraudulent fast, but Ahab's sincerity is illustrated through a genuine fast (ṣôm) when he hears the word of Elijah. Ahab is an emotive character to be sure, but this scene indicates that he takes the Israelite faith more seriously than may have been supposed; otherwise, his reaction would be closer to Jehoiakim in Jer 36:24 who hears the words of the scroll but shows no fear. But Ahab's surprising response pales in comparison to God's shocking reaction, and through a self-disclosure to Elijah commends the king's penitence and announces a deferred punishment until the next generation, though whether Ahab is ever acquainted with this delay is unclear. God's word to Elijah is reminiscent of Gen 18:17

---

[22] On Elijah's expansion of the divine oracle, see Wray Beal, *1 & 2 Kings*, 276, and Walsh, *1 Kings*, 331. Note also the similar dynamic in 2 Kings 9:1–10.

("Should I hide from Abraham what I am about to do?"), although in 1 Kings 21 Ahab's repentance becomes an object lesson for the prophet, and, by extension, the reader. On the positive side, God's response to Ahab suggests divine openness to human repentance, not mitigating the prophetic word but always allowing for the possibility of transformation. For audiences in exile and beyond, the notion that Ahab – despite his atrocities – can prompt God to look with favor is surely a powerful moment. Yet on the negative side, judgment on Ahab's house cannot be endlessly postponed and remains inevitable, and consequently the expropriation of Naboth's vineyard serves to anticipate the exile itself in 2 Kings 25: just as the kings of Israel and Judah steal land and possessions from their citizens, so the kings of Assyria and Babylon will take land and possessions. In light of such systemic failures, various prophetic texts such as Isaiah 42:1 unfold a messianic vision of a just ruler: "Behold my servant, whom I uphold, my chosen one in whom my soul delights; I have placed my spirit upon him, and he will bring forth justice to the nations" (cf. Jer 23:5).

There is scant evidence of Ahab's repentance in the long chapter of 1 Kings 22, where hostilities with Aram are renewed and Ahab's blood – as forecast in 21:19 – is finally consumed by dogs, though in Samaria rather than Jezreel. The southern king Jehoshaphat is formally introduced at the end of the chapter, but appears early on in deliberations with Ahab, and we later discover he has made a marriage alliance (2 Kgs 8:18; cf. 2 Chr 18:1) that causes much damage and is nearly fatal for the Davidic line. As it stands, the quarrel over Ramoth-Gilead gives rise to a number of theological questions and conundrums, such as the issue of true versus false prophecy, the possibility of divine deception, and the fulfillment of Elijah's word concerning Ahab's doom. In the opening scenes of the chapter, Jehoshaphat hardly seems to have a choice when Ahab invites him to reclaim Ramoth-Gilead, but his request for a genuine oracle – rather than the enthusiastic affirmation of Ahab's four hundred sycophants – raises the issue of the group's legitimacy. No explicit identification of the group as Baal prophets is provided, but the number four hundred is suspiciously reminiscent of Mount Carmel, and Zedekiah's patronymic ("Chenaanah") forms a soundplay with Canaanite. In yet another unexpected turn, Ahab acknowledges in v. 8 that there is a true prophet, "But I hate him, for he does not prophesy good things about me, only evil: Micaiah, son of Imlah!" While Micaiah is fetched, attention turns to the tableau on the threshing floor, and this is not an incidental spatial setting, as it underscores the separation of "the wheat from the chaff" in the prophetic realm: "In Hos 9:1–2, for instance, prostitution on threshing floors is associated with the worship of other gods and the polemic against Baʿal, the deity responsible for the land's fertility. Threshing floors suggest hybridity, the miscegenation of Canaanite and Israelite, the antithesis, in other words, of Yahwistic purity."[23]

Micaiah's repartee with Ahab indicates previous hostilities and doses of sarcasm, but when his oracle is unveiled, it is a unique vision within the Deuteronomistic History. Not without irony, Ahab adjures Micaiah to speak the truth "in the name of the LORD," and Micaiah unfolds his utterance: he reports the striking of Israel's shepherd on the mountains, and then, after Ahab complains to Jehoshaphat, Micaiah describes a lying spirit dispatched from the celestial council to entice Ahab by means of his

---

[23] Francis Landy, "Threshing Floors and Cities," in *Memory and the City in Ancient Israel*, ed. Diana V. Edelman and Ehud Ben Zvi (Winona Lake, IN: Eisenbrauns, 2014), 79–97 (80).

own prophets to his death in battle at Ramoth-Gilead in vv. 19–23. Some interpreters might be uneasy about God using deception to forward an agenda, but that is exactly what is happening here: under the aegis of divine sovereignty, even lying spirits can be dispatched for judgment against a wayward king.[24] For an audience in exile and beyond, this scene presents a new angle on the horizons of God's power, as even false prophets can be co-opted to accomplish the divine will. Ahab, of course, is now informed outright that he is being deceived by Zedekiah and his gang of sycophants, which the reader suspects he knows already, thus raising the stakes in the public arena. But Micaiah's boldness in confronting Ahab earns him a slap in face from the iron-horned Zedekiah, and his further prophecy about Zedekiah hiding in an inner room evokes memories of Ben-Hadad's hiding in 20:30.

---

[24] Cf. the lengthy discussion in Fretheim, *First and Second Kings*, 126–28. Note also Seow, "The First and Second Books of Kings," 167: "The most profound, if also confounding, theological message in this passage is that God may not fit our preconceived image of unimpeachable goodness. The passage jolts us into the realization that such a notion of deity, ironically, is too limiting for God. Such a god would be an idol, a god of our own creation. Rather, the passage forces us to deal with a God who is sovereign, a God who is absolutely free to use any means – even those contrary to human reason or standards of morality – in order to bring divine purpose to fulfillment. The God of the Bible is a sovereign deity who oversees all that goes on in the world, darkness as well as light, woe as well as weal (Isa 45:7). The biblical God may harden people's hearts so that they do not respond to God aright (Exod 4:21; 9:12; 10:1, 20, 27; 11:10; 14:8; Deut 2:30; Isa 6:10; Rom 9:18), incite people to do wrong and then condemn them (2 Sam 24:1), deceive people (Jer 4:10), or send lying spirits (2 Thess 2:11)." For a perspective of the divine that further considers the mysterious and inscrutable on a broader canvas, see J. J. M. Roberts, "Does God Lie? Divine Deceit as a Theological Problem in Israelite Prophetic Literature," in *The Bible and the Ancient Near East: Collected Essays* (Winona Lake, IN: Eisenbrauns, 2002), 123–31.

Ahab has been informed that he will die in battle, but his defiance is unyielding as he imprisons Micaiah and is determined to survive the fracas with the Arameans at Ramoth-Gilead. Jehoshaphat must rue his alliance with the north when he has to enter the battle as a highly visible target arrayed in his royal robes, while Ahab – with shades of Saul and Jeroboam – enters the fray in disguise, attempting to thwart Micaiah's oracle.[25] Yet the manner of Ahab's demise is equal to his wily machination, as an Aramean soldier fires an arrow at random that just happens to pierce the disguised Ahab between the joints of his armor. The narrative does not explicitly announce that God has directed the arrow, but the reader is invited to conclude that a hidden guidance system is at work. Ahab's body remains propped up in his chariot, sardonically continuing the theme of deception in this chapter, but when his blood is lapped up by the dogs, Elijah's earlier oracle and Micaiah's recent prediction are brought to fulfillment, as Ahab belatedly discovers that outmaneuvering the prophetic word is a difficult proposition. Jehoshaphat, meanwhile, manages to survive the battle despite his royal robes and close call in vv. 32–33, but a concluding notice in 22:48–49 outlines a failed naval expedition, a fitting metaphor for Jehoshaphat's alliance with the north that nearly shipwrecks the house of David as the long central section of the book of Kings continues.

FIRE AND WATER

The death of Ahab results in the accession of his son Ahaziah, whose fleeting tenure is distinguished only by a string of failures: Jehoshaphat refuses a maritime partnership (22:49), Moab rebels

---

[25] Cf. R. Coggins, "On Kings and Disguises," *JSOT* 50 (1991): 55–62.

(2 Kgs 1:1, a thread that is resumed in 2 Kings 3, where Jehoshaphat also resurfaces), and Ahaziah himself suffers a serious injury in an ignominious fall from the upper chamber (*ʿăliyāh*). Appreciating that the division between 1 and 2 Kings is usually deemed by scholars as somewhat arbitrary, it nonetheless is interesting that 2 Kings 1 begins in the same way as 1 Kings 1: a monarch confined to his bed with an uncertain future that creates a succession issue.[26] Ahaziah has inherited his father's predilection for heterodoxy (see 1 Kgs 22:52–53) and opts to consult Baʿal-zĕbûb, a name that many experts believe originally is the more lofty Baʿal-zĕbūl (meaning "Prince Baʿal") but satirically corrupted to "lord of the fly/flies."[27] It is curious that a Philistine deity is beseeched, but Ahaziah would have been better served by calling on Elijah, who in 1 Kgs 17:19–24 raises the widow's son from death in an upper chamber (*ʿăliyāh*).[28] Ironically, Ahaziah does get an answer, but neither the one that he wanted nor from the deity he consults; instead, his messengers are intercepted by Elijah on orders from an angel of God. Ahaziah sent his delegation to make an inquiry, but Elijah provides his own rebuking inquiry ("Is it because there is no God in Israel?") as his last confrontation with the house of Omri begins to unfold in 2 Kgs 1:3–4. Adding insult to injury, it is announced that Ahaziah will never recover from his mishap or leave his bed.

---

[26] Leithart, *1 & 2 Kings*, 165.
[27] E.g., John Day, *Yahweh and the Gods and Goddesses of Canaan*, JSOTSup 265 (Sheffield: Sheffield Academic Press, 2000), 79–80; on Beelzebul as the prince of demons in the New Testament, see Matt 12:24, Mark 3:22, Luke 11:14–20.
[28] On the idea that Ekron (*ʿqron*) forms a wordplay with the verb "to be barren/childless" (*ʿqr*) that highlights Ahaziah's lack of a son to succeed him, see Moshe Garsiel, *From Earth to Heaven: A Literary Study of the Elijah Stories in the Book of Kings* (Bethesda, MD: CDL Press, 2014), 147.

Elijah's visage must be well known because the king recognizes him from the description brought back by his messengers, "an owner of hair" (*ba'al śē'ār*). On the basis of Zech 13:4, it is possible that the description here refers to a hairy cloak worn by the prophet, probably the same one previously thrown in Elisha's direction (1 Kgs 19:19).[29] The mantle reappears in the next chapter, but, for the moment, Ahaziah's failed inquiry is comically rendered through a wordplay: the owner of hair (*ba'al śē'ār*) triumphs over the lord of the flies (*ba'al zĕbûb*). Ahab once clothed himself in sackcloth after hearing Elijah's excoriation, but Ahaziah responds to the prophetic word by sending companies of soldiers to arrest Elijah on top of a mountain, where the troops are repeatedly consumed by fire until the third captain is able to survive by pleading for mercy. The fire from heaven not only recalls the events at Mount Carmel, but also glances forward to Elijah's incendiary departure in the next chapter. Ahaziah repeatedly attempts to control the prophetic word, but his death in v. 17 confirms that he is not equal to the task; the sterility of his reign is further underscored by the fact that he has no heir, and so his brother Jehoram inherits the throne. Confusingly, there are now two kings of the same name (see 1 Kgs 22:50), but this is an apt comment on the similarities of the two kingdoms because of the marriage alliance between north and south. As for the northern Jehoram, he has received a kingdom in decline: the reference to the ships in the previous chapter indicates less seafaring reach than Solomon, while the Moabite rebellion points to waning external influence, and, in the context of the narrative, perhaps heightening divine judgment in keeping with rising apostasy.

---

[29] Mark J. Boda, *Haggai, Zechariah*, NIVAC (Grand Rapids, MI: Zondervan, 2004), 492.

Almost all of the attention in Ahaziah's reign was devoted to the story of his death, and in contrast his brother Jehoram will receive much more press (2 Kings 3–9). But Jehoram's career is held in abeyance in 2 Kings 2 as the narrative turns to a more impressive succession narrative, and the downward fall of Ahaziah forms a dramatic antithesis to the ascension of Elijah. In a rare occurrence, no monarchs are present in 2 Kings 2, as they seemingly are thrust aside to make way for a dramatic transfer of prophetic authority, perhaps to highlight a greater power than kings and their agendas.

At three different moments in 1 Kings 19, Elijah asks God to "take" (*lāqaḥ*) his life; in 2 Kings 2 God evidently obliges, an event that is foreshadowed even in the opening verse. In Gen 5:24, Enoch is famously taken (*lāqaḥ*) by God, but that event is much more laconic and cryptic than Elijah's fiery transport in this chapter. Apart from Elijah, a starring role is finally given to Elisha, who has not been heard from since having the mantle thrown at him in 1 Kgs 19:19–21. Immediately the apprentice displays the twin qualities of persistence as he follows his rather frenetic master and patience in dealing with the continual stream of inquiries from the "sons of the prophets," a group that makes various kinds of appearances in this sector of the book of Kings. On the positive side, they are faithful in dark times and work to keep the flame alive in an era of Omride accommodation; on the negative side, we will have occasion to observe that they are prone to misadventure and even in this chapter display only a partial grasp. But the sons of the prophets have clearly been informed somehow about Elijah's imminent departure, and various companies are encountered as Elijah and Elisha travel around, following a geographical itinerary that resembles the early conquest narrative of Joshua 3–8 (including crossing the Jordan on dry ground).³⁰ Significantly, Elijah invites his apprentice to ask for a parting gift, and Elisha's request for a "double portion" of his master's spirit is frequently interpreted as a reference to the inheritance rights of a firstborn son and heir.³¹ By means of this forthright request, Elisha is about to become the most elaborately drawn prophetic figure in the book of Kings, as he continues what Elijah starts: dismantling the house of Omri. Furthermore, it can be argued that over the course of his career Elisha doubles or enhances the miracles of his master, strongly suggesting that he is bequeathed a double inheritance of Elijah's spirit.³² The condition imposed on Elisha's request, however, is that he has to "see" Elijah's departure, a qualification that is met as Elisha has a front-row seat when Elijah is caught up in the tempest accompanied by a chariot of fire. Such an unprecedented departure cries out for a second act, and the manner of Elijah's heavenward ascent created expectations for his return as a "harbinger of the 'day of the LORD' (Mal 4:5)" and other associations with the messianic age, most prominently his appearance on the mountain of transfiguration in the synoptic gospels (e.g., Mt 17:3; Mk 9:4; Lk 9:30).³³

---

[30] Fretheim, *First and Second Kings*, 137. [31] Wray Beal, *1 & 2 Kings*, 304.
[32] Robert L. Cohn, "The Literary Structure of Kings," in *The Books of Kings: Sources, Composition, Historiography and Reception*, ed. Baruch Halpern, André Lemaire and Matthew J. Adams, VTSup 129 (Leiden: Brill, 2010), 107–22 (119).
[33] Seow, "The First and Second Books of Kings," 179. For Nelson (*First and Second Kings*, 163), the chariots and horse provide an allusion to Deuteronomy 20:1: "The replacement of one word for horse (v. 11) with another (v. 12, translated 'horsemen' by RSV) may point back to Yahweh's classic defense of the people in the exodus (Ex 14:9, 17, 18, 23, 26, 28) and to the Deuteronomistic and prophetic insistence that Israel's true defense never lies in the horses of Egypt (Dt 17:16; Is 31:1). Israel's secret defensive weapon was God (cf. Eph 6:10–17; Rom. 8:37–39)"

Witnessing his master's departure becomes a defining moment for Elisha: he emerges as a character with uncommon insight into the divine realm, and he will have his own moments with chariots and fire later in the narrative (see 6:17), formidable weapons beyond the reach of any earthly monarch. Upon picking up his master's mantle in 2 Kgs 2:13, Elisha's first act is to traverse the Jordan as a kind of new Joshua, who sets out to continue the (re)conquest of the land set in motion by Elijah (who is, in this light, the Moses figure of the wilderness) after the policies of Canaanization by the house of Omri.[34] Nonetheless, the sons of the prophets insist on sending out a search party, much to Elisha's consternation, and in this regard they are akin to the disciples in the gospels, with various degrees of doubt and diverging agendas. After the fruitless search, attention shifts to an emergency at Jericho (vv. 19–22), as its famed water supply has turned "evil" and causes bereavement, as though the land itself is reacting in protest to the sterile domestic policies of the Omrides. Summoning the prophet Elisha proves to be a wise decision, as he throws salt in the water, just as Moses once threw wood into a bitter pool with the same result (Ex 15:25): the waters of Jericho are healed, and there will be no more bereavement or death through miscarriages. The next episode in Bethel (vv. 23–25) – where Elisha curses a group of boys for an insult about his bald head and a pair of she-bears tear forty-two of them apart – has proven unsavory for many modern readers: "This murderous response to the boys' mockery is morally scandalous. Is it meant to suggest that Elisha does not make responsible use of his prophetic powers,

---

[34] Rachelle Gilmour, *Juxtaposition and the Elisha Cycle*, LHBOTS 594 (New York and London: T. and T. Clark, 2014), 82–87.

that after turning death to life at the spring he now spreads death?"³⁵ Surely the deaths of children (*yelādîm*) would be an obstacle for any interpreter, but it is curious that the same language in v. 23 for "small lads" (*neʿārîm qeṭannîm*) is also found in Solomon's self-description (1 Kgs 3:7), and he is hardly a child at the time. Furthermore, Rehoboam's cronies "who grew up with him" are labeled "children" (*yelādîm*) in 1 Kgs 12:8, but given that Rehoboam is forty-one years old (see 14:21), the text seems to be providing a comment on their juvenile behavior. Instead of children, then, it is entirely possible that the description in this scene reflects the immaturity of their insult, and thus the narrative is structured to form a contrast: Jericho's citizens treat the prophet with respect and the land is healed of bereavement, whereas Bethel experiences bereavement when the prophet is mocked. Far from being random, the number forty-two recurs in 2 Kgs 10:14 where it points to the end of Ahab's line, and so these opening scenes in Elisha's public career form an overture and a warning to the rest of the nation.³⁶ Burke Long provides a thoughtful summary:

> If Moses-Joshua represent a paradigm of transition for an earlier formative period in Israel's history, then Elijah-Elisha appear to serve a similar purpose for the DtrH. As Moses-Joshua stand for continuity in Yahweh's faithfulness and *tôrâ* giving, and constancy in obedient partnership, so Elijah-Elisha represent steady voices for Jerusalemite-styled Yahwistic allegiance in a kingdom laboring under the pernicious shadows of Jeroboam and Ahab. It

---

³⁵ Alter, *Ancient Israel*, 731. Cf. Mobley's caution: "the prophets in the books of Kings refuse to conform to our projections of ideal ethical heroes" ("1 and 2 Kings," 131). In some respects, the character of God might be similarly difficult for modern readers to accept, if God does not conform to projections.

³⁶ Dietrich, "1 & 2 Kings," 249.

was probably a long view from exile which took up this sweeping panoramic vision and suggested such special enhancement of Elisha's status. The pausal moment between reigns gave the opportunity for such analogical image making, and constrained the reader to make new associations with the paradigms that had always made theological sense of national memory.[37]

After the unique pause to narrate the prophetic succession that will prove decisive in ending the Omride dynasty, the storyline returns to Jehoram in 2 Kings 3 and begins with an appraisal of his reign: he initially appears in a better light than Ahab and Jezebel by removing the "Baal Pillar," but since it later needs to be demolished by Jehu in 2 Kgs 10:27 when the temple is turned into a latrine, it must have just been put into storage; therefore, an aura of ambivalence surrounds Jehoram's character. If his brother and predecessor Ahaziah "portrays a typical apostate, embodies the sickness of Israel, and typifies the struggle between the adherents of the Lord and Baal for the soul of God's elect," then Jehoram is representative of those who are unwilling to fully submit to God's kingship over the nation, and so the spiritual struggle of Israel is variously refracted through the portraits of these two monarchs.[38] The bulk of the action in 2 Kgs 3:4–27 revolves around the coalition assault on Moab because of the rebellion mentioned in 2 Kgs 1:1, and has been of interest to historians in more recent days because of background data supplied by the Mesha Stele.[39]

---

[37] Burke O. Long, *2 Kings*, FOTL 10 (Grand Rapids, MI: Eerdmans, 1991), 31.
[38] Fretheim, *First and Second Kings*, 139.
[39] For an overview of the Mesha Stele in context, see Kyle Greenwood, "Late Tenth- and Ninth-Century Issues: Ahab Underplayed? Jehoshaphat Over-Played?" in *Ancient Israel's History: An Introduction to Issues and Sources*, ed. Bill T. Arnold and Richard S. Hess (Grand Rapids, MI: Baker, 2014), 286–318.

Several movements within this chapter are particularly relevant for our study, starting with an acute water crisis: Jehoram recruits the king of Edom in the campaign against Moab, but, rather than cross the Jordan, he opts for the southern route through the Edomite desert, and over a seven-day period no water is found. Furthermore, Jehoshaphat has also been commandeered – locating this episode within the six-year overlap between the two allied kings of north and south – and sounds exactly as he did in 1 Kings 22 with Jehoram's father Ahab, including the call for a prophet after Jehoram's exclamation of despair in v. 10. An Israelite servant knows that Elisha is present, and designates him as the one who "used to pour water" on Elijah's hands; this description is not only appealing in light of the present crisis, but also anticipates Elisha's prediction. Like Elijah and Micaiah before him, Elisha is sharp with the king of Israel, and his prophetic response – even closer to Micaiah with his deceptively straightforward utterances – may be more complex than it seems. Owing to the presence of Jehoshaphat, Elisha is willing to comply and asks for a musician (see 1 Sam 10:5). His oracle in vv. 16–19 sounds encouraging: not only will the valley be filled with water but the Moabites will also be given into the hand of the coalition, extending grace once again to an heir of Omri.

For the second time during his ill-fated alliance with the north, Jehoshaphat has landed in an unenviable predicament: earlier he had to enter the theater of war dressed in his royal robes (1 Kgs 22:30), and now in the Edomite desert, he is dying of thirst. But Jehoshaphat survived the battle of Ramoth-Gilead, and now he survives the desert crisis because, as Elisha forecasted, the land is suddenly filled with water. This event occurs as an antithesis to Jehoram's misguided theological utterance in v. 10 ("Alas! For the LORD has called these three kings to give them into the hand of

Moab"), and it is certainly not the last histrionic outburst in his career. The temporal setting for the miracle is during the morning "about the time of offering the sacrifice," and complements the time of the evening sacrifice in 1 Kgs 18:36 when the fire of God consumes the altar on Mount Carmel. In 2 Kgs 3:20–23, the miraculous water not only saves the coalition troops, but also serves to deliver the Moabites in their hands: tricked by the color of the water, the Moabites falsely assume – much like Jehoram makes false assumptions in v. 10 – that the coalition forces have turned on each other (cf. 1 Sam 14:20), and instead of hastening to the plunder, they are precipitating their own demise. The reversal of fortune is sealed with a wordplay: flowing from the direction of Edom (*ĕdôm*), the water appears red (*ădom*) like blood, and so the water is the catalyst for a larger triumph. The environmental despoliation appears to contradict the guidelines of Deuteronomy 20:19–20, but even more controversial is the episode's chilling dénouement: with his back against the wall, the king of Moab offers his own son, the crown prince, as a sacrifice in v. 27. The "great wrath" against Israel is often thought to be divine (either the God of Israel or Chemosh of Moab), but since later Israelite kings such as Ahaz (2 Kgs 16:3) and Manasseh (21:6) are guilty of the same crime and there is no "great wrath," it is possible to interpret the anger as belonging to Moabite soldiers.[40] The withdrawal of the coalition has prompted some scholars to accuse Elisha of false prophecy, but as Raymond Westbrook points out, Elisha had merely announced in v. 19 that the cities would be "struck."[41]

---

[40] Note the comparative theological reflections of Christopher B. Hays, *Hidden Riches: A Sourcebook for the Comparative Study of the Hebrew Bible and Ancient Near East* (Louisville, KY: Westminster John Knox Press, 2014), 198.

[41] Raymond R. Westbrook, "Elisha's True Prophecy in 2 Kings 3," *JBL* 124 (2005): 530–32.

Consequently, Jehoram fails to complete the task of subduing Moab, the kind of half-heartedness that will mark his career until his final demise in 2 Kings 9. At the heart of the episode stands a sacrificial contrast, since the miracle of water occurs at the time of the morning sacrifice but the sacrifice of the prince of Moab is an abomination, and so, like the wounded Ahaziah, the king of Moab now loses his heir.

ELISHA ACTS

In the initial episodes of his career, Elisha appears every bit as confrontational as his lately departed master, as the divine curse against the Bethelites or the scathing words for Jehoram in 3:13 illustrate: "Go to the prophets of your father and to the prophets of your mother!" Yet the earlier scene with Elisha in Jericho reveals a life-giving capacity, and when the prophet is honored, healing occurs and the future is much less bleak. There are two major sections in 2 Kings 4, and no monarch is present in either, and for any audience under the sway of kings or paralyzed by royal fiat, this chapter illustrates that the prophetic word is more enduring. Reminiscent of Elijah in Sidonian territory (1 Kgs 17:9–16), the first scene of this chapter features a widow in crisis. By contrast, this widow is not a foreigner, but rather the wife of a deceased member of the sons of the prophets, and she has the wisdom to call on Elisha when a creditor threatens to take her two sons (2 Kgs 4:1–7). Following orders that may not seem immediately obvious, the widow and her sons not only survive the credit crisis, but their longer-term survival is assured when Elisha instructs them to live on the remainder of the oil. The wealthy woman of Shunem has a similar experience in the next episode (4:8–17), but her crisis is not financial. Despite the obvious

Prophets and Apostasy 139

economic disparity between the two women, there is some thematic continuity in the two episodes. Elisha's peripeteia allows him to occasionally enjoy the hospitality of this unnamed woman and her husband, who are examples of steadfastness in the north despite the promotion of Baal by the house of Omri. Building an upper chamber (*'ăliyāh*) for Elisha is a kind gesture, but is slightly ominous as well given the disasters previously associated with this spatial setting in the careers of Elijah and Ahaziah. When Elisha is in conversation with his servant Gehazi – who plays a prominent role in the next chapter – the reader belatedly discovers that the woman's crisis is less obvious: she has no son, a need that cannot be satisfied in any financial way. In a variation of the "type-scene of the barren wife," the woman conceives and bears a son during the next season according to the word of Elisha.[42] Based on the convention of the type-scene, we expect the son to be an important figure in the narrative; however, he remains anonymous, suggesting that he is a symbolic representative of the people of Israel, and one who stands to "inherit" the land.[43] Meanwhile, the citizens of Jericho, Jehoshaphat of Judah, the widow, and the Shunnamite woman all now have something in common: unlike the kings of Israel, the prophetic word is able to meet their needs and transform their circumstances.

In the second major section of 2 Kgs 4:18–37 – again following in the footsteps of Elijah – there is an emergency: the son has grown up and can assist with the harvest, but suffers an injury or

---

[42] For an overview and extended discussion of the type-scene, see Timothy D. Finlay, *The Birth Report Genre in the Hebrew Bible*, FAT II/12 (Tübingen: Mohr Siebeck, 2005).

[43] On the poetics of anonymity, see Adele Reinhartz, *"Why Ask My Name?" Anonymity and Identity in Biblical Narrative* (New York: Oxford University Press, 1998).

sudden illness, and, in the arms of his long-suffering mother, he dies. The northern couple were granted an heir through Elisha's intervention – in contrast to the lack of an heir for Ahaziah and the Moabite king – yet in v. 20 it appears that death has triumphed. In dire straits, the woman conceals her journey to the prophet from her husband, much as God has concealed the reason for her distress from Elisha, and so this episode contains ample divine mystery. Earlier in v. 16 she had implored the prophet not to deceive her when he announced that she would give birth, and she reminds Elisha of this when she approaches him in v. 28. But after the marathon return trip from Mount Carmel, in Elisha's upper chamber (*'ăliyāh*), the boy is brought back to life: in the wake of the horrifying child sacrifice of the previous chapter, a promised son is resurrected in Israel, and the great woman of Shunem – unlike Ahaziah and the king of Moab – again has an heir. The boy's seven sneezes correspond to the seven times that Elijah's servant is ordered to check for rain clouds on Mount Carmel in 1 Kgs 18:44 and further enhances the notion that Elisha is continuing the work of his predecessor. When the Sidonian widow's son is given new life in 1 Kgs 17:24, she says to Elijah, "Now I know that you are a man of God, and that the word of the LORD in your mouth is truth." In 2 Kgs 4:37, there is no confession from the woman, only a silent bow, because her actions testify that she already believed that Elisha was a man of God, and hence she stands as an exemplar for any community of faith: when the prophetic word is involved, exile and even death are not necessarily the end of the story.

The two anecdotes at the end of 2 Kings 4 continue these themes, beginning with a scene in vv. 38–41 that returns us to the sons of the prophets. At the start of the chapter there was a widow, and so the reader may conclude that the sons of the prophets (and their families) lead a precarious existence. Here the threat of starvation is palpable: not only do the Omrides pose dangers, but now v. 38 describes a regional famine that makes life even more challenging for this overtaxed crew. With memories of Ahab, the group is reduced to foraging: "Though nothing is made of it here, the famine-drought circumstance evidences continuity with the Elijah narrative (1 Kgs 18:1–6), and continues the attestation that the Omride kings are ineffective in their public responsibility."[44] Under Elisha's orders, a well-meaning acolyte is dispatched to collect herbs, but unwittingly – and this is becoming a familiar pattern for this prophetic guild – brings back poison that threatens the lives of all. Yet as with the Jericho salt, Elisha's use of flour (1 Kgs 17:12) brings relief, and on a larger scale than the Shunammite's son the entire community is rescued from death. Second, in vv. 42–44 the famine is evidently over, because a farmer brings a gift of firstfruits as a gesture of support for the prophets. Unexpectedly, there is a voice of skepticism – parallel to Jehoram in 2 Kgs 3:10 – from within, the prophet's own (here unnamed) servant who doubts that the meager quantity of supplies can feed the multitude. But even a little might be enough when an authentic gift is offered to God (cf. Mk 12:42), and in v. 44 Elisha's utterance counters the skeptical murmuring, thereby reminding readers to never underestimate the prophetic capacity to feed and sustain. For New Testament readers, the leftovers in this episode foreshadow the twelve baskets to come during the messianic era (e.g., Jn 6:13), courtesy of a figure whose deeds transcend even those of Elisha himself, and where feeding the multitude, rescue from tyrannical oppression, and ultimately resurrection loom large.

---

[44] Brueggemann, *1 & 2 Kings*, 325.

The skeptical servant of Elisha prepares the way for further role reversals in 2 Kings 5, a long narrative that begins with an introduction to Naaman, the commander of the Aramean forces: he is a powerful warrior but leprous, and thus disqualified from various kinds of social interaction (see Leviticus 13–14). There are a pair of stunning theological developments in the opening verses, beginning with the notice that through Naaman, God has granted victory (or salvation) to Aram against Israel. Allowing victory for Aram is reminiscent of the days of the Judges when God allowed foreign armies to invade a wayward people (e.g., Judg 2:14; 3:8; 4:2), and this not only militates against any sense of entitlement Israel may have, but also anticipates the later use of larger superpowers as instruments of divine chastisement. Second, an unlikely voice is heard in v. 3, as a captured Israelite slave girl proclaims that Naaman can be cured through the hand of a prophet in Samaria: instead of bitterness toward her captor, she speaks words of life despite her "exilic" status. The kings of Aram and Israel have bit parts in this chapter – primarily as foils for the other characters – and by means of their diplomatic correspondence, it is obvious that neither king realizes that the prophetic word is not constrained by political boundaries or royal agendas. Although the Aramean brings considerable gifts (perhaps including plunder stolen from Israel?), Elisha later refuses to take anything but duly instructs Naaman in how to be rid of his leprosy in accordance with the words of the Israelite girl. Having made the trek, the reader may have thought that Naaman would follow Elisha's orders, but he has a tantrum and evidently desires a spectacular miracle. If not for the wise counsel of his servants, Naaman probably would have departed with his leprosy uncured, but he does eventually submit to the prophetic word, unlike the kings of Israel, and experiences healing. Indeed, v. 15 features a remarkable confession from an enemy of the state – "now I know that there is no God in all the earth but in Israel" – and in the process there a deep irony: the leaders and the people of Israel are spiraling deeper into idolatrous compromise even as a foreigner is healed and pledges to honor only the God of Israel. Naaman's newfound commitment is manifested in a request grounded in his former worldview: he asks for a load of Israelite soil, and asks for forgiveness when accompanying the king into the temple of Rimmon. Opting not to engage in a polemical discourse or correct Naaman's nascent misconceptions about the nature of Israel's God, Elisha simply dismisses him in *shālôm*.[45] Naaman feels shame at the prospect of having to enter an idolatrous temple in the line of duty, whereas such installations are proliferating in the very heart of Israel.

Elisha's aide de camp Gehazi is last seen in 2 Kgs 4:29–31 when he is unable to awaken the dead son of the Shunammite, and in 5:19–27 he again makes an appearance in the aftermath of another healing. Elisha has just refused any gift from Naaman after extending mercy to the foreign military leader – here anticipating the increasingly international scope of Israelite prophecy (e.g., Isa 2:2–4) – but Gehazi runs after Naaman, determined to acquire something. His ruse plays on the poverty of the sons of the prophet that the reader has already noticed, and Naaman – perhaps relieved that Gehazi's errand is not more serious – gladly complies. When Gehazi hides the loot in a house at the citadel (usually associated with a king's palace), Naaman's deception is complete, but this time God has apparently not concealed

---

[45] Cf. Wray Beal, *1 & 2 Kings*, 335: "No judgment is levelled against the foreigner and he is free to set the worship of YHWH into the complex demands of his existing allegiances, even though they are tied to foreign worship practices."

anything from Elisha (see 4:27).[46] Despite Gehazi's denial that he did not go anywhere, Elisha's searing questions are prefaced with an unmasking ("Did not my heart go when the man turned from his chariot to meet you?") followed by a penalty: at the beginning of the chapter, Naaman the outsider is leprous, but in a radical reversal the leprosy is transferred to Gehazi the insider, and he and his descendants will forever carry a reminder of the ill-advised decision to act treacherously. Here there is a contrast between Gehazi (*na'ar*) and the servant girl (*na'arāh*), as each has a completely difference approach to both Naaman and Elisha: even though Gehazi has presumably spent many hours with Elisha, he still tries to manipulate the prophet, whereas the captured Israelite girl has the highest respect for the prophet and compassion for an afflicted foreigner. The exiled captive manifests theological insight despite her adversity and remains an unsung hero in the Deuteronomistic History.

Not so long ago, prophets were reduced to hiding in caves during the aggression of Jezebel, but at the outset of 2 Kings 6, there is a need for a larger residence; they are still poor and need to borrow tools for the job, but the fortunes of the sons of the prophets are at least mildly improving. The spatial setting for the new residence is in the vicinity of the river Jordan – where Naaman was just healed – perhaps implying that the iron grip of the Omrides is weakening and the "re-conquest" of the land is gaining traction. Imploring Elisha to join the project could signal their appreciation of him and the need for strong leadership among the company; alternatively, they could be plagued with some doubts – given their previous record of crises – and need Elisha in the case of emergency. To be sure, a crisis shortly ensues as a borrowed ax

---

[46] Provan, *1 and 2 Kings*, 193.

head is lost in the river, but Elisha's intervention with a stick (again, shades of Moses) allows the iron to float, and the crisis is averted. Elisha instructs the man to "raise up" the floating iron in v. 7, and the only other places in Genesis–Kings where this particular form of the verb (*hārem*) occurs are Exodus 14:16 and Joshua 4:5, important moments of the story when the Red Sea and the river Jordan are crossed and both Egypt and the wilderness are left behind.[47] As a group, this is the last appearance of the sons of the prophets, and apart from a supporting role by a younger member in 2 Kgs 9:1–10, they gradually fade from view. After the house of the Omri is destroyed, the mission of the sons of the prophets – a provisional movement that evidently arises as a reaction to that dynasty – seems accomplished. Perhaps it is symbolically appropriate that the completion of the new residence is never recorded in the text, and the reader does not hear about it again.

ROYAL ENTANGLEMENTS

In the next major sector of the narrative, the monarchs return to prominence, and most of the later accounts of Elisha in 2 Kings 6–8 include various interactions with royal figures. Compared to his master, Elisha is a more urban prophet and has complex relationships with a number of leaders. There is also a more international scope to his words, as is evident in 6:8–14 where the narrative shifts from the banks of the Jordan to the foreign court of the king of Aram. In response of Naaman's leprosy, the

---

[47] See W. Brian Aucker, "Putting Elisha in His Place: Genre, Coherence, and Narrative Function in 2 Kings 2–8" (Ph.D. diss., University of Edinburgh, 2000), 164.

king of Aram wrote a letter in 5:5–6 asking the king of Israel to cure Naaman, but in this next sequence he will personally discover that there is a remarkable prophet in Israel during a crisis of his own: he suspects a traitor within his ranks because the king of Israel is continually warned about the location of the Aramean war camps. When Naaman is healed, he articulates a confession about the incomparability of Israel's God (5:15), and in 6:12 a member of the Aramean court somehow knows that Elisha has divine insight that penetrates the king's very thoughts. Elisha's own servant Gehazi learned a difficult lesson about the prophet's supernatural insight, yet here this anonymous member of the Aramean court recognizes the uncommon power of Elisha's vision. When the king of Aram issues the arrest order – it is unclear how anyone knows Elisha is in Dothan or why he would stay there if the king is about to apprehend him – he resembles his Israelite counterparts, as Ahab was angry and searched for Elijah while Ahaziah likewise sent troops to seize him. Elisha is increasingly becoming a prophet whose words and actions have implications beyond the territory of Israel, and the king of Aram is now seemingly under his jurisdiction. Ironically, it is obvious in vv. 9–10 that Jehoram chose to listen to Elisha's advice and so avoids the Aramean troops: when he submits to the prophetic directive, he is much more successful at home and abroad.

The king of Aram has scant appreciation of his subordinate's comment about Elisha's auditory prowess, and instead musters a host and deploys his forces under the cover of night. The situation is risibly disproportionate, as a massive host is sent to arrest a single prophet, but the king's order to his troops to go and "see" (*rā'āh*) where the prophet is introduces a very important thematic plot movement in vv. 13–23. Indeed, an evocative and theologically rich set of scenes unfolds in Dothan, initially refracted from the perspective of Elisha's unnamed servant who innocently gets up in the morning and sees (*rā'āh*) the immense Aramean host.[48] Yet the servant's cry of despair is met with a prayer of Elisha to open the lad's eyes, and thus he is able to see that they are far from outnumbered: "Then the LORD opened the servant's eyes and he saw (*rā'āh*), and look, the mountain was full of horses and chariots of fire all around Elisha!" Having inherited a double portion of his master's spirit, the same fiery fleet that accompanied Elijah's translation now surrounds Elisha, and along with the servant, the reader is given a glimpse into a rarely seen world: to paraphrase *Hamlet*, there are more things in heaven and Earth than contained in the Omride philosophies. At a critical time in national history amid the darkness of the northern kingdom, the prophet is equipped with uncommon resources. Exilic readers may be invited to reimagine divine sovereignty when surrounded by similarly daunting foreign armies: combined with texts such as Isaiah 40 and Psalm 2 that outline both God's character and authority over the nations, the celestial host perceived by Elisha's servant could be unleashed at any moment, yet only is selectively unveiled. It could be argued that the nameless servant is a cipher in the story, representing the people of God who are encouraged to not fear when under visible threat – to believe in the prophetic word and trust that "twelve legions of angels" (Mt 26:53) are ever at the disposable of legitimate divine agents.[49] In 2 Kgs 6:18, it can

---

[48] Cf. Dietrich, "1 & 2 Kings," 251: "The city is quickly surrounded and there is no escape for Elisha. The reader sees through the eyes of the despairing servant what nobody else but Elisha can see: a heavenly host stands by Elisha, who also have horses and chariots, but theirs are made of fire (v. 17)."

[49] On characters such as Elisha's servant and the unnamed Israelite girl who speak in 5:3, see Mobley, "1 and 2 Kings," 134: "They constitute the faithful

be imagined that this celestial army – perhaps on standby, ready to enact the prophet's word – is responsible for activating Elisha's prayer to strike the Arameans with sudden blindness, the same word used in Gen 19:11 when the mob of Sodom surrounding Lot's house are similarly blinded. A stunning reversal thus occurs in Dothan, as a massive army arrived by night in order to arrest the prophet, only to be arrested themselves in the darkness of sudden blindness and subsequently led by Elisha right into the middle of Samaria. It is not stated if the king of Israel is surprised by this turn of events, but in v. 21 he is keen to destroy the enemy soldiers who have harassed the Israelites; like Elisha's servant when he sees the Aramean host in v. 15 and is full of fear, so the king's ebullient reaction is natural. However, the king is under the prophet's dominion here, and rather than destruction, Elisha views the matter differently and orders hospitality. Setting a table before one's enemies outlines a radical alternative to the typical ways of kings in the world, and consistent with the theme of new insight and vision in this chapter, Elisha's peaceful dismissal of the captured troops brings about a season of peace after contentious hostility.

Rather than lasting gratitude for his released soldiers, in 2 Kgs 6:24 the king of Aram prepares an even larger assault: with Samaria under siege, conditions in the city become desperate, driving mothers toward cannibalism (see Deut 28:53–57) and prompting Israel's king to utter a death threat against Elisha in v. 31. Not so long ago he called the prophet "father" (6:21), but

> remnant that the writing prophets always promised would make it through any disaster (Is 10:20–21; Jer 23:3; Am 5:15; Mi 2:12), the righteous who survive because of their faithfulness (Hb 2:4)." Cf. Brueggemann, *1 & 2 Kings*, 352: "The faithful are always deciding whether the hidden resources of God are an adequate ground for acting differently in a world of hostility and danger."

now he calls for his head, and it is conceivable that the king is furious because Elisha ordered clemency for the Aramean soldiers, only to have Arameans now besieging the city. But Ben-Hadad has recently discovered that Elisha can predict enemy movements and therefore is difficult to arrest, and even as the king marches toward his house, Elisha prepares for a confrontation. In 2 Kgs 7:1, Elisha issues a bold oracle before the king and the elders: although inflation is rampant in the besieged city – with a donkey's head fetching upward of eighty shekels – the prophet declares that the very next day will bring bargain prices for barley and flour at the gate of Samaria. In 6:33, there is a complaint that this "evil" situation is from God, but there is no stated reaction from the king about Elisha's startling forecast; instead, there is a voice of skepticism from the king's consigliere, who sarcastically remarks that even if God were to make windows (*'arubāh*) in heaven, such an event could not possibly happen! By responding to this incredulity with a retort that the officer will see it but not partake of it (7:2), Elisha reaffirms the forecast and rebukes the officer at the same time. It is important to note that Elisha announces a drastic reduction in prices at the *gate* of Samaria, the focal point of an ancient city "for security (Gn 19:1; Jgs 16:2–3), commercial transaction, (2 Kgs 7:1; Am 5:10, 15), and legal adjudication (Dt 21:15, 19; 22:24; 25:7)."[50] Control of the city gate thus emerges as a key issue here, for in each of these areas – security, economics and social justice – the kings of Israel have

---

[50] Carey Walsh, "Testing Entry: The Social Functions of City Gates in Biblical Memory," in *Memory and the City in Ancient Israel*, ed. Diana V. Edelman and Ehud Ben Zvi (Winona Lake, IN: Eisenbrauns, 2014), 43–59 (43); cf. Nelson, *First and Second Kings*, 191.

failed, yet now this pivotal spatial setting is on the threshold of transformation by the prophetic word.

It is hardly an accident that the story switches to the gate of Samaria for the beginning of the next episode of 7:3–20, as the reader is transported from the king storming Elisha's door to the utter outcasts of northern society: a fraternity of lepers ruminating on the certainty of death. Numerically, the "four" (*'arābāh*) lepers form a strategic wordplay with the "window" (*'arubāh*) mentioned by the skeptical officer, for these four lepers are the first witnesses of the window opened by God. Prior to their discovery, however, the lepers are fraught with despair: as diseased outsiders they have few options, and although they are inflicted like Naaman, they lack his status or access to royal channels. When they set out on their journey of surrender in v. 5 with a hunger that must rival the desperate mothers of 6:26–29, they could hardly have envisioned returning to the city gate with the announcement of an empty Aramean camp. For the second time in recent memory, lepers are the source of a testimony of reversal: Naaman is healed and confesses that no god is comparable to the God of Israel, while the lepers declare a day of good news in v. 10 and resolve to inform the royal household. The end of oppression along with provisions instead of scarcity certainly constitutes good news for besieged Samaria, perhaps anticipating later oracles of Isaiah where freedom is proclaimed to the captives and the year of the Lord's favor is announced (61:1–3). The Arameans were blinded in 2 Kgs 6:18, and now they have been acoustically confused by the God who subverts the mighty and utilizes the marginal to broadcast good news. Yet disbelief again prevails in the king's court as the lepers' testimony is not accepted immediately; only when a search party confirms the absence of Arameans – and therefore the end of the siege – do the residents of Samaria venture forth and proceed to gather the valuable plunder from the camp and the army in their headlong flight. The unexpected abundance results in a stampede for the bargain prices – in accordance with the word of Elisha – but carries with it some collateral damage: the cynical consigliere gets trampled in the gate, the place of justice, and his fate is symbolic of those oft-heard voices of doubt and rejection of the prophetic word in the northern kingdom.

As noted, the king of Israel is portrayed as an ambivalent figure during his recent conflicts with the Arameans, referring to Elisha as "my father" when the captive army is marched into Samaria (2 Kgs 6:21) but afterward issuing a death threat at the height of the siege (6:31) and attempting to arrest the prophet. Blaming Elisha for the siege – much as Ahab blamed Elijah for famine in 1 Kgs 18:17, labeling him the "troubler of Israel" – is typical of recent monarchs who refuse to acknowledge any personal culpability for the onset of national darkness. The king may have been clothed in sackcloth under his royal robes (2 Kgs 6:30), but no reaction is stated after a window is opened in a creative way by the God of Israel – enthroned high above all gods (Pss 97:9; 113:5) – rather than Baal the rider of the clouds. It is puzzling, therefore, that in the next episode of 2 Kgs 8:1–6, the king is asking about the great deeds of Elisha. The account begins with a flashback, as Elisha had informed the Shunammite woman to flee the land with her family and escape a seven-year famine. The woman then returns to the land and approaches the king at the very moment – in a miracle of timing and circumstance – that Gehazi is telling the story of how Elisha raised her son from the dead. There are several mysteries in this short episode (e.g., is it the same famine of the Aramean siege that the woman is warned about, and how exactly does she lose her property?), but also a pair of intriguing characters. First, the unnamed son of the Shunammite becomes a typological figure: he is poised to inherit the land that the king restores to the woman, and therefore represents every Israelite who might return from later exile and be granted an inheritance. Second, it is most surprising that Gehazi makes an appearance here, in light of his leprous sentence back in chapter 5. Ironically, Gehazi himself is one of Elisha's "great deeds," so it is surely appropriate that he testifies before the king, and evidently without bitterness. Just as the resurrected son is typologically configured to represent anyone who has experienced the trauma of death and dislocation but is restored to the land, so Gehazi becomes emblematic of the chastened sinner who tells the story of the prophetic word that turns death into life.[51]

When lepers brought good news to the king of Israel in 2 Kgs 7:10–12, there was immediate skepticism, but in 8:5–6 the king hears the story from another leprous figure and acts with magnanimity. Arguably, 2 Kgs 8:1–6 is Gehazi's finest hour, and Jehoram also appears in a positive light as he is willing to both listen to an account of great prophetic deeds and enact justice and economic equity, providing a glimpse of what could have been possible during his lengthy reign.[52] Yet when the woman of Shunem departs from the king's presence, the narrative abruptly switches to the spatial setting of Damascus where Elisha has mysteriously journeyed. Jehoram may be presented in a reasonably positive light as he restores the Shunammite's land, but the word of judgment spoken by Elijah in 1 Kgs 21:29 (where Ahab is

---

[51] Cf. Nelson's christological reading: "Stories about past mighty deeds now produce the faith that those deeds themselves once created. For the church, the stories of Jesus, who raised the dead and was himself raised, have power in themselves to solve life's problems" (*First and Second Kings*, 193).

[52] Cohn, *2 Kings*, 56.

told that evil will consume his house in the days of his son) is poised for fulfillment (cf. 1 Kgs 11:12). Hazael has not been mentioned since 1 Kgs 19:15, but he will be a major factor in the external oppression of the northern kingdom, and the abnormal circumstances of his crowning are narrated in 2 Kgs 8:7–15. The illness of Ben-Hadad has parallels to Ahaziah's illness and inquiry in 2 Kings 1 – with the Aramean ruler appearing more deferential to an Israelite prophet than his counterpart – but even more remarkable is the fact that Elisha is on foreign soil directing international affairs, an indication that God's reach and influence extend to other capitals and regimes as well as an expansion of prophetic jurisdiction. Furthermore, it could be argued that the prophet represents aspects of the divine character in this episode, nowhere more evident than in Elisha's tears when he reveals the forthcoming devastation against Israel to be wrought by the murdering Hazael. To be sure, the prophetic duplicity in this episode – Elisha instructs Hazael to tell Ben-Hadad that he will recover, but he will not – has disturbed some interpreters, with the king's murder being the first of Hazael's many atrocities: "If there is any meaning to be found in the holocaust of verse 12, it will not become clear until the fall of the Kingdom of Israel. It is not explicitly punishment for sin, at least not yet. Here the word of God impels a wicked deed for the strange purpose of bringing doom to Israel. Yahweh is not powerless, as some exiles were tempted to conclude, but rather one whose own purposes have made it necessary to declare war on the people of promise."[53]

---

[53] Nelson, *First and Second Kings*, 195; note also Seow, "The First and Second Books of Kings," 215: "The story of Elisha's role in the demise of Ben-hadad and the accession of Hazael is troubling to many modern readers. The man of God apparently tells Hazael to lie and, whether he had intended it or not, is complicit in the assassination of the king. Within the narrator's larger view

When Hazael suffocates his master and triggers a regicide, he at least follows the prophetic counsel and thus is a foil to the recalcitrant Israelite leaders and a preface to the Assyrian destruction shortly to come. Hazael's violence will be exceeded in scale and scope by a rapacious military that demolishes an entire nation along with its corrupt kings under the aegis of a tearful divine sovereignty.

Other than an appearance by Jehoshaphat in 2 Kings 3, there has been no sustained attention on the south since the end of 1 Kings 22. Yet after the account of Hazael's accession to the throne of Damascus, there are two brief regnal summaries in 2 Kgs 8:16–24, probably included here because the revolutionary events of 2 Kings 9 have lasting implications for Israel and Judah. Of course, the two nations have become intertwined through the marriage alliance brokered by Jehoshaphat, and that becomes a central pillar in southern Jehoram's indictment for traversing the path trailblazed by the house of Ahab. Such compromises would be enough to condemn the south if not for the divine guarantee – here inscribed with the metaphor of a lamp (see 1 Kgs 11:36; 15:4) – that allows for unmerited survival.[54] The promise to David is among the more pressing concerns of the interpreter, as the promise is sorely taxed as the narrative continues: in the shorter term, the southern kingdom will be vexed by Athaliah's terror

---

of history, however, this event fulfills the word of the Lord that promises an end to the horrible reigns of the apostate kings of the north. God's larger purpose will be worked out, it seems, even through human deceit (cf. 1 Kgs 22:1) and unjustified death. The story defies our moral logic, but the Bible as a whole tells the story of a God whose will is accomplished in ways that sometimes defy human logic and moral categories."

[54] On the nuance of political authority or dominion in the Hebrew term *nîr* in 2 Kgs 8:19, see Sweeney, *I & II Kings*, 319–21.

(2 Kings 11) and the northern invasion (2 Kings 18–19), and in the longer term through the toxic policies of Manasseh (2 Kings 21) followed by exile and dissolution of the institutional monarchy (2 Kings 25) before the gradual messianic recalibration of the promise (Amos 9:11; Jer 33:14–18; Isa 55:3; cf. Rom 1:3; Rev 22:16).

Edom's rebellion and reestablishment of its monarchy are the most documented events of Jehoram's southern reign (vv. 19–22). The revolt of this recent ally (2 Kings 3) together with the rebellion of the southwestern city of Libnah on the Philistine border serves to foreshadow later rebellions and loss of land, and underscores that the partnership with the northern Omrides produced less than desirable results overall.

There is no mention of any injury sustained in the Edomite conflict – in 2 Chron 21:18–19, Jehoram is inflicted with an incurable bowel disease – but he seems to die prematurely, hastening the accession of Ahaziah his son (2 Kgs 8:25–29). Ahaziah's dismal one-year (at most) reign is defined by his evil ways, and ominously, it is during his brief tenure that the initial strike of Hazael is recorded during yet another skirmish at Ramoth-Gilead involving a joint effort between north and south. The northern king is wounded during the fight, and during his convalescence Ahaziah makes an ill-fated trip to visit his colleague: the wounding of the northern king by forces of Hazael sets the wheels in motion for the purge of Jehu (1 Kgs 19:16) about to be set loose. A considerable amount of narrative space devoted to the house of Omri is now drawing to a close, with countless opportunities for repentance and an extraordinary investment of prophetic resources. But after decades of divine perseverance and consistent unresponsiveness, the hourglass is drained of its sand as a new king assumes power.

CHAPTER 6

Upheaval and Reprieve

With the tumultuous days of the Omride dynasty rapidly drawing to a close, 2 Kings 9–19 narrates the end of not only the dynasty but of the entire northern kingdom as well. Since Elijah's theophany on Mount Horeb, we have been anticipating the arrival of Jehu to overthrow the regime, and he scarcely has an equal in terms of zealous energy and revolutionary drive. But the end of the northern dynasty is not without implications for Judah, and the south has had its own struggle with apostasies since the schism at Shechem. As an element within his constructive proposal for Old Testament theology, Walter Brueggemann remarks that "an affirmation of covenant with its stipulations and requirements is a subversive claim against a world of autonomy in which relationships are sustained only by convenience, and not fidelity, in which duty and responsibility are overridden in self-indulgence that devours self, neighbour, and environment."[1] Yet the next installment of the story reveals that it is not only the Omrides who are guilty of covenant betrayal, since new monarchs such as Jehu in the north and Joash in the south have their own issues that prove destabilizing for both nations just as the Assyrian war machine is poised to arrive as a terrifying instrument of divine

---

[1] Brueggemann, "Old Testament Theology," 694.

justice. Prior to any Assyrian destruction, however, the reader witnesses the most violent scenes yet in the book of Kings, this time in the context of Israelites destroying each other.

SEDITIOUS APPOINTMENT

During the illness of Ben-Hadad, Elisha ventured to Damascus and empowered the usurpation of Hazael, and now with the king of Israel recovering from his wounds in Jezreel and thus removed from his military commanders in Ramoth-Gilead, Elisha is the architect of another usurpation.[2] In 2 Kgs 9:1, however, Elisha designates a young member of the sons of the prophets to anoint Jehu; there is no reason stated, but one suspects that speed is of the essence, and when the young acolyte is instructed to utter a terse oracle and flee, it is an apt introduction to one of the more frantic chapters in the entire Deuteronomistic History. Due to the clandestine nature of the task, it is appropriate that Elisha provides the lad with a flask of oil. Nonetheless, it is curious that the only other figure to be anointed with a flask is Saul (1 Sam 10:1), and thus Jehu is already associated with a failed king even before he begins his reign. Elisha's oracular instructions are terse, but the lad, who is the last recorded member of the "sons of the prophets" in Israel's royal story, certainly exits the narrative with a vengeance. Instead of any brief word, the youngster takes Jehu aside and unfurls a long and rabid oracle that details the eradication of Ahab's house, as occurred to the houses of Jeroboam and Baasha previously. Glancing ahead in the story, Jehu's dynasty will likewise fall on hard times, so in retrospect there will be a slight irony here. Jezebel is also singled out for destruction, and the character

[2] Dietrich, "1 & 2 Kings," 253.

of God presented by the young acolyte is bursting with retribution: "Only here in Kings is emphasis placed on Yahweh as an avenging God."[3] It is difficult to know whether the youngster is speaking of his own accord or with the (tacit) permission of Elisha, but his prediction of Jezebel's demise is accurate (9:37), his words overlap with the utterances of Elijah, and Elijah himself also expands God's own instruction (see 1 Kgs 21:17–24), so the acolyte should probably be given the benefit of the doubt. The military commanders refer to lad as a "lunatic" (cf. Hos 9:7; Jer 29:26), but they quickly dismiss Jehu's efforts to brush aside the visit. Perhaps there is oil still on his head, but when Jehu reveals he has been anointed king, they quickly proclaim Jehu as their ruler.[4] It is unclear whether these officers are ideologically opposed to the Omrides or merely opportunists seeking enhanced power, but their acclamation of Jehu – who shortly will be described as one who drives like a lunatic – intersects with the prophetic word as it moves toward its ferocious fulfillment with Jehu's wild chariot ride from Ramoth-Gilead to Jezreel.

Despite the wounding inflicted by Hazael, the king of Israel hitches his chariot to meet Jehu along with Ahaziah, and it is a portentous decision since the parties collide at the inheritance of Naboth: the arrow of Jehu pierces the son of Ahab on the same plot of ground where disaster was decreed to happen in the days of Ahab's son (1 Kgs 21:20–29). Even more intriguing than Jehoram's assassination is the utterance of Jehu in the wake of his regicide. Turning to his colleague Bidkar in 2 Kgs 9:25–26, Jehu

---

[3] Donald J. Wiseman, *1 & 2 Kings*, TOTC (Downers Grove, IL: IVP, 1993), 150.
[4] Cohn, *2 Kings*, 67. On the shout "Jehu is king," Wray Beal (*1 & 2 Kings*, 375) notes that this is not the usual shout of acclamation, but instead "it is that used when an individual seeks to establish a claim to the throne (2 Sam 15:10)."

claims that they were firsthand witnesses to the oracle of condemnation. As Alter states, "This is a piece of delayed exposition that sharpens our sense of Jehu's animus toward Jehoram: he and Bidkar were actually present when Ahab expropriated the field of Naboth after his judicial murder."[5] In a stroke, quite literally, Jehu is transformed into a theologically compelling character, assuming that his words are genuine. Is Jehu among the prophets? "It may be that Jehu is simply an ambitious, bloodthirsty, military killer. By this oracle he is transposed into a key player in a Yahwistic-prophetic drama much larger and more formidable than he as a military man could ever claim."[6] Through Jehu, the reader is acquainted with the report that Naboth's sons were also killed; this, combined with Jehu's excoriation of Jezebel in v. 22, serves to anticipate the violent fates of the rest of Ahab's sons and Jezebel in due course.[7]

Meanwhile, Ahaziah attempts to flee from Jehu and his arrows (vv. 27–28), but he too is struck and eventually dies in Megiddo (probably one of the cities for Solomon's horses and chariots; 1 Kgs 9:15; 19). On the one hand, Ahaziah pays a heavy price for his father's ill-advised alliance with the Omrides, and if Jehu understands his mission as being to purge the entire house of Ahab, then by extension Ahaziah is included. On the other hand, there is no specific prophetic warrant for his death, so Jehu might be guilty of a power grab as he ruthlessly eliminates every rival and exceeds his mandate (for which he is denounced in Hos 1:4–5).[8] Either way,

---

[5] Alter, *Ancient Israel*, 627. [6] Brueggemann, *1 & 2 Kings*, 387.
[7] See Peter D. Miscall, "Elijah, Ahab, and Jehu: A Prophecy Fulfilled," *Prooftexts* 9 (1989): 73–83.
[8] David T. Lamb, *Righteous Jehu and His Evil Heirs: The Deuteronomist's Negative Perspective on Dynastic Succession*, OTM (Oxford: Oxford University Press, 2007), 86–88.

the demise of Ahaziah creates a power vacuum in the south that ushers in the reign of Athaliah, the offspring of Jezebel, to whom we will return in due course.

Jehu evidently harbors deep antipathy for Jezebel, accusing her of spiritual prostitution and sorcery in 2 Kgs 9:22, yet she has a question for him in vv. 30–37 as he enters the gate of Jezreel. Her actions (adorning herself) and speech ("Is there peace, O Zimri, his master's murderer?") have been variously interpreted as a taunting gesture of defiance or an invitation to form an alliance, but Jehu answers with a question of his own ("Who is on my side?"), and Jezebel is promptly thrown from the window, where she is devoured in consonance with the prophetic word: a eunuch was involved in the restoration of the Shunammite's land, and now eunuchs are involved as Jezebel is evicted, as it were, from the land of Israel.[9] The theological configuration of Jezebel's demise merits at least two comments. First, it is possible that her final moments are a parody of the goddess whose worship she so vigorously sponsors. If Jezebel herself is presented as an embodiment of Anat, her final evisceration is a moment of poetic justice in the story: "Jezebel's 'skull' no longer laughs, nor do her 'hands' write false letters, nor do her 'feet' any longer walk on family land stolen away from murdered Israelites. Just as Anat sheds her enemies' blood, so Jehu sheds his enemies' blood. Readers even nominally familiar with the Baal-Anat cycle would have no problem grasping these parallels."[10] Second, for any community of

---

[9] See Janet S. Everhart, "Jezebel: Framed by Eunuchs?" *CBQ* 72 (2010): 688–98.

[10] Moore, "Jehu's Coronation and the Purge of Israel," 109. Cf. Appler, "From Queen to Cuisine," 68: "According to the Canaanite Baal myth, Anat had two symbols of power: her necklace of heads/skulls that she wore around her neck, and the hands that she wore around her waist as a belt (KTU 1:3). Jezebel leaves behind the symbols of her Canaanite goddess – her skull and hands."

faith wrestling with the theological significance of this text, Jezebel's invocation of Zimri carries an ironic edge, because she certainly wields power for more than seven days, but in the end suffers the same kind of ignominious fate as that earlier usurper. Jezebel destroys prophets, and ultimately is destroyed – a stone's throw from Naboth's inheritance that she helps her husband steal – by the creative efficacy of the prophetic word(s) spoken against her.

Jezebel's taunt about Zimri is summarily dismissed by Jehu, but it carries more meaning than he (or she) realizes, for even though Zimri reigned for merely one week, he still managed to walk in the sins of Jeroboam. Jehu purges the house of Ahab with uncommon zeal, and his reign is set to last for four generations, but he too will be guilty of walking in the sins of Jeroboam.[11] Indeed, Jehu becomes an increasingly ambivalent figure as 2 Kgs 10:1–16 unfolds, a carnivalesque stretch of text that presents several theological challenges for the interpreter. First, when Jehu sends letters that result in the death of Ahab's seventy descendants, the reader senses some epistolary retribution: Jezebel sent letters that result in Naboth's death, and now the guardians of her house respond to Jehu's letters with heads in baskets.[12] In this scene, Jehu emerges as one of the most Machiavellian political operatives in the book of Kings – once more citing the prophet Elijah as vindication – although his skullduggery has much in common with Ahab and

---

[11] Long, 2 Kings, 130.
[12] Commentators often point out that Jehu exploits the wordplay between "head" and "chief" in his letter; e.g., Leithart, *1 & 2 Kings*, 222: "Jehu plays on the ambiguity, instructing the elders to bring the 'heads' of the men to Jezreel. This might be taken as an invitation to parley, but it might also be taken as an instruction to decapitate Ahab's sons. Jehu retains deniability: 'I didn't mean literal heads,' we can hear him protesting on the evening news."

Jezebel. Second, as Jehu is en route to Samaria, he kills the forty-two relatives of Ahaziah, and while it could be that he slaughters this group in order to eliminate every rival, *forty-two* matches the number of Bethelites attacked by the bears in the wake of Elisha's curse in 2 Kgs 2:23, and thus suggests that the eradication of Ahab's house in the north is complete.[13] Jehu probably does not intend it, but this is only the beginning of the murderous mayhem that will soon engulf the southern kingdom in the near future (2 Kgs 11). Third, Jehu's recruitment of Jehonadab as he ventures to Samaria undoubtedly has a political component, especially since scholars often suppose that the Rechabites had origins among the Kenites (1 Chr 2:55; Judg 4:11–12) and were known for their austerity (Jer 35:1–16) and anti-establishment conservatism.[14] Their handshake forms another retributive symmetry in the narrative: just as Ahab invited Ben-Hadad into his chariot in order to procure an economic alliance (1 Kgs 20:33–34), so Jehu forges an ideological alliance in order to exterminate the initiatives of Ahab in Samaria. Regardless of Jehu's motives for aligning with Jehonadab, the presence of the Rechabites subtly reveals other pockets of resistance to fertility religion and related syncretism, as judgment against Ahab's administration is being accomplished through a number of unexpected channels.

Jehu promises Jehonadab a spectacle of fervency, and 2 Kgs 10:17–28 has no shortage of zeal as attention turns from the house of Ahab to the house of Baal in Samaria. Just as Jehu uses double-edged language in his letters, his invitations to a massive Baal celebration are likewise laced with ambiguity: he informs the northerners that he is about to host a great Baal sacrifice, along

---

[13] Cf. Sweeney, *I & II Kings*, 337.   [14] Wiseman, *1 & 2 Kings*, 153.

with a soundplay on the terms "serve" (*'bd*) and "destroy" (*'bd*).¹⁵ Such linguistic ambiguity is an intrinsic component of the narrative artistry in this sector of the story, but there is also a theological point, because Jehu's polyvalent use of language anticipates the narrator's ambiguous evaluation of Jehu at the end of this chapter. Jehu's actions in v. 22 likewise are cunningly duplicitous: the adherents are jammed in "mouth to mouth" and outfitted with cultic vestments that serve to identify them to the assassins, and are then promptly destroyed (along with the Baal pillar); in a scatological twist, the facility is turned into a latrine. For long-oppressed Yahwists who have suffered under decades of Omride tyranny, this has to be construed as a remarkable victory in a strikingly compressed amount of time, but the final summary of Jehu's reign in vv. 29–36 problematizes his assault against the Baal infrastructure of Samaria: even as he emerges as a colorful and interesting figure in the narrative, his character in the end is decidedly equivocal. On the one hand, God actually speaks words of commendation to Jehu in 2 Kgs 10:30, a rare intrusion into the narrative, as the eradication of Ahab's house is consonant with God's mind.¹⁶ On the other hand, Jehu is only rewarded with a four-generation dynasty (the same as Omri, although Jehu's dynasty will last longer in terms of years), implying an overall upgrade but not an unqualified endorsement. Moreover, the narrator's comments that frame the divine speech identify substantial

---

¹⁵ Long, *2 Kings*, 139: "Jehu's declaration to the people, 'Jehu will serve [*'bd*] him [Baal] much,' may contain a pun. With a slight change in the sound of the first guttural consonant in the verb, Jehu can be heard to say that he will *destroy* Baal (*'bd*, 'destroy')."
¹⁶ Cf. Leithart, *1 & 2 Kings*, 223: "Further, Jehu accomplishes 'all that was in my heart' *through deception*. As in his other dealings with the twisted house of Ahab, Yahweh is twisted with the twisted, the infinitely cunning God."

areas of failure such as continuance with the golden calves and the sins of Jeroboam – metonymic for eschewing the Deuteronomic code and failing to recognize the centrality of Jerusalem – and the incursions of Hazael anticipate further loss of land in the days of Jehu's heirs and beyond. For any theological reading of Kings, the zeal of Jehu falls short because it is focused on too narrow of a bandwidth: the temple of Baal is destroyed, but other vestiges of idolatry remain.[17] The lingering image of Jehu's maniacal driving is poignant, for if he had attended to his personal faithfulness with same intensity as his obliteration of Ahab's offspring, then he surely would not have bequeathed such an ambivalent legacy to his own house.

CIRCLE OF TREASON

Jehu's selective zeal and blind spots prepare the reader for the later inability of Judahite leadership to discern its own fallibility during the Babylonian crisis, and after the tumult in the north, the narrative returns to the south in 2 Kings 11. In the wake of Ahaziah's murder at the hands of Jehu, Athaliah steps into the power vacuum with a chilling purge of the royal seed. The syntax of 11:1 suggests a simultaneous sequence of events, and at the same time that Jehu is ridding the north of Ahab's house and the Baal temple in Samaria, so Athaliah – in all probability the daughter of

---

[17] With an eye to a more contemporary scene, Brueggemann (*1 & 2 Kings*, 404) cautions: "When religious passion is transposed directly into political-revolutionary action, violence driven by religious passion becomes a terrible enterprise. In that regard, the massacre by Jehu is a harbinger of the many and strange ways in which religion fuels political revolution in our own time."

Ahab and Jezebel – destroys her own flesh and blood in Jerusalem.[18] Athaliah's motives are not fully disclosed in the narrative, but the promise concerning David's throne is deeply threatened by her aggression. Yet the murderous rampage of Athaliah is countered by the courageous act of treason by Jehosheba – perhaps even the very daughter of Athaliah herself, although the text remains silent on their relationship – who hides the infant Joash within the inner precincts of the temple. It is reported in 2 Chronicles 22:11 that Jehosheba is the wife of Jehoiada the priest, and a poignant inversion can be glimpsed: just as an ill-advised alliance resulted in the toxicity of Ahab's house infecting Jerusalem, so a different alliance between the temple and palace offsets the malignancy and allows the Davidic line to survive. The name Jehosheba means "Yah(weh) swears," and through her actions, the divine oath to David remains secure in an enclave of faithfulness.[19]

The motif of a vulnerable infant hidden from the carnage of a tyrant has been seen before in the Hebrew Bible, and scholars often note some compelling similarities between the hiding of Joash and the earlier account of Moses' rescue in Exodus 2, stories that feature a child of promise daringly concealed from a death-dealing parental figure.[20] In the gloom of Egyptian slavery, a

---

[18] On the question of Athaliah's lineage, see Patricia Dutcher-Walls, *Narrative Art, Political Rhetoric: The Case of Athaliah and Joash*, JSOTSup 209 (Sheffield: Sheffield Academic Press, 1996), 27–28.

[19] Leithart, *1 & 2 Kings*, 225.

[20] E.g., Provan, *1 and 2 Kings*, 221: "This is not the only time in the Bible when God's promises hang by the slender thread of a baby boy whose life is threatened by wicked rulers. Moses is hidden away in the midst of Egyptian genocide, growing up unrecognized for who he is, under Pharaoh's very nose (Exod. 2:1–10). Jesus, himself a 'son' of David, is removed from Herod's dominion in the face of a similar threat (Matt. 2:13–18). He, too, grows up, his true identity concealed, under the gaze of other 'kings of the Jews.'" Cf. Fretheim, *First and Second Kings*, 180.

future deliverer in the chain of God's promise is preserved; likewise, at a most critical hour for the Davidic house, an unheralded character defies monarchic tyranny. Much further down the line, a later descendant of David will be protected from a genocidal purge in the land of Egypt, of all places (Matt 2:15–16). Each of these narratives has quiet individuals capable of great faith, and for the authors of the book of Kings, there is every reason to believe that God continues to operate in this manner and use everyday virtues and convictions to further promises and counter oppression.

Few details are disclosed about Athaliah's reign, but while she wields power in the land, the young Joash is secretly reared in the temple, and the queen could hardly have been expecting the conspiracy orchestrated by an unlikely revolutionary, Jehoiada the priest. The timing of the priest's coup is notable: on a seventh day during the seventh year, after careful planning, the Davidic scion is publicly unveiled.[21] For the second straight chapter, there is a temple plot thick with deception, although this one takes place in the Jerusalem temple with the true king taking over from the usurper and offspring of Baal worshippers. Joash's legitimacy is underscored with a number of symbolic accoutrements, including the shields that belonged to King David (defending the rightful heir) and what is called a copy of "the testimony" (*hā'ēdût*), a Hebrew term that is "used elsewhere in the Bible for covenant documents (e.g., Exod 25:16, 21; 31:18; 32:15; 34:29; 40:20) and occurs in conjunction with David's kingship in Ps 132:12."[22] One guesses that Athaliah is not in the habit of observing the Sabbath,

---

[21] See Wray Beal, *1 & 2 Kings*, 388: "The notation is a common trope that introduces a climactic event in a series (one thinks of the seventh day of creation, or the seventh march around Jericho)."

[22] Seow, "The First and Second Books of Kings," 230.

but when she hears the commotion and sees the crowned king, she twice utters her only word in the narrative ("Treason"), although it is uncertain whom she is addressing. Athaliah's ancestor Omri came to power because he had the support of the army, but as the last Omride, Athaliah is destroyed when the army opts for the Davidic heir and follows the orders of the priest. Executing Athaliah outside the temple foreshadows its cleansing and repair efforts under Joash and also links her death in the horse entrance with the earlier demise of Jezebel. In this case, no one commands that Athaliah be given a burial, and the glaring absence of any regnal formula seals her ignominy. The only other recorded casualty is the deviant priest Mattan; scholars often suspect that this name is a truncated form of *Mattaniah*, and if so, it is striking that the divine name is excised from Mattan just as Athaliah tried (and failed) to axe the seed of David.[23] The Baal temple in Samaria becomes a latrine, whereas the temple in Jerusalem is about to be restored by Joash, who, after a covenant renewal ceremony, begins his forty-year reign as the legitimate heir of David in the most elaborate coronation narrative since Solomon.

The temple in Jerusalem has not been a prominent spatial setting for a long time in the narrative, but it looms large in the story of Joash: he was hidden within the temple as an infant, and a lengthy repair project is the centerpiece of his reign, presumably neglected while Athaliah and Mattan wielded power. Nevertheless, the career of Joash contains more ambivalence than may have been expected after such an auspicious beginning. Joash may act uprightly all the days that he is instructed by Jehoiada (12:2), but

---

[23] A similar truncation occurs with the name Micahyahu/Micah in Judges 17:1–13; see E. Aydeet Mueller, *The Micah Story: A Morality Tale in the Book of Judges*, Studies in Biblical Literature 34 (New York: Peter Lang, 2001), 76.

that remark sounds a faintly ominous note, for what will happen after the priest dies? The high places are not removed – in this context they appear to be a rival to the temple, the place of Joash's coronation – and the opening verses amount to a qualified commendation at best. A colossal apostasy after Jehoiada dies is narrated in 2 Chronicles 24, but in 2 Kings 12 the bulk of the attention is focused on Joash's efforts to repair the temple. Such initiative is laudable, and according to v. 4, the restoration appears to be ordered early in his reign. It seems odd, therefore, that Joash fails to notice that the repairs have not happened until his twenty-third year; the matter finally gets straightened out – and there is a long digression about priestly responsibility and workers' compensation – but the delay causes the reader to wonder if the temple is the king's highest priority. Either way, the extensive fundraising over many years is obviated when Hazael sets his sights on Jerusalem after he destroys the Philistine city of Gath: Joash then empties the same temple that he has just restored in order to pay off Hazael. Like Asa before him (1 Kgs 15:18) and surely foreshadowing the Babylonian despoliation, this is neither the first nor the last time that temple treasures will be carried off by foreign kings. But for Joash, the humiliation of draining the temple presages his own clouded demise, as he is struck down by two of his servants in 2 Kgs 12:20–21. The details are obscure, but Joash appears to be assassinated while traveling to an unspecified location, probably suggesting Joash's bribe of Hazael did not meet with universal approval. There may have been great expectations surrounding Joash, but he has a less than stellar finish: "Joash was able to refurbish the temple, but in the end had to rob it. Rescued from death as a baby, he was struck down forty years later by his own servants. Heir to God's gracious promise to David, he received the testimony of the law and was a partner in the

Upheaval and Reprieve

covenant between God and the people. Yet he failed to live up to the precepts of that covenant."[24] An ironic circle thus encloses the career of Joash, as he is preserved and enthroned by means of a conspiracy against the house of Ahab, but in the end falls victim to a conspiracy within his own ranks.

LOSING GROUND

Before turning to the reign of Amaziah, the narrative switches to the north as the careers of two descendants of Jehu are recounted in 2 Kings 13. But even as the nation hurdles toward oblivion, this chapter is a provocative site for theological reflection. The first of Jehu's heirs is Jehoahaz (vv. 1–9), who opts to walk in the sins of Jeroboam and suffers the now-familiar harassment of Hazael and his son Ben-Hadad as a consequence. Yet in a stunning development, Jehoahaz responds to the manifestation of divine anger by entreating the favor of God, a remarkably uncommon move in the northern kingdom. There is a structural comparison with Joash of Jerusalem, as both kings face an Aramean crisis but have different reactions. As Hazael marched toward Jerusalem in 2 Kgs 12:18, Joash – after previously confronting the priests for mismanagement of the temple – opts for the tenuous security of a bribe and empties the treasuries.[25] Despite persisting in the sins of

---

[24] Nelson, *First and Second Kings*, 214.
[25] Gina Hens-Piazza, *1–2 Kings* (Nashville, TN: Abingdon, 2006), 317: "The threat of Hazael's assault on Jerusalem is the litmus test as to whether or not Joash's public persona of virtue and covenant fidelity was founded upon a deep interiority and attention to the Lord or not. His rapid willingness to trade all of the temple treasures for security lays bare where his real trust lies. Such crises in life confront us as well with the depth or shallowness of our own virtue and the steadfastness, or lack thereof, for our own commitments."

Jeroboam, at the height of the Aramean crisis Jehoahaz does not accommodate but rather cries out in prayer, with echoes of earlier days in the book of Judges. Equally intriguing is God's response, as God hears and sees (*rā'āh*) the plight of Israel. Whether God responds because of the king's intercession or because Jehu has been given a guarantee of four generations is not stated, but a "savior" is sent to allow the people to escape Aram and live in their tents. Ample speculation about the identity of the savior can be found in the scholarly literature, but the vagueness must be intentional in order to underscore that God is willing to send other saviors in the future (and causing the reader to wonder what would have happened if Joash entreated the face of God rather than plundered the temple). At the outset of a very bleak time for the people in this next stretch of the book of Kings, God is pictured as intensely active and responsive. It is disappointing, therefore, when Israel's response to the unnamed "savior" in v. 6 is to default to the transgressions of the past rather than write a fresh script, and so instead of inaugurating a new era, Jehoahaz bequeaths a divided legacy to his successor Jehoash.

The career of Jehoash in 2 Kgs 13:10–25 is hardly distinguishable from that of his father, other than a conflict with Amaziah of Judah that receives further attention in the next chapter. By far the most riveting events in his reign come after the report of his funeral, starting with a flashback to a meeting with Elisha prior to the prophet's death. Elisha has not been heard from since the anointing of Jehu; it may have been presumed that his career was over, but now he reappears on his deathbed as he receives a visit from the king of Israel. Jehoash's father cried out in prayer, and now Jehoash himself cries out to the prophet. Despite his deviance (or perhaps because of it), the king's utterance ("My father, my father! The chariots and horsemen of Israel!") amounts to a confession that the true power of Israel resides in God through the instrument of the prophetic word. Elisha tests Jehoash with arrows, but as with Jehu's reform, there is only partial success: "Jehoash had a chance to succeed fully; he failed, and in effect determined his own future. It is likely that this failure has such effects, not simply because of this one test, but because the test reveals the shape of a life."[26] Hazael inflicts damage on Israel but is not allowed to destroy the nation, because according to v. 23, God extends compassion on account of his covenant with the ancestors – the only such occasion in Kings where the ancestral promise is invoked. Furthermore, v. 23 also states that during the era of Jehoash, God was not willing to "cast" Israel (*šlk*) aside, although this divine patience is finally exhausted in 2 Kgs 17:20 when the nation is "cast" (*šlk*) from God's presence. Such casting will be catastrophic, but not the end of the story. In the last cameo of Elisha the prophet, there is a reminder of hope in the midst of trauma. A seemingly random event is narrated in vv. 20–21 about life after death: when Moabite raiders interrupt a funeral, the pallbearers hastily "cast" (*šlk*) the corpse in fear, but it touches the bones of Elisha and the man springs to life. Assuming that death is a metaphor for exile, the larger point of this section of 2 Kings 13 emphasizes that despite the tomb of captivity, the possibility of resurrection exists because of God's commitment and promise.[27]

---

[26] Fretheim, *First and Second Kings*, 183–84. Three victories are noted in v. 25.
[27] Provan, *1 and 2 Kings*, 231: "Yet even in exile, there is hope. If contact with the great prophets of the past is maintained, through obedience to their teachings (we presume), death may yet be followed by unexpected resurrection (cf. Ezek. 37:1–14), defeat by victory. For God's love is ultimately strong enough to overcome death. It is no coincidence that the first allusion in Kings to exile as an aspect of Israelite experience appears in a chapter that

In the wake of Joash's assassination in Judah, the narrative formally turns to the reign of Amaziah his son in 2 Kings 14, although the northern kingdom features prominently. His qualified commendation is followed by taking revenge for his father's death and selective obedience to the law of Moses, and, in a strange irony, Amaziah acts within the constraints of Deut 24:16 (stating that children should not be put to death because of fathers), but he himself is later murdered for his own misdeeds in v. 19, strongly suggesting that he pays a high price for his military folly.[28] Officially, the high point of Amaziah's career has to be the assault on Edom with a host of casualties and the renaming of the city of Sela (which some believe to be Petra) as Joktheel as a sign of subjugation.[29] Yet the hubris of Amaziah leads to disaster: buoyed by this success, he focuses his aggression on northern Israel and issues a brash challenge, but Jehoash is an increasingly complex figure and warns Amaziah to desist in a thinly veiled parable (cf. Jotham's fable in Judges 9:7–20). Whether Amaziah desires to prevent the south from further northern entanglement or is merely taking advantage of the Aramean decline is not indicated, but he takes no heed of Jehoash's figurative peroration, and their showdown in Beth-Shemesh results in substantial (and apparently unnecessary) losses for Judah and Jerusalem. As it stands, this sequence of misplaced pride, invasion, a broken wall, a plundered temple and a king taken into captivity forms a dress rehearsal for the

---

contains the first mention of the covenant with the patriarchs. Only a promise like that can offer Israel any comfort in the midst of the devastation that is shortly to come." On the verb "throw," see Gilmour, *Juxtaposition and the Elisha Cycle*, 208.

[28] Cohn, *2 Kings*, 99.
[29] On the location of Sela, see Sweeney, *I & II Kings*, 365.

Babylonian offensive shortly to come, and therefore is a warning that the royal court would be wise to hear: "This proleptic exile of Judah is fittingly carried out by Israel, ironically enough, since it was by following the example of Israel that Judah turned from the way of Yahweh in the first place."[30] Amaziah might rename a foreign city, but the embarrassment of a looted capital is trumped by his own murder by conspiracy some years later, indicating growing factions and foment within Jerusalem's political circles.

Amaziah is the victim of a machination, but his son Ahaziah (or Uzziah) replaces him, consistent with the Davidic dynastic promise. But Jehu's dynasty continues in the north, and its penultimate king Jeroboam II is the immediate focus in 2 Kgs 14:23-29. Jeroboam II's reign lasts forty-one years, but comparatively little space is devoted to his career, which is slightly ironic since he recovers so much space for Israel by overseeing a territorial enlargement of Solomonic proportions (cf. 1 Kgs 8:65). Geographic expansion takes place under the prompting of Jonah son of Amittai, known otherwise only through the prophetic book that also bears this name, where the Assyrian capital of Nineveh is the surprising object of divine compassion, much to Jonah's chagrin. Jonah is angry that God extends mercy to the undeserving citizens of Nineveh, and curiously 2 Kgs 14:26-27 lyrically reflects on the quality of divine grace dispensed on the wayward northern kingdom. The reader may have expected the prophets Amos and Hosea – active during the reign of Jeroboam II, and acutely concerned with rampant apostasy and injustice – to receive mention, but in the wider canonical tradition, it is not inappropriate that Jonah features here since the book of Jonah

---

[30] Leithart, *1 & 2 Kings*, 240.

presents a challenging view of God's global concern that extends even to the cattle of Assyria. The success of Jeroboam II should be attributed less to his geopolitical acumen, then, and more to God's ongoing involvement: "In the end, the entire episode is governed by Yahweh's verb 'save' in v. 27. Yahweh saves Israel. Jeroboam is Yahweh's agent. Biblical, prophetic faith has a characteristic way of recruiting into Yahweh's work those who are unaware of selection, but who act unwittingly and effectively."[31] Jeroboam II's real estate acquisition is against the grain in the recent narrative, but like Jehu's dynasty, it will not last as the northern kingdom continues to resist the offer of divine grace that is evidenced in vv. 26–27.

In the south, Azariah/Uzziah embarks on a fifty-two-year reign, placed on the Davidic throne at sixteen after his father's demise. He does what is right, but the short space allocated to his career in 2 Kgs 15:1–7 is clouded with ambivalence. The high places are not removed, and either the king lacks the necessary spiritual discernment to realize they are a stumbling block, or he finds it politically expedient to allow them to remain. Furthermore, this failure is compounded with a divine affliction of leprosy that leads to the king's confinement and co-regency with his son Jotham. The Chronicler's narrative attributes the leprosy to the king's overweening pride and brazen entry into the temple (2 Chr 26:16–20), but in 2 Kings 15 the attention falls elsewhere: in structural terms, Uzziah is afflicted but the Davidic promise continues, a marked contrast to the dizzying string of northern monarchs with varying degrees of ineptitude that follow in 2 Kings 15, beginning with the last of Jehu's house, Zechariah. As the fifth king in Jehu's line, Zechariah occupies an unenviable position, and other than

---

[31] Brueggemann, *1 & 2 Kings*, 445.

walking in the sins of Jeroboam, the only noteworthy event of his six-month reign is a public execution at the hands of the obscure Shallum.[32] Whether there are political motives for Zechariah's murder, it is an ironic end for Jehu's dynasty, which itself began with a series of public executions. Consequently, a period of relative dynastic stability is replaced by disorder, an indication of what happens in the absence of any divine guarantee or after the expiration date of God's assurance, and this chaos should serve as a potent reminder to the Davidic house in Jerusalem.

The murder of Zechariah acts as an overture for the next sequence in the chapter that overflows with seditious schemes: Shallum conspires against and assassinates Zechariah, only to be murdered in turn by Menahem after one month. There are only hints, but a number of scholars have argued that these overthrows are politically motivated, with some sectors of the northern constituency opting for an alliance with Assyria and others preferring partnership with Aram. Menahem rules for ten years, and if his barbaric rampage in v. 16 is any indication, he owes his longevity to violence more than any other factor. Specious pragmatics also play a role, as evidenced by Menahem's payment to Pul – another name for Tiglath-Pileser III king of Assyria – through taxation levied against the wealthier citizens in order to cement his hold on the kingdom. This is an indirect and starkly minimalistic introduction for an empire that is such a dominant and fearsome predator in the coming chapters, with no elaboration of the

---

[32] Cf. Robert Althann, "Shallum," in *ABD* 5:1154: "The prophets Amos and Hosea allude to these events. Amos foretells Zechariah's murder (7:9, 11) and Hosea speaks of royal assassinations (7:6–7, 16). Both see them as signs of the corruption that will take Israel into exile. These strokes plunged the country into civil war shortly before the renewed advance of Assyria into the West." Note also Mobley, "1 and 2 Kings," 139.

history or logistics of perhaps the greatest military power seen on earth to this point.³³ Of course, more details can be found later in Kings and elsewhere in the Hebrew Bible (for example, the approaching machinery that is poetically inscribed in Isa 5:28, "Whose arrows are sharp, All his bows are taut. The hoofs of his horses are reckoned like flint, And his wheels like the whirlwind"), yet the reader wonders why the first official mention of Assyria in the book of Kings is a footnote in the reign of Menahem.³⁴ The immediate effect is that Assyria is configured as a formidable opponent, but perhaps not the central adversary of Israel, and so the reader will be led to conclude that Assyria is an instrument of divine chastisement under the purview of God's control. Before long, Assyria will inflict a vast amount of damage, and therefore Menahem's payment is an investment that will yield no long-term return; but God is a more daunting antagonist, and so far Menahem has done everything to ensure divine disapproval for his self-serving policies. Ironically, Menahem's name means *comforter*, but all he offers is temporary respite and ultimately only false comfort for the north. When Pekahiah the son of Menahem succeeds his father in v. 22 after ten years, it is an exception to the recent run of usurpations, but the conspiracy of his military officer Pekah in v. 25 resumes the chaotic trend of violent overthrows. Pekah's twenty-year reign might be longer than most in recent memory, but it is also fraught with Assyrian incursions, carrying lasting implications for north and south: Tiglath-Pileser's land acquisitions and northern deportations are

---

[33] See Peter Dubovský, "Tiglath-Pileser III's Campaigns in 734–732 B.C.: Historical Background of Isa 7, 2 Kgs 15–16 and 2 Chr 27–28," *Biblica* 87 (2006): 153–70.

[34] Peter Machinist, "Assyria and Its Image in the First Isaiah," *JAOS* 103 (1983): 722.

a preview of what Israel can soon expect on a larger scale. For the theological interpreter, Pekah's demise and Hoshea's treachery take the nation to the edge of a precipice, and the following chart illustrates both a striking historical symmetry and a diagrammatic parable of repeated futility as the Icarian demise of the northern kingdom draws near:

A Jeroboam I
  B seven kings
    C seventh king: Ahab
      D Jehu (destroys Ahab's house)
A´ Jeroboam II
  B´ seven kings
    C´ seventh king: Hoshea
      D´ Assyrian invasion.[35]

Far from being immune to the mounting international pressures, Judah will have its own challenges as the narrative resumes with the career of Jotham in vv. 32–38. Chronological details are not immediately clear, but after Uzziah's death, Jotham reigns on his own, and the architectural centerpiece of his career is rebuilding the Upper Gate of the temple: his son will engage in an extensive building program in the next chapter, but it will be a dark antithesis. Jotham's efforts are laudable, although overshadowed by a heightening crisis epitomized in v. 37 where God sends Rezin of Aram and Pekah of Israel against the land of Judah. Often referred to as the Syro-Ephraimite alliance and given more press in Isaiah 7, the reader of 2 Kings 15–16 can conclude that these are testing times for Jotham and his successor Ahaz, and their responses to this maelstrom reveal the quality of their

---

[35] Leithart, *1 & 2 Kings*, 238.

faith. After a rapid parade of monarchs, considerably more narrative space is allocated to the career of Ahaz in chapter 16, but he is given a negative evaluation from the outset: beyond tolerating the high places, Ahaz burns incense there and engages in the abominable ritual of child sacrifice (cf. Deut 12:31). Ahaz's domestic compromises are a prelude to his approach to external conflict, and just as he eschews Israel's law at home, so he follows a similar course abroad. Syro-Ephraimite tensions are introduced during Jotham's reign, but come to a head for Ahaz in events that are of great interest to historians but are also important for any theological reading. Rezin and Pekah are threatening Ahaz – to the point that Judah loses control of the southern port of Elath and an assault is launched against Jerusalem – to join an anti-Assyrian alliance, but Ahaz refuses and instead opts for Assyrian assistance against the coalition. There may be no outright condemnation of Ahaz's decision in the narrative, but he condemns himself through his language of submission to the Assyrian king, who has just wreaked havoc in the north despite Menahem's earlier payment. Walter Brueggemann notes that Ahaz's verbs in 2 Kgs 16:7 ("come up" and "save") are usually requests made to God, but since Ahaz has rejected traditional confidence in the LORD, he directs his cry for help to a different master and thereby misappropriates the roles of son and servant: "From the rigorous Yahwistic perspective reflected in our narrative, the Davidic king can only be son and servant of Yahweh (see Ps 2:7; 2 Sam 7:14; Ps 89:20, 26). Thus the submission of the king to Tiglath-Pileser is a direct repudiation of the identity of the Jerusalemite king and a rejection of the only theological rationale for the Davidic kingdom."[36]

---

[36] Brueggemann, *1 & 2 Kings*, 501.

The king of Assyria's response to Ahaz is swift and sure, and in the aftermath of Damascus's destruction, Ahaz makes a trip that alters the future.[37] It is unstated if religious obligations were expected of Assyrian vassals, but it is quite plausible that Ahaz sends instructions to redesign the Jerusalem altar on the basis of a new prototype because he is enamored with the idea of redefining the image of the king of Judah. His father Jotham rebuilt the Upper Gate of the temple, but instead of relying on or trusting in the one whom the temple honors, Ahaz opts for an extensive refurbishing that places himself front and center, with echoes of Jeroboam from an earlier era. Ahaz intends to "make inquiry" on the bronze altar (2 Kgs 16:15), and it appears that he sends further tribute to the king of Assyria, much like he pilfers the treasury and squanders the future for the hope of immediate relief from the short-term threat of the Syro-Ephraimite alliance. Uriah the priest evidently does the king's bidding, and in his eagerness to please his master he is an alter ego of Ahaz himself. When Ahaz dies, he is succeed by Hezekiah – one of his sons not passed through the fire (see v. 3; *contra* Deut 12:31) – who inherits a legacy of Assyrian accommodation and will painfully discover that his father drains the treasuries only to purchase an unreliable ally.

---

[37] The humiliation of Damascus foreshadows the later fate of Jerusalem; cf. Provan, *1 and 2 Kings*, 245: "Tiglath-Pileser descends upon Damascus and captures it and removes both Rezin and its inhabitants, though by different means (cf. the reverse 'exodus' implied by deportation to Kir, the original Aramean homeland according to Amos 9:7)." See also Antoon Schoors, *The Kingdoms of Israel and Judah in the Eighth and Seventh Centuries B.C.E.*, trans. Michael Lesley; Biblical Encyclopedia 5 (Atlanta, GA: Society of Biblical Literature, 2013), 16–17.

BEHIND THE CURTAIN

Hezekiah will be confined like a bird in a cage in due course, but the lengthy 2 Kings 17 first narrates the woeful story of northern decimation in three sections, where the voice of the narrator is more comprehensively heard than at any previous point in the book, as though stepping forward to address the audience directly with a high concentration of Deuteronomistic language: "A network of evaluative nerves from all over the Book of Kings gathers into a central ganglion at this point. Here there are echoes of the language used by the narrator's editorials and the judgment speeches made by the prophets and by God."[38] However, before any address from the narrator, vv. 1–6 describe Hoshea's fateful last steps: he enters the narrative with a treacherous overthrow, and departs the same way as his conspiracy to escape from Assyrian vassalage with Egyptian help is somehow discovered. The identity of So, king of Egypt, has been subject to ample speculation, but as it stands, Hoshea is a meager pawn on the imperial chessboard, and even for a king who is evaluated as modestly better than others, his situation is hopeless: he is imprisoned, and Samaria is besieged for three years before it is destroyed and the population deported into various parts of the Assyrian empire. It is quite ironic, therefore, that Hoshea's name means *savior*, and there is no record of his fate as he departs the narrative with only a failed alliance as his legacy, emblematic of his people, and a warning for the future:

> Hoshea turns traitor against Assyria by trying to form an alliance with Egypt. Trusting in Egypt, or in any power other than Yahweh, is disastrous, a breach of covenant because it is a breach

---

[38] Nelson, *First and Second Kings*, 228.

Upheaval and Reprieve 181

of faith. These events too foreshadow the later exile of Judah: Jehoiakim, like Hoshea, rebels against an overlord (24:1), provoking Nebuchadnezzar to invade. Within this parallel there is an important contrast: Hoshea is taken to exile and disappears from history, while Jehoiachin, who becomes king during Nebuchadnezzar's march toward Jerusalem, is lifted up at the end of 2 Kings 25. David will be restored; not so Hoshea, the false savior.[39]

The last northern king Hoshea vanishes into oblivion without any regnal summary of his reign, but there is a dirge for the northern kingdom as the narrator begins a long homily in vv. 7–23. Assuming that the Deuteronomistic History is a national autopsy conducted in the wake of exile, this section of the story is an important moment of extended spiritual reflection, and the tone is set with the opening line: "This came about because the descendants of Israel sinned against the LORD their God – who brought them up out of Egypt from under the hand of Pharaoh king of Egypt – and they feared other gods."[40] Although there are a plethora of transgressions, violation of the first commandment regarding other gods stands at the top of the catalogue. Foregrounding the exodus event has a particular effect within the indictment, for even as the Israelites are disobedient to the God who brought them into the land of Canaan, now they are driven

---

[39] Leithart, *1 & 2 Kings*, 251.
[40] On elements of theodicy in this passage, see Sweeney, *I & II Kings*, 389–90. Barton ("Historiography and Theodicy in the Old Testament," 31) creatively posits a public setting for a recitative performance: "I wonder, however, whether Noth's theory that it is punctuated by the great speeches placed in the mouth of leading figures (rather than by the later chapter and book divisions) might suggest its use over a period of several days, each concluding with the appropriate speech."

out like the previous occupants in whose ways they have followed.⁴¹ Lest the audience pin the blame on kings and leaders exclusively, this litany of sins underscores a corporate guilt and collective iniquity, with deportation as the consequence. Years earlier, Ahijah of Shiloh had warned Jeroboam's wife that Israel would be uprooted and scattered beyond the river, and now – after centuries of walking in the sins of Jeroboam – judgment has arrived from a nation beyond the river. Israel is driven out with an absence of divine partiality, and it is hardly an accident that in v. 19, Judah is also mentioned in a thinly veiled warning in the aftermath of Assyria's devastation of Samaria and the northern kingdom.

Deportation of northern citizens by the Assyrians is only half the story, as the concluding section of the chapter (vv. 24–41) outlines a resettlement initiative: other conquered groups are imported into the northern territories along with their religious proclivities. Lions have already appeared in 1 Kings 13 and 20 as agents of judgment, and when God dispatches lions against the new northern population, it is consistent with the warning in several texts from the *tôrāh* (e.g., Lev 26:21–22; Deut 32:24, "the teeth of beasts I will send upon them"), but paradoxically illustrates ongoing divine interest in the north even after devastation.

---

⁴¹ Fretheim, *First and Second Kings*, 192, citing Deut 9:5, "It is not because of your righteousness or the uprightness of your heart that you are going in to occupy their land; but because of the wickedness of these nations the LORD your God is dispossessing them before you, in order to fulfill the promise that the LORD made on oath to your ancestors, to Abraham, to Isaac, and to Jacob" (NRSV). Cf. Martin Noth, *The Deuteronomistic History*, JSOTSup 15 (Sheffield: JSOT Press, 1981), 91: "For Dtr then the demand for observance of the divine law has as its background the fact that God has manifested himself and acted at the beginning of Israelite history and has repeatedly intervened to help."

The lions also prompt an intervention from the Assyrian king himself, who proposes to send back an exiled priest: Jeroboam had earlier disenfranchised the priesthood, and so sending a northern priest back results in new versions of syncretism.[42] In terms of the larger narrative, the northern demolition recounted in 2 Kings 17 is an important theological moment: "The thrust of this claim of justification for the destruction is to insist that history – in its large, international scope – is ordered by Yahweh according to ethical, covenantal norms. That is, history in all its parts – including the deployment of Assyria, the superpower – moves according to the intention of Yahweh, so that Assyria here does not at all undertake any autonomous, imperial action."[43] For those readers in Babylonian exile at the end of 2 Kings 25, there is an encouragement to believe that catastrophe is not the final verdict. However, the Assyrians are not done with the land of Judah, and for the time being, the juggernaut appears poised to destroy Jerusalem as well.

STAY OF EXECUTION

With Hoshea unenviably buffeted between the superpowers of Egypt and Assyria, Hezekiah begins his career in Jerusalem with all the dubious baggage of his father Ahaz behind him. Like his northern counterpart, Hezekiah will face his own torrent of international pressures. Yet his twenty-nine-year reign begins on

---

[42] Cf. James R. Linville, *Israel in the Book of Kings: The Past as a Project of Social Identity*, JSOTSup 272 (Sheffield: Sheffield Academic Press, 1998), 216: "Ironically, because of the attempts to appease the angry god, the Assyrians are actually worthy of a better reputation than the Israelites they replaced, since there is no story of Israelite attempts to please Yahweh."

[43] Brueggemann, *1 & 2 Kings*, 485–86.

an optimistic note, and even as the Assyrians are dismantling the north, so Hezekiah dismantles the high places and related installations in the south, efforts that earn him a rare commendation in 2 Kgs 18:5 as one who trusts in the LORD without peer. Included in his housecleaning is an unexpected object of affection: the reader belatedly discovers the bronze snake (called Nehushtan) of Num 21:4-9 has become an item of veneration, and so a sign that pointed to God's healing capacity in an episode of wilderness rebellion is now an aberration that Hezekiah smashes as part of his reform. Furthermore, his western victories over the Philistines evoke memories of David – to whom Hezekiah is favorably compared – and his rebellion against Assyria is a stunning contrast to his father's capitulation. Based on the speeches below (e.g., vv. 21, 24) it would seem that a coalition with Egypt is the form of rebellion, and in light of the northern experience reiterated in vv. 9-12, any kind of alliance is a risky enterprise and certainly proved fatal for Hoshea. Jerusalem has been faced with threats and incursions before, but neither on the Assyrian scale nor with the fires of northern destruction smoking in the background, and readers have just arrived at a critical point in the theological plot of Kings as Hezekiah is put to the sternest test yet faced by any descendant of David.

Sennacherib's entrance into Judah features an overthrow of the fortified cities, a strong message that Jerusalem will soon be targeted. If immediate success is expected because of Hezekiah's piety, such is not the case, inviting the interpreter to perceive a different divine agenda at work here in the midst of Hezekiah's ordeal as his suffering exceeds that of Ahaz, his accommodating predecessor. With his political rebellion uncovered, Hezekiah's confession of sin and plea for withdrawal come with a heavy price, but because of the folly of previous kings, there is not enough gold in the temple treasuries to meet the Assyrian requirement even when the door frames are stripped. It is unclear if Sennacherib is angered by the payment or is engaging in some diplomatic treachery, but in v. 17, a high-ranking delegation is dispatched from Lachish – the siege of which is memorably depicted on a wall relief from an Assyrian palace – and they take their stand at the conduit of the upper pool, with ominous warnings of an impending siege: "That they could get so near to Jerusalem's water supply suggests that this would be a major worry in the defense of the city."[44] Statistically, the speeches of the Rabshakeh – usually understood as the field commander of the Assyrian army – represents the most multilayered theological utterance by any foreign character in the book of Kings: prior to any military action against Jerusalem, the city is besieged with a verbal assault, the memories of which carry lasting significance.[45]

The Rabshakeh presumably lacks the physical dimensions of Goliath, but his rhetorical strength is far superior, and his opening gambit in vv. 19–25 includes an array of stylistic tactics and agile shifts. Deploying a series of questions at strategic intervals, the overarching theme of the speech is signaled early as he draws attention to the issue of trust and successively undermines each pillar of Jerusalem's resistance: they are relying on mere words that are no match for the Assyrian war machine, it is folly to place confidence in Pharaoh who will prove to be an unstable ally, and

---

[44] Roger Tomes, "1 & 2 Kings," in *Eerdmans Commentary on the Bible*, ed. J. D. G. Dunn and J. W. Rogerson (Grand Rapids, MI: Eerdmans, 2003), 275. On the payment issue, see Paul S. Evans, *The Invasion of Sennacherib in the Book of Kings: A Source-Critical and Rhetorical Study of 2 Kings 18–19*, VTSup 125 (Leiden: Brill, 2009), 143–51.

[45] See Peter Machinist, "The Rab Šāqēh at the Wall of Jerusalem: Israelite Identity in the Face of the Assyrian 'Other,'" *HS* 41 (2000): 151–68.

any hope in God is misplaced because the Rabshakeh makes the striking claim that the Assyrians have come under God's direction.[46] By deprecating Hezekiah's reforms, the Rabshakeh aims to drive a wedge between king and people, creating factions that turn the city against itself and create internal confusion to match the external turmoil: "Are the Judeans wise, the commander questions, to trust in the unseen LORD, when the all too visible Assyrian army stands at the gates with overwhelmingly superior numbers (v. 23)?"[47] Imploring the Assyrian to use Aramaic must be an attempt at damage control by the three Judean officers – a counterpoint to the Assyrian triumvirate dispatched by Sennacherib – but far from complying, the Rabshakeh amplifies his voice in Hebrew and more directly addresses the citizens within earshot of the wall. In 2 Kgs 6:24–29, the Aramean offensive against Samaria illustrates the grim realities and dietary disgust of a protracted siege, and according to the Rabshakeh, the prospects for Jerusalem are hardly more appetizing. The concluding movement of his speech in 2 Kgs 18:28–35 causes the interpreter to strongly suspect that the Rabshakeh is trying to internally divide the city, and as he adopts the tone of a prophet, he variously assails the integrity of Hezekiah and claims that the king of Assyria offers a better deal in a new land of promise, painting a picture of eating figs and drinking clean water that sounds decidedly more attractive than filth and urine. Alongside

---

[46] Cf. Brueggemann, *1 & 2 Kings*, 496: "Assyria has been dispatched by none other than Yahweh, because Yahweh wants recalcitrant Jerusalem to be destroyed, a point long anticipated by the prophets of Israel (18:25). This is the most daring taunt imaginable, that Assyria is a tool of Yahweh against Yahweh's own people" (citing Isa 10:5, "Ah, Assyria, the rod of my anger – the club in their hands is my fury!").

[47] Provan, *1 and 2 Kings*, 256.

a diminution of Hezekiah is the claim that other gods have been powerless to resist the Assyrian advance, and therefore the LORD cannot be considered as having adequate power to deliver Jerusalem: "Now the real issue becomes clear. Sennacherib is in effect claiming to be God's rival for the loyalty of Judah, one who can in reality give what God is apparently unable to provide: security, land, life. As in the struggle between Pharaoh and God in Exodus or between Baal and God in I Kings 18, the stakes have reached the ultimate limit. Is the God of Israel really God alone, or can Sennacherib demote God to just another empty divinity?"[48] Asserting that confidence in Hezekiah and God are woefully misplaced, there is nonetheless a curious "response" to the Rabshakeh in v. 36, as the citizens of Jerusalem are silent in accordance with the king's order. At earlier points in Israel's royal history, factions and divisions were usually fatal, but here the uncommon unanimity is constructive and must betoken the respect of the citizens for Hezekiah. Nonetheless, in light of having just destroyed the larger and stronger northern kingdom, the Rabshakeh is hardly uttering idle threats, and therefore the self-controlled response of silence must be challenging in the face of such intimidating rhetoric.

[48] Nelson, *First and Second Kings*, 239. The key lineaments of the confrontation are also nicely summarized by Dominic Rudman, "Is the Rabshakeh Also Among the Prophets? A Rhetorical Study of 2 Kings XVIII 17–35," *VT* 50 (2000): 110: "The Rabshakeh couches his mixture of threats, admonitions and promises in 'prophetic' language, aiming thereby to make the Jerusalemites abandon their covenant with Yahweh to form a new one with Sennacherib. Thus, the narrator of the siege account depicts a confrontation between the Assyrian king as false god and Yahweh as true God, mediated by their respective 'prophets,' the Rabshakeh and Isaiah. Caught in the middle of these duelling antagonists is Hezekiah, whose choice will determine whether the remnant of Judah will remain Yahweh's people, or follow Israel into oblivion."

Depicted as an active reformer earlier in his career, Hezekiah is passively offstage during the taunting speeches of the Rabshakeh until he returns to the narrative spotlight at the start of 2 Kings 19 clothed in sackcloth after hearing his officers' report. Recalling once more the siege of Samaria in the days of Elisha, the northern king was likewise clothed in sackcloth and seemingly without options (2 Kgs 6:30–31), and he responded by calling for the prophet's head. In the midst of a crisis involving a superior opponent, Hezekiah's reaction is categorically different, for in 2 Kgs 19:2–4, he sends his courtiers to Isaiah the prophet with a request for prayer using a childbirth metaphor that seems to express despair and uncertainty for the next generation.[49] Equally important is the place where Hezekiah sends his appeal: earlier he had plundered the temple and stripped the gold in an unsuccessful attempt to placate the Assyrians (18:15–16), but now in chapter 19, he enters the temple and entreats the prophet to pray. Isaiah has not been mentioned before, but in the narrative context seems to be sufficiently well known, and the king probably expects some kind of response. Isaiah's immediate oracle in vv. 6–7 begins with an encouragement for the king not to "fear," and declares that God will cause the Assyrian king to hear a report that prompts his retreat. Although positive, the oracle seems threatened when there are further troop movements to Libnah in v. 8, and Sennacherib appears concerned with the arrival of Tirhakah (who might be represented as something of a false savior in the story). Sennacherib's self-aggrandizing letter to Hezekiah asserts that trust in

---

[49] Note the study of Katheryn Pfisterer Darr, "No Strength to Deliver: A Contextual Analysis of Hezekiah's Proverb in Isaiah 37.3b," in *New Visions of Isaiah*, ed. Roy F. Melugin and Marvin A. Sweeney; JSOTSup 214 (Sheffield: Sheffield Academic Press, 1996), 219–56.

Upheaval and Reprieve 189

God for Jerusalem's deliverance is futile: the king of Judah is commended for his trust in 18:5, but he now finds that his trust is sorely tested by the Assyrian onslaught. As it turns out, the name *Isaiah* means "salvation of the LORD," and when Hezekiah lays out Sennacherib's letters before God in the temple, Isaiah's unsolicited oracle forecasts a startling reversal.

Hezekiah's prayer in response to Sennacherib's letter is fraught with theological significance, with a marked emphasis on the creative power and potency of Israel's God compared to other deities in a manner that evokes memories of the confrontation with Pharaoh in Egypt (Exod 9:14–16). In other words, Hezekiah's prayer frames the present crisis as an assault on God's character, inviting the reader to perceive Sennacherib as a new Pharaoh "who does not know the LORD" and the people of Israel in desperate need of divine rescue. Hezekiah implores God to "open his eyes," language that is similar to 2 Kgs 6:17 when the eyes of Elisha's servant were opened and he glimpsed horses and chariots of fire before the army of Aram was diverted from their destructive mandate. Hezekiah also asks that God would hear (*shāmaʾ*) the words of ridicule sent by Sennacherib, only to have Isaiah arrive in v. 20 to report God's declaration: "Your prayer to me about Sennacherib king of Assyria I have heard (*shāmaʿtî*)." In the longest poetic oracle in the book of Kings (vv. 21–34), the bellicose speeches of the Assyrians are countered as Isaiah unfolds an image of a different kind of ridicule: the blaspheming king who has boasted about scaling the heights of mountains with his myriad chariots and drying up the streams of Egypt with the soles of his feet is now mocked by a young maiden – who remains a virgin because she was not raped by the empire's lackeys – contemptuously tossing her head at him as he is shamefully led away as a prisoner with a hook in his nose. Rather than the king's recent initiative, God long ago ordained that cities would be destroyed by the Assyrians, but Sennacherib's raging has run its course, and in a remarkably personal word he can expect nothing but disaster. Hezekiah, by contrast, is given a sign about forthcoming harvests, suggesting that a remnant will survive and not be accosted by Sennacherib again. The concluding affirmation ("For I will defend this city to save it, for my own sake and for the sake of my servant David") does not indicate that Hezekiah's piety is the rationale for rescue; rather, Jerusalem will escape because of the divine character (recently insulted by the Assyrians) and the antecedent promise to David. Later in the narrative, Jehoiachin will be in Babylon prior to the invasion (2 Kgs 24:15), and so the survival of the Davidic line continues despite Jerusalem's destruction.

Isaiah's oracle of salvation does not indicate precisely how or when Jerusalem's rescue will take place, but the manner and the timing must be a relief to the beleaguered king and the citizens of the city: upon waking up the next morning, behold (*hinnēh*) lifeless corpses! It is unclear if the citizens – whose point of view is refracted in v. 35 – are aware that the divine angel is responsible for the liquidation of the army, but commentators often point out that the nocturnal temporal setting and the scale of deliverance evokes memories of the liberation from Egyptian slavery and from the pursuit of Pharaoh and his hordes in the days of the exodus: "The Passover that destroys Assyria brings new life for Judah," says Peter Leithart, "as Yahweh again shows himself, as he did against Egypt, to be incomparably greater than all gods and all emperors."[50] The episode could have certainly concluded at this point, but the denouement in vv. 36–37 featuring Sennacherib's return to Nineveh and subsequent assassination by his sons

---

[50] Leithart, *1 & 2 Kings*, 259.

illustrates that divine payback is hard to avoid: Hezekiah prayed to God in the Jerusalem temple and experiences deliverance, whereas Sennacherib's god evidently does not protect his supplicant in the temple of Nineveh.[51] Even at this moment of exodus-style triumph, however, the reader should bear in mind that Sennacherib is not the last monarch in the book of Kings to be guilty of misplaced confidence in a temple. Judah's last monarchs are likewise tempted to be overly comfortable with the notion that the daughter of Zion who mocked the imperial power will never be violated, regardless of circumstances or covenant infidelities. Sennacherib may not be the only victim of hubris either, for Hezekiah himself faces further challenges in 2 Kings 20, and the concluding portion of his reign cautions that inner complacency can be more dangerous than any external threat.

---

[51] Christoph Uehlinger, "Nisroch," in *Dictionary of Deities and Demons in the Bible*, 2nd edn., ed. Karel van der Toorn, Bob Becking and Pieter W. van der Horst (Leiden: Brill, 1999), 631: "Sennacherib who attempted to challenge the one universal god (2 Kgs 19:15, 19) is personally punished. Murdered by his own sons while praying to 'his god' who cannot help him, he meets a destiny which was decided and announced by Yahweh (2 Kgs 19:7). Sennacherib's forlorn trust in a powerless god marks a final counterpoint to Israel's trust in the one true god."

CHAPTER 7

Demolition and Exile

In the midst of Solomon's long prayer at the temple's dedication, a clear warning is sounded: persistent failure will trigger divine anger that will inexorably lead to expulsion and captivity in a foreign land (1 Kgs 8:46). Not only is this warning personally reiterated by God in 1 Kgs 9:6-9, but after the division of the kingdom, Ahijah of Shiloh forecasts that Israel will be uprooted from the good land of their ancestors and scattered beyond the Euphrates (1 Kgs 14:15). These earlier warnings are realized when the northern kingdom is annihilated in 2 Kings 17, and in this concluding section of the Deuteronomistic History, the southern kingdom of Judah likewise faces its own day of judgment. As Sandra Richter reminds us, Joshua–2 Kings is a theological history predicated on the tenets of Deuteronomy: "narrated from the platform of a covenantal understanding of Yahweh's relationship with Israel, this epic work accounts for Israel's successes and failures as the predictable outworkings of Israel's faithfulness to the *bĕrît* articulated at Sinai." Richter concludes: "Hence, from the Plains of Moab to the Plains of Jericho (2 Kgs 25:5), from Moses to Jehoiachin, the history's overarching agenda is to explain Israel's covenant relationship with God, and how the failure of this relationship eventually leads to the nation's demise at the hands of the Neo-Babylonian Empire in 586 BCE."[1] Hezekiah and Jerusalem survive the Assyrian crisis in 2 Kings 18-19 with an unparalleled stay of execution, but even as the threat of Sennacherib is vanquished, other dangers lurk as the book of Kings draws to a close. And yet, despite the devastation at the end of the story, it can be assumed the sweeping narrative of the Deuteronomistic History is composed in the wake of exile in order to rebuild the faith of Israel and declare that divine promises have not been nullified, for out of Jerusalem's ruin, a new chapter of God's faithfulness is poised to begin.

VISITING TIME

Hezekiah emerges from 2 Kings 19 with vindicated trust, but 2 Kings 20 presents two episodes that provide a more ambivalent perspective and together point toward Judah's forthcoming downfall. The first episode, in 20:1-11, begins with a temporal reference ("In those days") that, when combined with the surrounding context, locates Hezekiah's illness before the reprieve and in the midst of the Assyrian crisis: Isaiah's terse announcement of death is met with a prayer from Hezekiah, followed by the prophet's abrupt return and an assurance of fifteen more years of life, sealed with a sign of the shadow. The larger narrative is structured in a parabolic fashion, and by means of this flashback the reader is afforded an opportunity to reflect on Hezekiah's double crisis, for not only is the city under threat, but also the king himself is on the verge of death: his body is besieged by illness as the city is

---

[1] Sandra Richter, "Deuteronomistic History," in *Dictionary of the Old Testament: Historical Books*, ed. Bill T. Arnold and H. G. M. Williamson (Downers Grove, IL: InterVarsity, 2005), 220.

threatened by the Assyrian military. Yet both cases illustrate the efficacy of Hezekiah's prayer, and in the face of mortal dangers, the king calls on God, and through the mediation of the prophet, each threat subsides. Within the theological macroplot of Kings, prayer and the prophetic word can overrule the power of the empire, and, just as surprisingly, a divine reversal can add years of life.[2] At this point, the narrative emphasizes divine freedom but also underscores the efficacy of human prayer in changing or shifting God's action. Hezekiah is evidently suffering from some kind of "boil" (v. 7, *shehîn*), the malady of Job and an affliction mentioned in Leviticus 13, perhaps explaining why the king is unable to enter the temple precincts. More acutely, boils "are among the plagues of Egypt (Exod. 9:8–12) and among the curses of Deut. 28:27. Hezekiah's boil is a sign that Judah is threatened as Egypt was and that its king is threatened with disfiguring skin disease. He is healed, and Israel is delivered once again from 'Egyptian' diseases. Hezekiah is healed with a cake of figs, for instead of pestilence and boils the land will be filled with vineyards and fig trees."[3] On the one hand, then, Hezekiah's illness is a picture of Judah's ailment, as God is willing to suspend the sentence and directs the prophet Isaiah to deliver a word

---

[2] Cf. Seow, "The First and Second Books of Kings," 273–74: "For the individual, as well as for the people of God as a larger community, there is hope in trusting God, even if no hope seems possible (20:6). Even if the shadow has been cast and it has lengthened ten times, God can reverse it (20:8–11). This is the kind of trust that the text challenges the reader to have. The grace of God through faith makes it possible for death to be overcome (Rom 3:21–31; 4:2–4; Gal 2:1–10). This is at the heart of the gospel story in the New Testament." Within a wider biblical theology, Seow's comments are certainly appropriate, although life-threatening circumstances during Hezekiah's tenure pose dramatic challenges for the community.

[3] Leithart, *1 & 2 Kings*, 260.

of liberation. On the other hand, there is an implicit warning that time is running out: fifteen more years are added by grace, but how will this gift be received?[4] It is suggestive that the shadow sign takes place on the steps of Ahaz, implying that Hezekiah is not bound by the sins of the past and can pray for an alternative future. Even if the nation of Judah is buried in the grave of exile (cf. 2 Kgs 13:21), it is possible that God can raise the nation back to life.

There are grounds for assuming that the second episode in 2 Kgs 20:12–19 – where Hezekiah entertains the Babylonian embassy and hears Isaiah's dire prognostication – is also presented as a flashback and is correlated with events prior to the Assyrian deliverance. The agents of Merodach-Baladan (cf. Isa 39:1) ostensibly arrive to offer a gift to Hezekiah upon his recovery from illness and are treated to an extensive tour of the treasuries (presumably before they are emptied in 18:15–16). No exact motives are stated for the visit, although a gift and letters (sĕpārîm) from the king of Babylon suggest that an alliance is sought: "The word sĕpārîm likely refers to an official letter; the same word was used earlier to denote what Hezekiah received from the messengers from Assyria. It is ironic that just after Hezekiah is assured by YHWH that Jerusalem will not fall, the king of the nation that ultimately conquers Jerusalem

---

[4] Moberly, *The Theology of the Book of Genesis*, 17: "The theological interpretation of scripture – its reading with a view to articulating and practicing its enduring significance for human life under God – involves a constant holding together of parts and a whole which is regularly reconfigured." Indeed, nowhere is this truer than in the Hezekiah narrative, where the king should either be commended for keeping his options open or chastised for seeking Babylonian assistance.

appears bearing gifts."[5] The paucity of details about the timing and purpose of the Babylonian visit means that reader's attention is focused on Hezekiah's decisionmaking process, and for the second time in 2 Kings 20, he faces an internal crisis: first his illness, and now this seductive temptation to secure a deal that might resolve the Assyrian crisis. Consequently, this episode complicates our view of Hezekiah. Earlier he is commended for his trust (18:5), but now it appears that trust is more challenging than may be supposed, for "while he was seeking Yahweh's aid (see 19:19), Hezekiah sought to protect Jerusalem by agreeing to an alliance with Babylon."[6] The king's trust is now assailed – as it were – by both the Assyrians and the Babylonians, and in the longer term, the apparently peaceful delegation from Merodach-Baladan represents more danger than the Assyrian war machines presently devouring the land of Judah. These scenes thus illustrate the inherent difficulties of trust, and even as Hezekiah implores God and hears Isaiah deliver a prophetic word about Sennacherib's retreat (see 19:6–7), he is not without inner tension. Perhaps it is easier to negotiate an alliance than imagine the fulfillment of an unlikely prophetic word, but the picture that emerges here is that trust involves an acknowledgment that God has the capacity to intervene and transform circumstances.

While it might be tempting to reduce this narrative to the simple formula *piety = deliverance*, an audience in exile is invited

---

[5] Cohn, *2 Kings*, 144.
[6] Long, *2 Kings*, 244; cf. Hens-Piazza, *1–2 Kings*, 372: "Babylon just might be the means to finally be rid of the persistent Assyrian menace that is hovering over Jerusalem." Note also Dietrich, "1 & 2 Kings," 262: "It seems that Hezekiah wanted to win him over as an ally and thus tried to impress his envoys by putting his military might and his war-funds on display (he might have even passed some of this on to Babylon)."

to a higher degree of engagement, and when hearing Isaiah's word, there is an opportunity to believe that more are with us than with them (cf. 2 Kgs 6:16) and so to resist the inclination to conclude otherwise and plan accordingly. Through the lens of Hezekiah, one learns that trust is not robotic, but instead is a disciplined, imaginative choice to rely on the character of God instead of on more expedient alternatives. Moses warned the Israelites about making alliances with the foreign nations (Deut 7:2; cf. Exod 34:12), and the Deuteronomistic History has numerous examples of the folly of jettisoning this principle, so a further element of trust is enacting the wisdom of the *tôrāh* over and against a convenient argument for eschewing the faith of Israel. It is noteworthy that the Babylonian envoys are shown the spices of the kingdom, for the only other place the term occurs in Kings is during the reign of Solomon (1 Kings 10), a king who opted for ill-fated alliances. Hezekiah is initially presented as a new David, but he is here inching toward the template of Solomon, therefore suggesting that Jerusalem faces its most subversive threats from internal compromises rather than external aggressions.

If there was nothing amiss with the Babylonian visitors, Isaiah probably would not have arrived in v. 14 to interview the king, but he approaches Hezekiah with questions ("What did these men say, and from where have they come to you?"), for which, like sightless Ahijah with Jeroboam's wife, he already knows the answers. Some dissonance can be perceived between king and prophet, and Hezekiah's initial evasiveness probably reveals a measure of culpability. Back in 2 Kgs 5:25 Elisha posed a straightforward question ("Where have you been, Gehazi?") before unleashing an oracle of doom about his servant's descendants. After Hezekiah concedes the provenance of his visitors, Isaiah declares that not only will the treasures be exported forcibly to

Babylon, but the king's own descendants will accompany the treasures under duress to a foreign palace where sterility awaits them.[7] The city of Jerusalem has just been delivered in accordance with the promise to David, but now the reader is prepared for another disaster in the days ahead. Such an announcement foreshadows the apostasy of the next chapter and creates suspense as the audience wonders how the Davidic line will survive. Meanwhile, Hezekiah's bifurcated response to Isaiah's oracle is painfully short-sighted, as his public acquiescence ("The word of the LORD that you have spoken is good") is offset by a private soliloquy ("Will there not be peace and security in my days?"). Hezekiah's hospitality to the Babylonian delegation is somewhat reminiscent of his father Ahaz in 2 Kgs 16:7–8 currying favor with the Assyrians, while his conflicted reaction to Isaiah's objurgation is a harbinger of how the last kings of Judah will respond to the prophetic word: "Hezekiah's response to the prophet is curious. Whether naïve or foolish, the king takes comfort in the prophet's word. It seems that Hezekiah is willing to exchange whatever it takes to acquire peace and security in his time. However, his willingness to engage Babylon indicates his utter lack of understanding regarding the long-term cost of this new courtship."[8] Some commentators find it puzzling that Hezekiah does not pray in response to Isaiah's oracle; after all, when Isaiah announces his imminent death, the king cries out to God, who duly orders the prophet to return with an announcement of an additional fifteen

---

[7] On the eunuchs, see Alter, *Ancient Israel*, 669: "Although *sarisim* sometimes may refer to court officials who are not necessarily castrated, one suspects that the core meaning that involves castration is invoked here: there could be no greater curse for a king than to have his sons turned into eunuchs, incapable of begetting offspring."

[8] Hens-Piazza, *1–2 Kings*, 373.

Demolition and Exile 199

years of life. The reader might conclude that Hezekiah does not pray in response to the oracle about his later descendants becoming eunuchs in the palace of Babylon because he is not personally affected, and therefore his portrait in Kings ends on a note of ambivalence.[9] We can adduce that Hezekiah lives out the rest of his years in relative security, but also with awareness of the grim future for his successors. It is not without irony that his obituary notice in v. 20 recounts his aquatic legacy popularly known as Hezekiah's Tunnel, an engineering feat that channeled water into the city to survive the exigencies of an invasion.[10] This water supply will be needed urgently in the days ahead when the Babylonians – as anticipated by Isaiah – return without gifts and Hezekiah's descendants find themselves under siege. As with most of the narratives in the book of Kings, the Hezekiah story does not offer a tidy package of spiritual truisms, but instead dramatizes a confrontation of faith and its alternatives in the midst of tense political conflicts and military incursion. Paradoxically, the same trust in the prophetic word that God will deliver Jerusalem from Assyria is required to believe that God will actually allow Jerusalem to be destroyed by Babylon in the closing phases of Kings.

MANASSEH'S MEMORY

Areas of scholarly consensus are hard to find in our narrative, but it is (almost) a truth universally acknowledged that Manasseh is

---

[9] Fretheim, *First and Second Kings*, 208.
[10] For background, see Mary K. Y. H. Hom, "Where Art Thou, O Hezekiah's Tunnel? A Biblical Scholar Considers the Archaeological and Biblical Evidence Concerning the Waterworks in 2 Chronicles 32:3-4, 30 and 2 Kings 20:20," *JBL* 135 (2016): 493-503.

configured as the worst of the Davidic line whose fifty-five-year reign ushers in an era of unprecedented apostasy, which is catalogued in 2 Kgs 21:1–18 along with searing indictments for leading Israel astray and shedding innocent blood.[11] Hezekiah invested energy in dismantling and breaking high places and deviant objects (18:4), whereas Manasseh rebuilds the high places and retrofits the sanctuary with Baalistic appurtenances: in the same temple precincts where Hezekiah prays when confronted with the Assyrian crisis, his successor erects an Asherah image and exceeds the dispossessed nations of Canaan for iniquity. After the recent focus on external aggression in various forms throughout 2 Kings 17–20, Manasseh's career is notable for its absence of any obvious adversary; instead, there is a plethora of detail regarding his deviance from altars to soothsaying. Naturally, the question arises as to why Manasseh embarks on this program, and some interpreters have theorized he seeks to appease the Assyrians as a vassal: there are scant grounds for doubting that a political opportunism motivates Manasseh's domestic policy – in other words, he found it advantageous to aggressively reverse the policies of his father and must have help from certain sectors of the population – but in 2 Kings 21, these reasons are subordinated

---

[11] See further Schipper, "Hezekiah, Manasseh, and Dynastic or Transgenerational Punishment," 81–105. It should be noted, however, that Manasseh is characterized differently in 2 Chron 33:12–16; see Philippe Abadie, "From the Impious Manasseh (2 Kings 21) to the Convert Manasseh (2 Chronicles 33): Theological Rewriting by the Chronicler," in *The Chronicler as Theologian: Essays in Honor of Ralph W. Klein*, ed. M. Patrick Graham, Steven L. McKenzie and Gary N. Knoppers; JSOTSup 371(London: T. and T. Clark, 2003), 89–104; Ehud Ben Zvi, "Reading Chronicles and Reshaping the Memory of Manasseh," in *Chronicling the Chronicler: The Book of Chronicles and Early Second Temple Historiography*, ed. Paul S. Evans and Tyler F. Williams (Winona Lake, IN: Eisenbrauns, 2013), 121–40.

to the overriding theological implications of such choices, and these choices hurtle Judah toward its doom.¹² The comparison to Ahab suggests that both kings opt for political expedience over covenant loyalty, and just as Ahab's action results in dynastic punishment, so Manasseh's failures procure an irreversible decree of destruction against Jerusalem that God "has chosen" (v. 7). Overall, Manasseh's name ("forget") carries an ironic sting as he embarks on a sequence of action in 2 Kings 21 that ignores the recent deliverance, much like the nation as a whole is guilty of amnesia since the events of the exodus (v. 15), and enhanced culpability is thus attached to a people who disregard "God's ongoing gracious action on their behalf."¹³

The reign of Manasseh is structured so that a collective prophetic utterance – anonymously voiced in vv. 11–15 with a dense cluster of figurative language – is the pivotal point of the chapter. It is apparent that Manasseh has been confronted with the prophetic word on numerous occasions yet has consistently rejected it, and it is plausible that these prophets are part of the innocent blood that fill the streets of Jerusalem (v. 16). During Hezekiah's recent crisis, there is an illustration of divine grace that turns back time, but here God's patience has seemingly reached its breaking point, and Jerusalem's forthcoming calamity is explained by detonating a pair of explosive metaphors in v. 13. First, God will personally use a measuring line and plumb line recycled from the days of Ahab to destroy Jerusalem as Samaria was destroyed

---

[12] On the political factors at work, see Sweeney, *I & II Kings*, 427–30. For a recent assessment of Asherah (*'ashērah*) symbolism and its connection to blessedness (*'ashērê*), note John J. Collins, "Israelite Religion: The Return of the Goddess," in *The Bible after Babel: Historical Criticism in a Postmodern Age* (Grand Rapids, MI: Eerdmans, 2005), 99–129.

[13] Fretheim, *First and Second Kings*, 210.

previously: "The city will be assessed by the divine building inspector (cf. the use of the measuring line in Isa. 34:11; Lam 2:8), and, like a dangerous building, condemned."[14] Manasseh's building projects that reverse the efforts of Hezekiah will now be systematically dismantled under God's direct supervision. Second, the city of Jerusalem will be wiped out like a dirty dish after a meal, picturing its despoliation and complete overturning: "To wipe a dish and turn it upside-down to drain signified the depopulation of the land (cf. Jer 51:34)."[15] At the same time, Richard Nelson points to a possible flicker of light after the darkness of exile and upheaval: "If there is any hope at all beyond that exile, it is of the very thinnest, implied perhaps in the homey metaphor of the dish. The dish that is Jerusalem will be wiped clean of its inhabitants and turned over, but it is at least not broken, as is so often the case with these ceramic metaphors (Ps 2:9; Eccles. 12:6; Jer 19:11)."[16] As Nelson suggests, because the dish is not smashed, there are hints it might be used again, and this tension between Jerusalem's status as the dwelling place of God's name forever and the notice of its destruction in v. 7 is balanced in v. 8, an antecedent divine word that emphasizes the conditional nature of land tenure. For now, the meal is over but the dish is not broken, and perhaps there are hints of restoration even after the trauma of exile.

Yet any thoughts of restoration are best held in abeyance, as this announcement of judgment is described as *ear-tingling*, an expression last heard in the days of Eli when an anonymous man of God declared the termination of that priestly dynasty (1 Sam 2:27–36). God's anger at the cultic malfeasance in Shiloh – in fact,

---

[14] Provan, *1 and 2 Kings*, 267. [15] Wiseman, *1 & 2 Kings*, 231.
[16] Nelson, *First and Second Kings*, 251.

where we are controversially told in 1 Sam 2:25 that God delights (*ḥāpēṣ*) in the death of Eli's sons – is now manifested during Manasseh's long career in Jerusalem. The narrative of Manasseh, therefore, is of great theological significance, especially if one of the key questions in the book of Kings is: what provokes divine anger to the point that Israel is expelled from the land?[17] An allusion to Eli's flawed leadership is germane, for just as that house was judged and a new order emerged, so something similar could take place during a period of exile from the land. Even as God's sense of exasperation is palpable during Manasseh's kingship, divine grace is not so easily extinguished. A case might be made that God is presented as the ideal king in the book of Kings, with a passion for justice and a profound vision for the future of the community.

Listed among the legion of Manasseh's transgressions is passing his son (LXX, *sons*) through the fire, though it is not stated whether he does this to placate a deity (cf. 2 Kgs 3:27; 23:10) or perhaps as a cynical ploy designed to send a chilling message to his constituency that he will brook no opposition. Regardless, Manasseh's son Amon should consider himself fortunate to be alive, but he is not afforded any direct speech during his unimpressive two-year reign in 2 Kgs 21:19–26. It increasingly appears as though the phrase "did evil in the eyes of the LORD" includes an attitude the king takes with respect to the faith of Israel and a posture the king adopts in relationship to divine kingship.

---

[17] Cf. Barton ("Historiography and Theodicy in the Old Testament," 28) on the larger theme of the Deuteronomistic History: "Its purpose was theodicy, the explanation of the disaster that had befallen Israel in terms of the justice of God. The work was meant to convince its readers that the disaster of exile was a fully justified punishment by the God of Israel of his own people because of their constant backsliding and apostasy."

By refusing to walk "in the way of the LORD," Amon – like many before him from the wilderness generation onward (cf. Num 32:13; Judg 2:11) – asserts his autonomy and disregards the path of covenant faithfulness (Deut 5:33). The only exciting event in Amon's career is his murder by his own courtiers: "The coup against Amon probably has tangible realpolitik behind it, but here it is juxtaposed to Amon's cultic sins as if in direct response to them."[18] After a half-century of his father's rule, Amon may have been prudent to chart his own course rather than be a pale derivative of Manasseh and fall prey to a factionalism that consumes him "in his own house" – a throwback to the instability of the north in the aftermath of the schism (1 Kgs 16:9–22) and a foreshadowing of turbulence that will soon engulf the land of Judah. No motives for the assassination are provided, but there is a double conspiracy, as those courtiers are in turn executed by "the people of the land." It should be recalled that the people of the land are actively involved in the overthrow of Athaliah – who, Manasseh-like, is willing to consume her own offspring – leading some scholars to suggest a religious motivation. Because young Josiah, a figure who will decisively break from the policies of predecessors, is subsequently installed, it is argued that a modest revolution is under way: "But then something surprisingly hopeful happens: 'The people of the land' – the same political group who brought about the downfall of the 'evil' queen Athaliah, enabling the 'good' king Joash to come to power (2 Kgs 11:18, 20) – intervene to punish the king's murderers and place a certain Josiah on the throne. The struggle between loyalty and disloyalty to YHWH, and thus between the existence and destruction of the kingdom of Judah, has taken an unexpected turn."[19] On the one

---

[18] Wray Beal, *1 & 2 Kings*, 492.   [19] Dietrich, "1 & 2 Kings," 263.

hand, Joash inaugurates a period of renewal and cleanses the temple in 2 Kings 12 after Athaliah's reign of terror, and so there are great expectations surrounding Josiah, who is installed by the people of the land at the conclusion of 2 Kings 21. On the other hand, the untimely death of Joash (12:20) might prompt the reader to raise questions about how the career of Josiah will end and to wonder if any reform movement can mitigate the prophetic decree of disaster.

LOST AND FOUND

Both Manasseh and Amon are buried in the garden of Uzza, and although scholars have put forth several proposals for this cryptic locale, the most intriguing theory posits a connection with the ill-fated Uzzah in 2 Sam 6:6–8.[20] In that cautionary tale, God strikes Uzzah when he stretches forth his hand to steady the ark, a cultic infraction that prompts David to temporarily abandon the relocation project. It is not without irony, therefore, that the massive defilements of Manasseh and Amon accompany them in their gravesite, but their place of interment is also a segue to the career of Josiah, in which issues of defilement soon take center stage. Rarely has a character been more anticipated than Josiah, as his name is first mentioned in the context of cultic defilement during the man of God's apostrophic excoriation of Jeroboam's altar at Bethel in 1 Kgs 13:2, centuries before Josiah's arrival here in 2 Kings 22. It is significant, therefore, that the narrative of Josiah's career

---

[20] E.g., Sweeney, *I & II Kings*, 432: "Earlier commentators identify Uzza with King Uzziah, but the name refers to Uzza in 2 Sam 6:8." Cf. the discussion in Francesca Stavrakopoulou, "Exploring the Garden of Uzza: Death, Burial and Ideologies of Kingship," *Biblica* 87 (2006): 1–21 (4–5).

begins in medias res as a repairer of the temple; and, in the absence of any hints to the contrary, the reader assumes he has been at it for some time. Josiah is immediately portrayed as a reformer, and with the prophetic word of 1 Kings 13 in mind, it is expected that he will finally dismantle Jeroboam's idolatrous apparatus, which has been a stumbling block for all. No monarchic voice has been heard in the text since Hezekiah's fateful words in 2 Kgs 20:19, but Josiah is differentiated from his predecessors by means of his speech. His first words (spoken in the eighteenth year of his reign, at twenty-six years of age) betoken an upright posture before God, addressed to the high priest on the subject of the people's votive gifts and fair payment to the workers.

No background data are provided for Hilkiah (who evokes memories of Jehoiada during the reign of Joash), but along with characters such as Shaphan, there is an indication of a more faithful court than in previous eras. The main event is not, however, the restoration of the temple, but rather a most startling discovery revealed by Hilkiah during the routine business: "I have found the scroll of the *tôrāh* in the house of the LORD" (2 Kgs 22:8). At this point an important matter of narrative criticism arises, because the only report of the scroll is Hilkiah's disclosure in a private conversation with his colleague Shaphan, and any further comment from the narrator is withheld. At the very least, the reader is invited to wonder if Hilkiah has in fact stumbled upon the scroll or had kept it concealed during the recent darkness, and is now testing the waters to determine if it is safe to bring the scroll back into circulation. These scenes certainly feature some cautious treading by both Hilkiah and Shaphan, implying a period of political danger in advocating any kind of covenantal claims. Waiting until Josiah's eighteenth year to reveal the scroll may seem excessive, but after more than a half-century of apostasy under Manasseh and Amon, perhaps Hilkiah is understandably circumspect given Josiah's genetics. I might suggest that Hilkiah is configured as an agent of preservation who patiently subverts the previous tyrannical regime; Josiah is the subject of the ancient prophecy, but within the larger theological plot, it is vital to note that he does undertake his reforms alone. Jehoiada, the only other high priest in the book of Kings besides Hilkiah, similarly waits until the time is right and carefully plans with his allies before unveiling the long-secreted scion within the temple precincts – hidden, like the scroll, from a rogue monarchy.

The content of the scroll has generated considerable debate within the secondary literature, but many scholars assume that at least some portions of Deuteronomy are included owing to the subsequent stress on repentance, eradication of Canaanite religious practices, centralization of worship, public reading of the law, and observation of Passover.[21] Since a reticence surrounds the precise lineaments of the scroll, attention is directed to the king's response to Shaphan's reading in vv. 9–10 instead.[22] When Hezekiah receives the report of the Rabshakeh's words, he tears his clothes and consults with a prophet (19:1–2); likewise, when Josiah hears the words of the scroll, he tears his clothes and calls for an inquiry that leads to consultation with Huldah the prophetess, suggesting that the present threat against Jerusalem is just as dire

---

[21] For background discussion, bibliography and compelling thoughts on the relationship between Josiah, Deuteronomy and the scroll of 2 Kings 22, see Brent A. Strawn, "Reading Josiah Reading Deuteronomy," in *Reading for Faith and Learning: Essays on Scripture, Community, and Libraries in Honor of M. Patrick Graham*, ed. John B. Weaver and Douglas L. Gragg (Abilene, TX: Abilene Christian University Press, 2017), 31–47.

[22] On the effect of ambiguity surrounding the scroll, see Cohn, *2 Kings*, 153–56.

as the Assyrian incursion. Royal voices are not always trustworthy in the book of Kings – as Solomon's bombast in 1 Kgs 5:4 or Ahab's bravado in 1 Kgs 22:27 variously illustrates – and so it is a rare moment of the highest lucidity when Josiah personally gives utterance to a theodicy after hearing the scroll: as though addressing numerous audiences at the same time, Josiah confesses that divine wrath is merited because the written words have not been treated with care. Without any attempt to evade responsibility, Josiah is presented as a figure of uncommon theological maturity as he acknowledges a longstanding attitude of disobedience from the ancestors to the present, and calling for a second opinion to confirm his interpretation of the scroll certainly heightens his credibility.

According to 2 Kgs 23:2, there are other prophets around, and it is not explained why Huldah the prophetess is sought by Josiah's delegation.[23] Apart from any other significance, her residence is given, and her husband's description would seem to designate him as a temple official, so presumably she is a well-known figure, which is why Hilkiah and the other officers seek her out.[24] There is no indication of Huldah's age, but evidently she has survived the turmoil of previous regimes, and so, akin to

---

[23] The only other named prophetess in the Deuteronomistic History is Deborah; see H. G. M. Williamson, "Prophetesses in the Hebrew Bible," in *Prophecy and Prophets in the Hebrew Bible*, ed. John Day; LHBOTS 531 (New York: T. and T. Clark, 2010), 65–80. Among the many studies, note Renita J. Weems, "Huldah, the Prophet: Reading a (Deuteronomistic) Woman's Identity," in *A God So Near: Essays on Old Testament Theology in Honour of Patrick D. Miller*, ed. Brent A. Strawn and Nancy R. Bowen (Winona Lake, IN: Eisenbrauns, 2003), 321–39.

[24] Claudia Camp, "1 and 2 Kings," in *The Women's Bible Commentary*, ed. Carol A. Newsom and Sharon H. Ringe (Louisville, KY: Westminster John Knox Press, 1992), 115, notes a haunting symmetry between the consultation of Huldah and the earlier visit of Jeroboam's wife to Ahijah: "The story of the

Hilkiah, she is a person of influence shrouded in mystery and one of the faithful in the land whose legacy is memorialized in these pages. Hilkiah brings the scroll to the forefront of the royal conscience, while Huldah unfurls its relevance in a densely packed oracle with two parts. First, vv. 16–17 confirm both the collective prophetic word in the era of Manasseh and Josiah's instinctive response in 22:13 about Judah's state of imperilment, and it is striking that "Huldah's oracle of judgment contains no conditional qualification, no suggestion of escape, no summons to repent."[25] It is clear that God is on the verge of bringing evil against Jerusalem, and reconciling this catastrophe with the endurance of the Davidic line and the centrality of the temple is a challenge for the interpreter. Second, 2 Kgs 22:18–20 concern Josiah personally, with a commendation for his penitent response and an announcement about his future: he will be gathered (*'āsaph*) to his grave in peace and spared the sight of Jerusalem's destruction. Through Huldah, the reader is given another perspective of Josiah's contrition – he also wept, a detail not mentioned earlier – and God's own acoustic confession, "I have heard": after centuries of God's people not hearing, Huldah's oracle reveals that God is neither remote nor missing and is intimately bound up with the book of the law. Moreover, for the second time, Josiah is the subject of a prophecy that involves death. In 1 Kgs 13:2, the man of God declares that Josiah will one day sacrifice the priests of the high places, and now Huldah forecasts Josiah's own burial. Interweaving these two prophetic words reveals that even as the vestiges of Jeroboam's idolatrous

divided kingdom begins and ends with words of women, words of prophets, words about a single life saved, words about a nation doomed."

[25] Brueggemann, *1 & 2 Kings*, 547.

machinery are purged, the city of Jerusalem is on the verge of destruction, just like the altar of Bethel in days of old. When Hezekiah heard Isaiah's gloomy forecast of his progeny's deportation to Babylon after his own peaceful retirement, he remains inert, with no recorded movement for the rest of his career. By contrast, Josiah hears Huldah's prophetic word about his own burial and the catastrophe that will befall Jerusalem, and he is positively frenetic: he gathers (*'āsaph*) the people for a public reading of the book of the covenant (as the scroll is now called) and enacts a covenant renewal ceremony with the rhythms of Joshua 24 (cf. Deuteronomy 29), leading the cause like Solomon but without the baggage. To be sure, the abhorrent installations of Solomon are nearing the end of their long career and are among the many idolatrous targets mentioned in 2 Kgs 23:4–20 as Josiah sets his sights on a comprehensive cleansing of the land. This detailed section provides a retrospective glance of the extent of the pollution, enumerating a range of high places and sites of child sacrifice, as well as chariots devoted to the worship of the sun and weavings for Asherah: Josiah turns not to the right or left except when it comes to destroying deviant appurtenances on the right and left. Amid the burning bones of Bethel – the spatial apogee of Josiah's reform – the undisturbed grave of the old prophet from Bethel in vv. 16–18 stands as a reminder that Jeroboam's altar would be destroyed by a descendant of David. Yet the fulfillment of this centuries-old word brings to mind Huldah's more recent oracle, and both Judah and Josiah are inevitably heading to their own different kinds of burials. As Josiah undertakes his dismantling of the northern shrines, there is "no reference to the foreign cult sites set up by the immigrants settled in Samaria by the Assyrians (17:29–32)," perhaps to indicate that the syncretism of Israelite kings represents a more palpable threat than any form of worship imposed by the empire.²⁶ However, Assyria may yet prove a menace for Josiah as it did for his ancestors, and even though its days as a geopolitical powerhouse are waning, this nation still has one more part to play in the fulfilment of Huldah's oracle.

For any theological analysis, a central question involves Josiah's motivation for this reform, since Huldah's word seems unequivocal and without flexibility. Perhaps the king is hoping for a reversal nonetheless: "In a desperate attempt to protect his people from divine wrath and certain ruin, Josiah undertakes a massive reform of Israelite religion."²⁷ An analogy would be King David in 2 Sam 12:15–23, when he fasts and weeps in a concerted effort to overturn Nathan's oracle about his child, later explaining his behavior to his baffled courtiers: "While the child was yet alive I fasted and wept, for I thought, 'Who knows, the LORD might be gracious to me and the child will live?' But now he is dead, so why should I fast?"²⁸ Alternatively, the reticence surrounding Josiah's motives raises the possibility that he is not attempting to stave off Huldah's oracle as much as simply leading the people and implementing what has been read aloud in the scroll. The reform of chapter 23 is an intricately detailed stretch of text, as layers of idolatrous accretion are scraped away as though preparing the

---

[26] Cohn, *2 Kings*, 158.
[27] Lauren A. S. Monroe, *Josiah's Reform and the Dynamics of Defilement* (New York: Oxford University Press, 2011), 3. Cf. David Janzen, "The Sins of Josiah and Hezekiah: A Synchronic Reading of the Final Chapters of Kings," *JSOT* 37 (2013): 364: "Huldah's prophecy raises the intriguing question as to why Josiah, having heard that the nation will be destroyed, and having already received a reward for the humility he has expressed before the prophetess delivers the oracle, decides to enact his repentance anyway."
[28] See Fretheim, *First and Second Kings*, 219.

land for a future generation that might perhaps be granted a fresh start after a period of chastisement. At the very least, within the narrative context of 2 Kings 23, the reforms operate as a preparation for Passover in vv. 21-23, sweeping the house in anticipation of the long dormant festival. Since it is otherwise only recorded in Josh 5:10-11, the Passover forms a lamentable *inclusio* in the Deuteronomistic History: just after Israel enters the land, Passover is celebrated, and now on the brink of expulsion, the deliverance from Egypt is remembered once more. Israel's tenure in the land is bracketed by these two Passovers – with a lengthy history of unforced errors in between – prompting the reader to conclude that collective amnesia is a major contributor to impending judgment.

The necessary conviction to embark on such reforms and observe Passover is surely what earns Josiah an incomparable commendation, yet it is not enough to offset the centuries of provocation that culminate in the reign of Manasseh. God was willing to relent somewhat to Ahab, but the lack of willingness to relent here underscores the enormity of guilt that is captured in the divine speech of v. 27: "Even Judah I will turn from my presence like I turned aside Israel, and I will reject this city – Jerusalem which I have chosen – and the house where I said, 'My name will be there!'" In the absence of any addressee or prophetic mediation, this divine utterance resembles a soliloquy, with a pathos that stems from covenant betrayal. There is a tension with prior promises and the commitment to Jerusalem, and yet one might hope for a loophole because God does not state that the rejection will last forever; perhaps there is a flicker of light in the midst of certain disaster. Furthermore, Josiah's sudden demise in 23:29-30 brings us back to Huldah's forecast ("You will be gathered to your grave in *shalom*"), held by some interpreters to mean a peaceful death and thus calling the prophecy into question.[29] To be sure, the circumstances are cloudy – Josiah is killed by Pharaoh Neco in Megiddo, with few details disclosed – but the king's servants do bring his body back for burial in his own tomb.[30] The untimely death of this most promising figure is regrettable, but it is a twist in the plot that does not exactly qualify as a false prophecy: unlike the days of Hezekiah, the shadow of judgment does not move backward, and Josiah's death between the superpowers ends his reform efforts, which were powerless to resist the rise of the Babylonians.

THE JOURNEY OF KINGS

In retrospect, we discover that Josiah had multiple wives (counter to Deut 17:17) – probably an effort to secure alliances against mounting geopolitical uncertainties throughout the region, but in the end as ill-fated as his venture to Megiddo to confront Pharaoh Neco. After Josiah's death, the people of the land – public leaders responsible for his coronation in 21:24 after killing Amon's conspirators – anoint a younger son, Jehoahaz, in his place. Is it a political gamble to anoint their own candidate, continuing the anti-Egyptian proclivities of Josiah?[31] If so, their action raises the ire of Neco, who demonstrates his hold over Judah by taking Jehoahaz to Riblah – not the last time a king of Judah will be marched there – and levying an indemnity (v. 33). During the heady days of Solomon, silver was worthless; now, it is all they have left, and the same people of the land are forced to pay a bill

---

[29] For arguments against a false prophecy, see Long, *2 Kings*, 254–55.
[30] Sweeney, *I & II Kings*, 450.
[31] Cf. Seow, "The First and Second Books of Kings," 288.

that is admittedly less than Hezekiah's tribute to the Assyrians (18:14), but only because of their reduced circumstances. When Jehoahaz is taken to Egypt where he dies, it further emphasizes the loss of any semblance of independence for Judah, as foreign monarchs now play a decisive role. The stark absence of God in this section of the text is part of the theological movement in the plot, illustrating what happens when the community abandons God: eventually, God withdraws from the community.

Installed by Neco with a change of name that is likely an assertion of subjugation, Jehoahaz's older brother, Jehoiakim, rules longer than his sibling but hardly fares better. Jehoiakim has an infamous cameo in Jer 36:22–24 when he burns the scroll of the prophet (prompting the reader to wonder how Josiah could have sired such contemptuous offspring), but the main event of 2 Kgs 23:36–24:7 is the gradual ascendancy of Babylon and the diminution of Egyptian control over Judah. Outside of any historical considerations, Babylon here arrives stealthily in the narrative, just as the delegation furtively arrived in Hezekiah's court bearing gifts that masked any motives or ambition. Back in 2 Kings 17, the narrator stepped out from behind the curtain to catalogue a lengthy indictment in the wake of the Assyrian invasion; in 24:2–4, the same voice uses a more compact canvas to unfold how God directs foreign raiders (including the *Chaldeans*, not mentioned since Gen 15:7) against Judah and brings the words of rejected prophets to fulfillment, owing to the final excesses of Manasseh. Regardless of his political maneuverings, Jehoiakim has little chance for success. Indeed, God is not the only one whom Jehoiakim disappoints, as he also rebels against Babylon – ostensibly to escape the Egyptian yoke – but the main form of reprisal comes against his son, Jehoiachin. Following the notice of Jehoiakim's death is a description about Babylonian territorial

Demolition and Exile 215

acquisitions in v. 7 – from the brook of Egypt to the Euphrates – and since the description corresponds to the reach of Solomon's empire in 1 Kgs 4:21, the reader is given the spatial dimensions of how far the nation has fallen and how much has been forfeited.[32] Not only has Solomon's empire been overtaken, but the last vestiges of his material legacy in the temple are also taken away by the Babylonians during Jehoiachin's three-month reign. Isaiah had warned that Babylon would cart away the treasures (20:17), and so their actions here are part of the larger framework of prophecy and fulfillment in the narrative tapestry.[33] The Babylonians have seized control of both the land and the calendar: Jerusalem's capture occurs in Nebuchadnezzar's eighth year (24:12), suggesting "that the chronological benchmark has now passed from Judah to Babylon."[34] Isaiah also declared that Hezekiah's descendants would be taken captive (20:18), and so they are. When Jehoiachin surrenders, he is led away with a multitude of nobles and artisans, and here begins the march toward exile: "As people used to come from all over the world to Solomon's court, so now all the notables of Jerusalem journey on an enforced pilgrimage abroad."[35] Does the comparatively quick surrender (cf. 25:1–2 for a longer siege) imply that Jehoiachin and the others are banking on a good deal or a speedy return from Babylon? If so, it is yet one more misstep in a litany of miscalculation from

---

[32] Wray Beal, *1 & 2 Kings*, 516.
[33] Cf. von Rad, *Old Testament Theology*, 1:340. In Moshe Weinfeld's classic formulation, the fulfillment of prophecy is one of a number of Deuteronomistic tropes (e.g., the idolatry battle, exodus and covenant, Davidic line election and *tôrāh* observance) that can be traced with the theological plot of the Joshua-Kings narrative. Moshe Weinfeld, *Deuteronomy and the Deuteronomic School* (Oxford: Clarendon Press, 1972).
[34] Cohn, *2 Kings*, 167.   [35] Provan, *1 and 2 Kings*, 278.

Judah's monarchs, for Jehoiachin will never have a successor on the Jerusalem throne, and only a long prison sentence awaits him in Babylon. It will be left to his uncle – whose name is changed to Zedekiah – to preside over the nation's final days during his eleven-year career. There are some parallels between Jehoiachin and his uncle Jehoahaz – each of them reigns for three months before a foreign potentate takes them into captivity – but while Jehoahaz is apparently alone, Jehoiachin is accompanied by thousands of others, suggesting that Egypt is a dead end while in Babylon there is the possibility of a remnant.[36] The death of Jehoahaz in Egypt is recorded in 23:34, yet no such fate is recorded for Jehoiachin, who is on life support but is alive in captivity.

Zedekiah – the third and last of Josiah's sons to sit on the throne – is sketched in minimal terms (24:18–25:12), but the few details that are included do not indicate a great deal of competence. His initial comparison with Jehoiakim is not flattering, implying political vacillations and a fruitless quest for alliances; the mention of rebellion against Babylon suggests a divided court and factions that Zedekiah is unable to control. And yet, even if Zedekiah was a worthy monarch, 24:20 unfurls the apex of the theological editorials in the book of Kings – underscoring that God's anger finally casts the people from the divine presence – and the remainder of Zedekiah's reign narrates how such an event took place: "The verdict, attributing exile to Yahweh, is a match for the summary statement of 25:21 that credits the deportation to Babylon. The narrator easily and without awkwardness appeals to

---

[36] Note Cohn, *2 Kings*, 166: "The parallel structure suggests that the Egyptian interlude is a kind of foreshadowing of the final end of Judah. The doubling of the motifs points to divine control even though in both accounts mention of direct divine involvement is absent."

double agency. It is no problem in prophetic horizon to credit exile to Yahweh (24:20) and to the empire (25:21)."[37] Zedekiah's rebellion is the catalyst for the beginning of the end. It is left to the reader to discern the shape of Zedekiah's actions or search elsewhere in the Hebrew Bible (e.g., Jer 37:16-21; 38:14-27), but for the narrative of Kings, these details are of less consequence.[38] What matters instead is that the Babylonian army surrounds the city, and desperate conditions result: the Aramean siege of 2 Kings 6 paints a dismal picture of such exigencies, so now as the city of Jerusalem runs out of bread in 2 Kgs 25:3, the graphic warnings of texts such as Deut 28:49-57 become realities.

When the city wall is finally pierced, Zedekiah attempts to escape from the siege that was prompted by his own rebellion. Not only is he captured by the pursuing army who somehow gets wind of his flight from Jerusalem, but also the grammar of 2 Kgs 25:5 allows for the possibility that Zedekiah is abandoned by his troops at his most critical hour.[39] Arguably, it is a fitting denouement for Judah's last king, for as Zedekiah departed from God on an evil path, so now his soldiers go their own way in the face of capture. Compounding the irony is Zedekiah's arrest in the vicinity of Jericho: that famous city was conquered when the people of Israel followed God's directions, but now in the wake of centuries of disobedience, it marks their captivity.[40] Jehoahaz had been

---

[37] Brueggemann, *1 & 2 Kings*, 580.
[38] On the differing portrayals of Zedekiah in the Masoretic Text and the Septuagint, see Shelley L. Birdsong, *The Last King(s) of Judah: Zedekiah and Sedekias in the Hebrew and Old Greek Versions of Jeremiah 37 (44):1–40(47):6*, FAT II/89 (Tübingen: Mohr Siebeck, 2017).
[39] Cf. Wiseman, *1 & 2 Kings*, 233.
[40] Within the larger framework of the Deuteronomistic History, see Fretheim, *First and Second Kings*, 224: "The king is captured near Jericho (the place where Israel entered the land 600 years or so before)"; Provan, *1 and 2 Kings*,

taken earlier to Riblah (23:33) as an Egyptian prisoner, and now the arrested Zedekiah is brought to the same place to face the Babylonian king who installed him and against whom he has rebelled. A bold interpreter might posit a metaphorical picture here, as Nebuchadnezzar could be a human cipher for God's judgment on Judah's last wayward king. Regardless, Zedekiah is forced to watch the execution of his sons before he is blinded, and for Peter Leithart, there are echoes of Eli's fate at the outset of Israel's monarchic history during the devastation at Shiloh: "At the battle of Aphek, the sons of the blind priest Eli are killed, and then Eli himself dies. But the most grievous aspect of that battle is that the Philistines capture the ark of the covenant of Yahweh. Here, a king witnesses the deaths of his sons and is then deported, and in the surrounding context the entire house of Yahweh is dismantled. The tragedy of Shiloh is happening all over again (Jer 7)."[41] Furthermore, when Zedekiah the captive is blinded and led away in bronze chains, there are echoes of Samson's fate in Judg 16:21–22. The hair on Samson's head began to grow back while he was grinding in the prison, and although Zedekiah has no hope, this allusion to Judges indicates that captivity might not be the end of the story.

Not long after Zedekiah loses his eyes, the temple loses its remaining treasures. Several long chapters are devoted to the construction of the temple earlier in the story, but only a handful of verses describe its burning and looting at the hands of the Babylonians: "A few words uttered by a man in a uniform, and the

279: "The site of Israel's first military victory in their new land (Josh. 6) thus becomes a place associated with their final defeat in it."

[41] Leithart, *1 & 2 Kings*, 276.

order of Creation collapsed."[42] Singled out among the debris is the Bronze Sea – that great symbol for God's subjugation of disorder – now broken by Babylon as a stark manifestation of the insurgent forces of chaos unleashed against Jerusalem. Moreover, tearing down the pillars of the temple is given extra attention, and as the symbolic gateway to the divine abode in the temple, the implication in vv. 16–17 is that God has departed and the sacred space has been consumed by foreign entities.[43] The long history of despoliation is concluded as both the temple and the fragile ideology of Zion's inviolability are dismantled: Nebuchadnezzar is at the end of a lengthy parade of invaders, and so others take the gold while he is left with the bronze. In a sad irony, the people of Judah accompany the bronze, the last tokens of their lost monarchy, into exile. Herein is what might be termed *the journey of kings*, as the Babylonian king ventures to Judah to take the king and people on a long march into captivity, thus reversing the journey of Abraham out of Ur of the Chaldeans. David Noel Freedman observes that there has been no mention of Chaldeans since the days of Abraham, and thus he argues that in the midst of obvious heterogeneity and diversity of the components within Genesis–Kings, it is possible to trace a unifying theme, with the end of the story returning us to the beginning: "How could those in captivity in Babylon, as described at the end of Kings, miss the point or fail to compare the story in Genesis with theirs?"[44] Abraham once set

---

[42] Elie Wiesel, *All Rivers Run into the Sea: Memoirs* (New York: Knopf, 1995), 70.
[43] See Carol Meyers, "Jachin and Boaz in Religious and Political Perspective," *CBQ* 45 (1983): 167–78.
[44] Freedman, *The Unity of the Hebrew Bible*, 8; he further notes: "Going from Babylon to Babylon may seem like a retrograde journey. After all the time and effort and devotion and dedication, there was precious little, if anything,

out from the land of the Chaldeans with only God's word. Now Abraham's descendants are once again in the land of the Chaldeans, but they still have the divine promise to Abraham that might inspire them with hope for a return journey that is based on the character of God. It was announced in Genesis 12 that through Abraham's offspring, every family on earth would be blessed, and this word has not yet reached fulfillment, nor has God ever indicated that the covenant with Abraham has been annulled.

Meanwhile in Judah, the landowners are sent away into exile, and the poorest among the citizenry are left behind to inherit the earth under the stewardship of Gedaliah, who is stationed in Mizpah (a prominent site in the days of Saul's precarious tenure), a makeshift administrative center in the wake of Jerusalem's burning. Gedaliah is presumably appointed because he is a Shaphanite (cf. 2 Kings 22, where Shaphan is intimately involved in the newly discovered scroll during Josiah's reign), and, because he is from a line of reasonable administrators who encouraged the community to submit to Babylon, there is every opportunity for this group to survive in the ravaged land of Judah. But the shocking scenes narrated in vv. 22-26 – with the murder of Gedaliah by Ishmael, a military captain of royal seed – should give any reader grave pause for expecting any revival of the institutional monarchy. As far back as 1 Samuel 8, the elders of Israel demand a king to "lead us in battle," and the penultimate image in the book of Kings is the last royal seed in the land in a self-consuming civil conflict, which invites reflection on how these

> to show for that struggle for independence and statehood. The exiles were back where they started! But it would not get worse, and when the signal from God came, they could start again. Babylon may have been where the dreams ended, but it is also where they could begin again, and they would one day begin again" (p. 9).

scenes function as a microcosm of Israel's monarchic history, with fanatical ideas trumping consistent obedience and assertion of privilege destroying humble responsibility. Ishmael's cascade of violence triggers a rash flight "for fear of the Chaldeans," setting the stage for a climactic irony: God brought them out of the land of slavery into the land of promise, and yet the final exile of the book of Kings is a voluntary one stemming from the crowning act of defiance and folly in the Deuteronomistic History.[45] It would be hard to imagine a sadder ending to Kings than this return to Egypt, but there is one more vignette that provides an alternative perspective on the royal seed in Babylon.

UNCHAINED PROMISE

Rather than terminating the story on a note of failure with the murders of Ishmael and the ignominious flight to Egypt, the book of Kings – and the larger Deuteronomistic History – ends with an unexpected and more open-ended conclusion.[46] Earlier in 2 Kgs 24:12–17, Jehoiachin surrenders and is deported to Babylon, and since his uncle is enthroned in his place, presumably he is never to be heard from again. On the surface, there seem to be parallels

---

[45] Provan, *1 and 2 Kings*, 279.
[46] "Abruptly and surprisingly the scene shifts from the refugees fleeing to Egypt from the Babylonians," writes Cohn (*2 Kings*, 172). "The exile of Jehoiachin opened a gap which only now, after the story of Judah has reached its dreadful end, does the writer fill in by making us recall that we do not know what became of the deported king. True to his regnal framework, the writer introduces his brief glimpse of Jehoiachin in Babylon by dating the event – not, however, by the year of his reign but by the year of his exile." Cf. Hens-Piazza, *1–2 Kings*, 400: "Thus, the narrator dates this final brief note not according to the reign of this king, but according to the event that has rewritten salvation history – his exile."

with Hoshea's unenviable fate in 17:4, as the last of the northern kings was arrested by Shalmaneser and placed in a "house of confinement" (*bêt kele'*), where he disappears from history. Likewise, Jehoiachin was seized and incarcerated by Nebuchadnezzar, but in the last paragraph of the book (2 Kgs 25:27-30), he returns to the stage and is released by the new king of Babylon from the "house of confinement" (*bêt kele'*). After all the mayhem of Jerusalem's devastation and Ishmael's treachery, vv. 27-30 narrate a comparatively pedestrian event as Jehoiachin is granted parole and given a royal allowance in Babylon: there is no hint of any return to the land or restoration of the Davidic throne in Judah, only this brief and underdeveloped note of survival. Over the past decades, there has been no shortage of debate over the meaning of these closing verses, with interpretations ranging from the pessimism of Martin Noth to the relative optimism of Gerhard von Rad, followed by the mediating position of Hans Walter Wolff with a stress on repentance, along with a number of other positions or theories.[47] For the purposes of this study, we will inquire briefly how the final episode of Jehoiachin's release concludes the

---

[47] A convenient bibliography and summary of major positions can be found in David Janzen, "An Ambiguous Ending: Dynastic Punishment in Kings and the Fate of the Davidides in 2 Kings 25.27-30," *JSOT* 33 (2008): 39-58. As one example, note his comments on p. 55: "Some scholars see here a parallel to the story of David's treatment of Mephibosheth in 2 Samuel 9. Like Mephibosheth, Jehoiachin is the surviving male scion of a dethroned house; like David, Evil-Merodach takes pity on his defeated enemy, and seats him at his table and provides him with food. If this is in fact the parallel that the author of 25.27-30 wants readers to see, then clearly his or her view of the future of the house of David is not an optimistic one, for the Davidides would thus appear like the Saulides: a defeated house that will not rule again." Janzen cites Jeremy Schipper, "'Significant Resonances' with Mephibosheth in 2 Kings 25.27-30: A Response to Donald F. Murray," *JBL* 124 (2005): 521-29.

theological plot of the book of Kings and provides a modicum of hope for the people of God.

Among the more innovative trends in recent research is the identification of allusions to the Joseph narrative within the closing lines of Kings. As Peter Ackroyd and others have pointed out, there are a number of linguistic and situational affinities between the experiences of Joseph in the book of Genesis and Jehoiachin at the end of Kings: both figures are the objects of imperial favor and are released from prison, both are outfitted in new clothes, and just as Joseph is given lavish gifts by Pharaoh, so Jehoiachin is granted an allowance and a place at the royal table for the rest of his days.[48] If this intertextual relationship is granted, a number of suggestive theological implications emerge, and a stronger argument can be made that there are grounds for optimism rather than pessimism as the book of Kings closes with the release of Jehoiachin. In the first instance, a more subtle level of divine involvement is apparent in each narrative, sagaciously expressed by Joseph himself in Gen 50:20 to his brothers: "Even though you intended to do harm to me, God intended it for good, in order to preserve a numerous people, as he is doing today" (NRSV). The brothers' experiences that eventually lead to reconciliation in Egypt resonate with the circumstances of Jehoiachin's survival in Babylon, and both episodes are situated in a foreign land where God – in the end, contrary to all appearances – has not abandoned them. Furthermore, at the end of both Genesis and

---

[48] Peter R. Ackroyd, *Exile and Restoration: A Study of Hebrew Thought of the Sixth Century B.C.*, OTL (Philadelphia: Westminster, 1968), 79–83; cf. John E. Harvey, "Jehoiachin and Joseph: Hope at the Close of the Deuteronomistic History," in *The Bible as a Human Witness to Divine Revelation: Hearing the Word of God through Historically Dissimilar Traditions*, ed. Randall Heskett and Brian Irwin; LHBOTS 469 (London: T. and T. Clark, 2010), 51–61.

Kings, there are anticipations of divine action that will result in a departure from these foreign lands: the exodus event is foreshadowed through Joseph's last words to his family in Gen 50:24–25 ("God will surely visit you and bring you up from this land"), while the release of Jehoiachin in his thirty-seventh year of exile carries its own set of potentialities. At the mercy of the Babylonian potentate, it would be a stretch to think that these lines point toward Jehoiachin's resumption of monarchic duties in Judah. Instead, like the people of Israel in the early portions of Exodus, attention is directed to God's activity toward those who are powerless in captivity:

> The Book of Kings achieves its denouement on a note of hope that, at some point in the future, Israel would again experience a second exodus and a new opportunity to live in the land. Similar open-ended endings, which not only lean into the future but also more specifically into a future that includes Israel's inhabitance in and inheritance of the land, are found elsewhere in the Hebrew Bible.[49]

There is a narrative potency in the allusions to Joseph and the exodus prelude at the end of Kings, therefore, but not because of any forthcoming miracle of departure so much as the expectations of a new beginning and the start of a promising journey. More than just deliverance from slavery in Egypt, the exodus story includes a long march through unfamiliar territory and testing

---

[49] Michael J. Chan, "Joseph and Jehoiachin: On the Edge of Exodus," *ZAW* 125 (2013): 575; he continues: "The exodus from Egypt, of course, is used elsewhere in the Hebrew Bible as a prototype for other, often future, salvific events – the most notable examples being from Deutero-Isaiah (see, e.g., Isa 43,16-21; 51,9-10; 52,7-12), with other occurrences of the theme elsewhere (Am 9,7; Mi 7,15, etc.). It comes as no surprise, then, that the Book of Kings would conclude with an echo of Israel's exodus."

in the wilderness, the struggle to build a sanctuary and learning to rely on God in hostile and sterile environments, along with all the attendant difficulties of possessing the land of promise. At the end of Kings, the people are faced with strikingly similar challenges, and they need to be prepared for a new chapter of obedience and self-control: "The conclusion to the book of Kings is, then, multivocal and even ironic, its import for and relationship to the larger story of Israel not so clearly stated. But so too is the ongoing exile and impending exodus, to which II Reg 25,27–30 alludes. Like remembering Davidic kingship, remembering exile and exodus is complicated. The exile/exodus, in Israel's story, symbolizes at once the people's oppression and its freedom, its failures and its successes, its struggle with apostasy and its devotion to Yahweh."[50]

When these various factors are considered, the hope at the end of Kings is also a call for commitment and an expression of gratitude. Consequently, Jehoiachin's release in the final scenes returns the reader to the Davidic dynasty promise once more, especially as there is no mention of any personal prospects or progeny for Jehoiachin himself, nor any hint of personal repentance or any sense of chastisement received; neither is there any regnal formula that provides a notice of death. As noted previously, the book of Kings begins with the aged king confined to his palace and uncertainty over succession looming in the background. Through a host of machinations and maneuverings, Solomon is ensconced as David's successor, but despite his deeply ambivalent legacy, he becomes an ironic voice of optimism in the

---

[50] Ian Douglas Wilson, "Joseph, Jehoiachin, and Cyrus: On Book Endings, Exoduses and Exiles, and Yehudite/Judean Social Remembering," ZAW 126 (2014): 527.

text when his prayer encourages the congregation that God hears penitent prayers even in exile, and that they might be objects of divine compassion even after a litany of sins (1 Kgs 8:46–53). At the end of Kings, confidence stems not from the institutional monarchy of the past, but from the God who has made a promise to David that will endure in a new iteration. The durability of the promise – regardless of how long the "wilderness" journey may last – appears to be subtly invoked with Jehoiachin's release, and it will probably require a good deal of creative and adventurous faith to discern the relationship between kingship and the anointed in the era of the restoration and beyond, which is to come.

CHAPTER 8

The Theology of Kings Past and Present

The theological interpretation of Scripture is not without its difficulties in our contemporary cultural climate, but this study has probed the theology of 1 and 2 Kings by providing a reading of the narrative that attempts to elicit some of the major theological themes and flashpoints within the sequential movements of the text.[1] Overall, the book of Kings is a fertile site for such analysis, not least because unique facets of the divine character are revealed in this narrative and because of the way that various actors in the story respond in accordance with (or at variance to) the basic

---

[1] For discussion of ways that a text's theology can be embraced while remaining respectful toward the narrative, see Tim Meadowcroft, "Theological Commentary: A Diversifying Enterprise," *Journal of Theological Interpretation* 7 (2013): 133–51. On the personal dimension of theological work in our day, note the challenging remarks of Michael Fishbane, *Sacred Attunement: A Jewish Theology* (Chicago: University of Chicago Press, 2008), 2: "No evasions should be permitted as we each ask, in what sense is God a living reality in our lives, or merely some abstraction of thought; and in what respect is religious life a matter of true engagement, or simply an expression of inherited behaviors?" Further, "it is also necessary to ask, in what way is the language of scripture real or true or compelling for us, given its personalized portrayals of God and divine dominion, or its particular picture of the world order and its spiritual entities? How do they jibe with our contemporary sense of language and spirituality and cosmos?" Note also the collection of essays in Craig G. Bartholomew and Heath A. Thomas, eds., *A Manifesto for Theological Interpretation* (Grand Rapids, MI: Baker, 2016).

tenets of Israel's faith traditions. Thus, when God communicates to Elijah that judgment on Ahab will be deferred because of his attitude of contrition (1 Kgs 21:28), or when Ahaz sends instructions for modifying the altar based on an Assyrian prototype (2 Kgs 16:10), there are a number of insights – involving the capacity for divine surprise or the recurring tendency for royal leaders to choose political convenience over covenant faithfulness – that can emerge for the reader interested in exploring the theology of Kings. Admittedly, this study has been more of a preliminary undertaking rather than purporting to be the final word, instead posing questions and sketching an outline of what theological analysis of Kings might involve within our current milieu and methodological diversity. Recognizing that the approach taken here is certainly not the only way and that much more remains to be done, this concluding chapter directs the reader to four other areas for further study in the theology of Kings: performing a comparison with another section of the Deuteronomistic History (i.e., the books of Samuel), evaluating the roles of the temple in Kings and Chronicles, comparing several scenes from the book of Jeremiah, and suggesting points of theological intersection with New Testament material that might be of interest for contemporary audiences.

LASTING GUARANTEE

Although Samuel and Kings are both major parts of the Deuteronomistic History, there are some immediate and striking differences in style and content between the two books.

For instance, 1 Samuel begins with an elaborate parable whereby Israel's forthcoming request for a king is refracted through the lens of Hannah's request for a son: just as having sons is a laborious enterprise, so giving birth to kingship carries considerable risks for Israel's polity. Furthermore, the "ark narrative" of 1 Samuel 4–6 is a story of exile and return: the capture of the ark and its subsequent restoration as God subdues a foreign oppressor anticipates Israel's own national journey of exile and return in 2 Kings 25 and beyond. Similarly, there is inordinate attention devoted to the expansive and painful biography of the inaugural monarch Saul, and the portrait of his descent into madness is quite unlike anything else in the pages of Joshua–Judges or Kings. While it is entirely possible that different tradents are responsible for various blocks of material preserved and compiled in Samuel/Kings – and scholars vigorously debate a range of compositional options – there are also compelling points of continuity, and undoubtedly Kings completes the story that the books of Samuel begin.[2] For the theological interpreter, these points of continuity present a remarkable opportunity, and one of the key questions that emerges surrounds the promise to David: how is this promise presented in Samuel, and how is it then treated in Kings? As Patricia Tull summarizes, in 2 Samuel 7 God articulates through Nathan the promise of an enduring house:

> Chapter 7 is a theological centerpiece not only of this book but of the Deuteronomistic History overall. David expresses to the prophet Nathan his wish to build a "house" for God. God relays through Nathan that, on the contrary, it is God who will build David a house – that is, a dynasty. Reaching both backward and forward in the story, God says of David's unborn son: "I will not take my steadfast love from him, as I took it from Saul. . . . Your house and your kingdom shall be made sure forever before me"

---

[2] A convenient summary of competing positions is found in Thomas Römer, "Deuteronomistic History," *Encyclopedia of the Bible and Its Reception* (Berlin: Walter de Gruyter, 2013), 6:648–53.

(7:15–16). Eli, Samuel, and Saul all failed to see their sons succeed them. This fourth time around, succession is assured.[3]

The irony is apparent as David desires to build a physical house for God in Jerusalem – and the reader is uncertain of his motives – but God surreptitiously intervenes and declares that David will be given an enduring dynastic house constructed with much stronger material. Throughout the remainder of the 2 Samuel narrative, this promise is sorely tested but never retracted, because, like the promise to Abraham, it is not predicated on exemplary human conduct: "The various intrigues involving a wayward David and his equally wayward sons indicate that politics (both sexual and power) posited on a calculating worldly wisdom leads only to disaster. Nevertheless, Yahweh's covenant grace prevails. Unlike Saul, David himself is not rejected (cf. 1 Sam 15:26), nor is Yahweh's promise done away with."[4] Despite the unconditional language directly uttered by God, the first mention of the promise in Kings, as we have observed, occurs in David's last speech to Solomon (1 Kgs 2:3–4). Here, however, David tells his son that occupying the throne is conditional ("If your sons guard their way, to walk before me in truth with all their heart and soul, there will not be cut off from you a man upon the throne of Israel") with no mention of an eternal house built by God. To be sure,

---

[3] Patricia K. Tull, "1 and 2 Samuel," in *Theological Bible Commentary*, ed. Gail R. O'Day and David L. Petersen (Louisville, KY: Westminster John Knox Press, 2009), 101–17 (111–12).

[4] Brian E. Kelly, "Books of Samuel," in *Dictionary for Theological Interpretation of the Bible*, ed. Kevin J. Vanhoozer (Grand Rapids, MI: Baker, 2005), 717–21 (719). It certainly could be argued that overall, David's conduct is worse than Saul's, but assurances such as 2 Sam 7:15 ("But my faithful love [ḥesed] will never be withdrawn from him as I withdrew it from Saul, whom I withdrew from before you") ensure the survival of his fallible and avaricious successor(s).

Solomon is not careful and becomes the first in a long line of Davidic successors to fall woefully short – culminating in dismissal from the land as God warned (1 Kgs 9:7) and the prophets made clear (2 Kgs 21:14) – and thus the narrative concludes with the people in exile and a king without a throne in Jerusalem.[5] And yet, the final scenes in 2 Kings 25 underscore that the line of David has been preserved, and so the reader is privy to a larger pattern in the story: whether it is during the dark days of Athaliah's tyrannical purge or with Jehoiachin's surprising parole at the end of the story, neither internal disaster nor the external tempest of Babylonian captivity extinguishes the lamp (2 Kgs 8:19) of Davidic promise. Just as the ark of the covenant returns from exile in a foreign land (1 Sam 6:10–16), so there is hope for the line of David to likewise experience release as 2 Kings finishes on an open-ended note.

THE TWO TOWERS

The architectural centerpiece of the book of Kings is the Jerusalem temple, and while Solomon's palace takes longer to build and is bigger – ostensibly to provide a residence for his staggering number of wives – the destruction of the temple finally receives more attention during the Babylonian offensive against Jerusalem.

---

[5] Cf. Iain W. Provan, "The Messiah in the Book of Kings," in *The Lord's Anointed: Interpretation of Old Testament Messianic Texts*, ed. Philip E. Satterthwaite, Richard S. Hess and Gordon J. Wenham (Grand Rapids, MI: Baker, 1995), 67–85 (72): "The promise to David, that he should have an eternal dynasty, appears in Kings in a curiously paradoxical form. For much of the narrative it provides us with an explanation as to why the Davidic dynasty survives, when other dynasties do not, *in spite of* the disobedience of David's successors (e.g., 1 Kgs 11:36; 15:4)."

An apparent rejection associated with the place where "God's name" is placed must therefore be construed as a monumental catastrophe, and at the end of the story there is no hint of any forthcoming rebuilding: "The postscript announcing Babylonian mercies to the exiled King Jehoiachin (2 Kgs 25:27–30) offers a glimmer of hope to anyone interested in the fate of the Davidides, but the same work offers no such good news about the Jerusalem cult. There are no prophecies predicting the shrine's restoration."[6] By contrast, the final sentence of 2 Chronicles does not refer to Jehoiachin's release but instead features the clarion call of Cyrus – whose spirit was stirred by God (2 Chr 36:22) – to rebuild the temple, and this conclusion is part of the reason that most scholars maintain (in a rare instance of academic agreement) that the temple is a major theme within the Chronicler's narrative.[7] There are a number of distinctive elements of the temple's configuration in the book of Chronicles, including the spatial setting. Whereas 1 Kgs 6:1 emphasizes the time of the temple's construction in relation to the exodus from Egypt, 2 Chr 3:1 correlates its location within defining moments in the lives of Abraham and David:

> Solomon began to build the house of the LORD in Jerusalem on Mount Moriah, where the LORD had appeared to his father David, at the place that David had designated, on the threshing floor of Ornan the Jebusite. (NRSV)

---

[6] Gary N. Knoppers, "Yhwh's Rejection of the House Built for His Name: On the Significance of Anti-temple Rhetoric in the Deuteronomistic History," in *Essays on Ancient Israel in Its Near Eastern Context: A Tribute to Nadav Na'aman*, ed. Yairah Amit et al. (Winona Lake, IN: Eisenbrauns, 2006), 221–38 (222).

[7] H. G. M. Williamson, "The Temple in the Books of Chronicles," in *Templum Amicitiae: Essays on the Second Temple Presented to Ernst Bammel*, ed. William Horbury, JSNTSup 48 (Sheffield: Sheffield Academic Press, 1991), 15–31.

The land of Moriah is the physical setting for the Akedah episode of Abraham in Genesis 22, the place where he is posed with the highest challenge of audacious trust. After passing the test involving the most costly sacrifice, God reiterates the words of the covenant promise not only about innumerable descendants, but also that "through your offspring all nations on earth will be blessed because you have obeyed me" (22:17–18). In the book of Chronicles, therefore, the Jerusalem temple is spatially connected with God's covenant with Abraham, carrying a unique set of implications. Some citizens may have demurred that the temple was too closely associated with the house of David and the ambitions of Solomon, undercurrents that can be perceived at various points in the Deuteronomistic History (e.g., 1 Kgs 12:16, 28). Turning to the Chronicler's account, however, the connection with Moriah projects a new set of possibilities: the temple site does not, so it would seem, originate with the Davidic monarchy but predates and outlasts institutional kingship, and certainly is given the last word in 2 Chronicles 36. Of course, a later constituency may lament that the second temple is lacking in grandeur compared with the legendary Solomonic edifice (see Ezra 3:12–13; Hag 2:3). Yet there is a much more valuable option available in Chronicles, for rather than opulence, the community is invited to concentrate instead on the great ancestral connections, and just as Abraham experienced the presence of God after passing the test in the land of Moriah, so the restoration community has the same site as a focal point for a similar kind of obedience.[8] In this discussion, I am assuming – again, with the majority of scholars –

---

[8] Louis C. Jonker, *Defining All-Israel in Chronicles: Multi-levelled Identity Negotiation in Late Persian-period Yehud*, FAT II/109 (Tübingen: Mohr Siebeck, 2016), 162–63.

that Chronicles is a later text than Kings, and provides a creative place for diachronic biblical theology and appreciation of the distinctive emphases within these vast historiographic works: "While there is overlap in how the temple functions within the two books, the temple in Chronicles is the vehicle for change, for hope, for new possibilities, and for the future of the community, as the past is reshaped by the Chronicler with different versions of how society should be constituted."[9] Additional angles of theological inquiry could be pursued – e.g., the height of the temple in Chronicles is five times higher than in Kings, perhaps as a towering antithesis to the hubris of Babel – and so there remain many areas of productive work for interpreters.[10]

OTHER INTERSECTIONS

Numerous points of connection can be discerned between the book of Kings and other poetic and prophetic works in the Hebrew Bible. Psalm 2, for instance, poetically intones a distinctive theology of kingship and the nations, while the book of Amos develops a strident critique of social injustice and related abuses during the era of Jeroboam II. The vision of Micah is temporally located during the reigns of Jotham, Ahaz and Hezekiah, and preserves another prophetic voice during this tumultuous period, while the theodicy of Job has both some parallels to and stunning

---

[9] Steven J. Schweitzer, "The Temple in Samuel-Kings and Chronicles," in *Rewriting Biblical History: Essays on Chronicles and Ben Sira in Honor of Pancratius Beentjes*, ed. Jeremy Corley and Harm van Grol (Berlin: de Gruyter, 2011), 123–38 (135).

[10] John Jarick, "The Temple of David in the Book of Chronicles," in *Temple and Worship in Ancient Israel*, ed. John Day, LHBOTS 422 (London: T. and T. Clark, 2005), 365–81.

divergences from the Deuteronomistic History.[11] In this section, we will narrow our focus to the book of Jeremiah, where the interpreter faces areas of overlap with the narrative of Kings, but also a number of backstories or episodes that provide new perspectives on events and characters. So, Jeremiah 40–42 has an extensive report on Ishmael's treachery and the murder of Gedaliah, a great deal more than the handful of verses in 2 Kgs 25:22–26. The book of Jeremiah also provides an alternative portrait of Jerusalem in the aftermath of Josiah's reform, and lengthy oracles such as Jeremiah's temple sermon reveal a corrosive attitude and widespread corruption among the populace despite the reformation. In addition, Jer 26:20–23 relates the escape of the prophet Uriah and his subsequent apprehension by the king's agents in Egypt; upon his forcible return to Jerusalem, he is executed by Jehoiakim personally, as the king wields the sword against Uriah, just as he wields the scribal knife against Jeremiah's scroll (Jer 36:23). This episode with Uriah has no equivalent in Kings, and the prophet is otherwise unknown. Consequently, the viciousness of Jehoiakim's treatment sheds light on the kind of hostility experienced by Jeremiah (and other prophets) during his eleven-year reign as the darkness of Babylon enveloped the nation. I would submit that such intertextual reflections can furnish the interpreter with a multidimensional and immersive theological experience.

Furthermore, the portraits of Zedekiah in Kings and Jeremiah are worth comparing. In 2 Kgs 24:17–25:7, Zedekiah, the last king

---

[11] For an example, see Raik Heckl, "The Relationship between Job 1–2, 42 and 1 Samuel 1–4 as Intertextual Guidance for Reading," in *Reading Job Intertextually*, ed. Katharine Dell and Will Kynes, LHBOTS 574 (London: Bloomsbury T. and T. Clark, 2013), 81–93.

to reign in the land of Judah, is delineated with minimal detail and an absence of direct speech: his doomed career begins with Nebuchadnezzar changing his name, and it concludes with that same potentate gouging out his eyes. But other than his negative evaluation, there is not much insight into Zedekiah's character in the book of Kings, as the story is focused relentlessly on the Babylonian destruction and its aftermath. The narratives of Jeremiah, on the contrary, contain a number of episodes where Zedekiah is prominent. To cite one particular case, in Jer 38:4–5, the court officials pressure the king to virtually kill the prophet by casting him into a cistern, and Zedekiah acquiesces: "Behold, he is in your hand, for the king can do nothing against you." Yet when he later consents to a secret mission to rescue the prophet by Ebed-Melech (38:10), this quiet authorization reveals a side of Zedekiah that serves to amplify any theological reading of Kings. Although Jeremiah is often in confinement, the real prisoner is the king, who seems to have a respect for the prophet (further manifested in his clandestine interview in vv. 14–28) but lacks the necessary resolution to oppose his officials.[12] As for the courtiers themselves, these scenes in the book of Jeremiah heighten the awareness of the stress and infighting during Zedekiah's decade on the throne, and even while the Babylonians are poised to demolish the city, an internal battle driven by rigid ideology and coercion is raging. During this decade, we can further surmise, there were opportunities for wiser decisions, but more often the citizens allowed themselves to be led astray by false prophecies

---

[12] Similarities between Zedekiah and Herod in the Gospel of Mark can certainly be pursued; on the latter, see Abraham Smith, "Tyranny Exposed: Mark's Typological Characterization of Herod Antipas (Mark 6:14–29)," *BibInt* 14 (2006): 259–93.

The Theology of Kings Past and Present 237

and self-serving oracles of political comfort that do not involve sacrificial choices. In general, it could be said that these two texts provide alternative perspectives, as Jeremiah opens a window on the internal chaos while Kings relentlessly unfolds the external turmoil. The judgment of 2 Kgs 24:19 that Zedekiah does evil in God's eyes – devoid of the courage required to stand on the prophetic word and lead the people beyond sectarian strife – is enhanced through the dramatic narratives of Jeremiah, and the reader is thus presented with an enriching cross-section of material that illustrates the breadth of theological witness.

THE LEGACY OF KINGS IN THE NEW TESTAMENT

The book of Jeremiah provides a convenient segue to consideration of how the book of Kings factors in the New Testament, as both Jeremiah and Kings in different ways fuel speculation about the advent of a future ruler. 2 Kings 25 concludes with Jehoiachin's release, a tantalizing episode that reveals little about his immediate prospects but does provide grounds for guarded hope. "Can such a hope," asks Iain Provan, "reasonably be described as 'messianic'? It is certainly a hope focused on the unforeseen future, a time which is not this time. There is no sense in the book of Kings that the king of the future is anything other than a distant prospect. It is equally clear that the king who is sought is an ideal king. The book of Kings always measures its monarchs in terms of the ideal, finding almost all of them wanting in serious respects."[13] The denouement of Kings highlights the

---

[13] Provan, "The Messiah in the Book of Kings," 76. Cf. Provan's conclusion and extension of the discussion in the book of Revelation (pp. 84–85), where he notes that salvation and "victory, rather than defeat, will be experienced at

survival of the exiled Davidic heir, and when the book of Jeremiah is brought into the equation, new intertextual insights emerge. On the one hand, Jer 22:28–30 articulates that Jehoiachin himself will never have a son seated on the throne in Judah, a bleak pronouncement that does not augur well for a revival of the institutional monarchy.[14] To be sure, there was ample opposition to Zedekiah and some partisan calls for the return of Jehoiachin in Jer 28:4 by Hananiah, but in the end such a stance was woefully misguided. On the other hand, Jer 23:5–6 unfolds an oracle that promises the later arrival of a Davidic offshoot who will reign wisely and execute justice: "In his days Judah will be saved, and Israel will live in security." The combination of the durability of the line at the end of Kings and the "branch" (*ṣemaḥ*) of David in Jeremiah's oracle, then, would advance the notion that the Davidic line will return from exile and contribute to a sense of messianic anticipation that is further developed in the gospel narratives.

Aside from any considerations of the Davidic genealogy (Matt 1:1–22; Luk 3:23–38), there are a number of references or allusions to the Kings narrative in the New Testament: for instance, a host of characters such as Solomon, the Queen of Sheba, and Jezebel are referred to by name, and the apostle Paul quotes the divine dialogue with Elijah on Mount Horeb in Romans 11:1–5 (cf. 1 Kgs 19:13–18), implying that it must have been a well-known story among the readership of the early church and thus instructive

---

Megiddo (=Armageddon, Rev. 16:16), as the nations are defeated and Babylon is brought low by the Davidic King (Rev. 16–19)."

[14] See Walter Brueggemann, "Heir and Land: The Royal 'Envelope' of the Books of Kings," in *The Fate of King David: The Past and Present of a Biblical Icon*, ed. Tod Linafelt, Timothy Beal and Claudia V. Camp, LHBOTS 500 (London: T. and T. Clark, 2010), 93–94.

for Paul's argument.[15] As a conclusion to this present study, there is a striking passage in Luke's gospel that feature a pair of episodes in the heart of the book of Kings. Not only do these references in Luke 4:25-27 testify to the circulation and influence of Kings, but they also illuminate how Kings was interpreted as theological literature; indeed, reflection on how the theology of Kings was negotiated in the New Testament may invite thoughts about the narrative's ongoing significance and contemporary relevance. The spatial setting of this episode in Luke 4 is the synagogue of Nazareth, and the immediate context is the discussion around a prophet's rejection in his hometown. Joel Green classifies this passage as parallelism that "underscores (1) the neediness of people in Israel, (2) the divine mandate under which Elijah ('was sent') and Elisha ('the prophet') worked, and (3) the exceptional character of the recipients of their ministries in these anecdotes," elegantly rendered as follows:

> But the truth is,
> there were many widows in Israel
> in the time of Elijah ...
> yet Elijah was sent to none of them
> except to a widow at Zarephath in Sidon.
> There were also many lepers in Israel,
> in the time of the prophet Elisha,
> and none of them were cleansed
> except Naaman the Syrian.[16]

---

[15] The correspondences between Elijah and John the Baptist are also manifold, perhaps including periods of frailty or discouragement (1 Kgs 19:3-10; Matt 11:2-3). For general remarks, see Craig L. Blomberg, "Matthew," in *Commentary on the New Testament Use of the Old Testament*, ed. G. K. Beale and D. A. Carson (Grand Rapids, MI: Baker, 2007), 78-81; Craig S. Keener, *A Commentary on the Gospel of Matthew* (Grand Rapids, MI: Eerdmans, 1999), 267-68.

[16] Joel B. Green, *The Gospel of Luke*, NICNT (Grand Rapids, MI: Eerdmans, 1997), 218. In terms of the larger context, Green further notes: "In Jesus'

Several texts in Luke's gospel draw on Elijah and Elisha – raised up as foils to the Omride dynasty in the northern kingdom – but our comments here will be limited to a few observations about these prophetic figures in 4:25–27 to conclude this study.[17] In Elijah's day, the famine in the land is a judgment for embracing the flawed ideology of fertility religion by king and country, and provides an opportunity to change direction and return to covenant faith. Ahab's hostility toward Elijah is juxtaposed with the Sidonian widow's hospitality, as she is bequeathed life and prophetic largesse while Ahab is continually frustrated. Applied to Luke's narrative, the rejection of Jesus at Nazareth is analogous to the antipathy toward Elijah, a motif that continues throughout the gospel account. But the irony of a better reception among foreigners must anticipate an equally important theme of the gospel, the inclusion of the Gentiles. The widow of Zarephath – surely among the most vulnerable of citizens in a time of famine – becomes an instrument of foreshadowing and an illustration of the reversal of expectation that is a hallmark of Luke's theological plot. A widow from Jezebel's territory receives what many Israelites do not, just as Naaman the Syrian is granted healing after listening to the affirmation of a captured servant girl

> address, the role of Elijah and Elisha as agents of healing to (and thus the exercise of God's grace among) outsiders is paramount. Elijah is sent to a woman, a non-Jew, a widow – surely a person of low status. Elisha encounters a non-Jew, too, a Syrian whose disease, leprosy, served as a further marker of his socio-religious distance from the community of God's people (Leviticus 14). With these examples, Jesus underscores that 'good news to the poor' embraces the widow, the unclean, the Gentile, those of the lowest status."

[17] For a collection of essays devoted to episodes alluding to these prophets such as the feeding of the multitude, healings and resurrection, see John S. Kloppenborg and Joseph Verheyden, ed., *The Elijah-Elisha Narrative in the Composition of Luke*, LNTS 493 (London: Bloomsbury, 2014).

and submitting to the word of Elisha. Miraculous signs in the book of Kings authenticate the prophets as agents of subversion who upend the regnant power structures and deliver an (unpopular) message of repentance, and the prophetic energy generated in these stories is subsequently reinvested in Luke's gospel.

Within Luke's economy, the prophetic careers of Elijah and Elisha serve to illuminate a paradox at the core of the gospel between rejection and embrace: "Throughout history, the gospel has always been more radically inclusive than any group, denomination, or church, so we continually struggle for a breadth of love and acceptance that more nearly approximates the breadth of God's love. The paradox of the gospel, therefore, is that the unlimited grace that it offers so scandalizes us that we are unable to receive it."[18] Returning to the Kings narrative, it is notable that neither the widow nor Naaman embraced the prophetic word without resistance, and so for Luke's readers, these examples might likewise function as a chance to reconsider the claims of Jesus. As evidenced in this passage from Luke, the book of Kings had an ongoing vitality and was interpreted as an integral scene within a dramatic performance, as God's promise about the line of David takes some peculiar shapes and turns with the arrival of a new son of David. Of course, only a single example has been canvassed here, but it nonetheless elucidates how the stories in Kings were remembered and theologically engaged by readers long after their composition. The prophets in the book of Kings ultimately become part of a larger narrative that points to radically reconfigured boundaries of inclusion and unveils testimony about the God who is not easily contained and reigns supreme

---

[18] R. Alan Culpepper, "The Gospel of Luke," in *The New Interpreter's Bible*, ed. Leander E. Keck et al., 12 vols. (Nashville, TN: Abingdon, 1999), 9:108.

over every earthly monarch. Earlier communities of faith were challenged and encouraged by these narratives that weave a tapestry of God's redemptive and transforming work, and so it comes as no surprise that the same continues to hold true for similar communities today.

Further Reading

The past several decades have seen an acute rise in studies on the book of Kings that attempt to integrate various historical, literary and theological aspects of the narrative. Although there are no shortage of difficulties in approaching the material, Kings remains a fruitful site for interpretive activity and of ongoing importance for contemporary readers struggling with not dissimilar issues faced by these ancient counterparts. The following list of books, articles and commentaries is by no means exhaustive, but is intended as a short introductory guide for further research into Kings and its place in the larger continuum of the Former Prophets.

Alter, Robert. *Ancient Israel: The Former Prophets: Joshua, Judges, Samuel, and Kings: A Translation with Commentary*. New York: W. W. Norton, 2013. Brief introductions and notes on Joshua–Kings from an influential literary critic of the Hebrew Bible.

Barton, John. "Historiography and Theodicy in the Old Testament." In *Reflection and Refraction: Studies in Biblical Historiography in Honour of A. Graeme Auld*, ed. Robert Rezetko, Timothy H. Lim and W. Brian Aucker, 27–33.

VTSup 113. Leiden: Brill, 2007. Overview of an important topic for theological reflection.

Brueggemann, Walter. *1 & 2 Kings*. Macon, GA: Smyth and Helwys, 2000. Fine resource for students and scholars alike.

"Old Testament Theology." In *The Oxford Handbook of Biblical Studies*, ed. John W. Rogerson and Judith M. Lieu, 675–97. Oxford: Oxford University Press, 2006. Accessible introduction to the task of Old Testament theology.

Cohn, Robert L. "The Literary Structure of Kings." In *The Books of Kings: Sources, Composition, Historiography and Reception*, ed. Baruch Halpern, André Lemaire and Matthew J. Adams, 107–22. VTSup 129. Leiden: Brill, 2010. Helpful survey of the architecture of the Kings narrative.

Conti, Marco, ed. *1–2 Kings, 1–2 Chronicles, Ezra, Nehemiah, Esther*. Ancient Christian Commentary on Scripture, Old Testament 5. Downers Grove, IL: IVP, 2008. Repository of insights from the patristic era in a user-friendly format.

Dietrich, Walter. "1 & 2 Kings." In *The Oxford Bible Commentary*, ed. John Barton and John Muddiman, 232–66. Oxford: Oxford University Press, 2001. Short commentary particularly strong on historical and comparative elements.

Fretheim, Terence E. *First and Second Kings*. Louisville, KY: Westminster John Knox, 1999. Suggestive points of application with a contemporary readership in view.

Goldingay, John. "The Theology of the Hebrew Bible/Old Testament." In *The Cambridge Companion to the Hebrew Bible/Old Testament*, ed. Stephen B. Chapman and Marvin A. Sweeney, 466–82. New York: Cambridge University Press, 2016. Another stimulating overview of the theological task.

Granowski, Jan Jaynes. "Jehoiachin at the King's Table: A Reading of the Ending of the Second Book of Kings." In *Reading*

Between Texts: Intertextuality and the Hebrew Bible, ed. Danna Nolan Fewell, 173–88. Louisville, KY: Westminster John Knox, 1992. Addresses the crucial final verses of 2 Kings on the fate of Jehoiachin.

Hens-Piazza, Gina. *1–2 Kings*. Nashville, TN: Abingdon, 2006. Thoughtful attempt to relate the narrative to the present interpretive milieu.

Janzen, David. *The Violent Gift: Trauma's Subversion of the Deuteronomistic History's Narrative*. LHBOTS 561. London: T. and T. Clark, 2012. Academic monograph that employs recent advances in trauma theory.

Leithart, Peter. *1 & 2 Kings. Brazos Theological Commentary on the Bible*. Grand Rapids, MI: Brazos, 2006. Strong contribution to a series dedicated to theological interpretation.

Levenson, Jon D. "The Temple and the World." *Journal of Religion* 64 (1984): 275–98. Seminal article on the temple in Kings and elsewhere in the Hebrew Bible.

Linville, James R. *Israel in the Book of Kings: The Past as a Project of Social Identity*. JSOTSup 272. Sheffield: Sheffield Academic Press, 1998. Some productive questions raised in this monograph that originated as an Edinburgh dissertation.

Long, Burke O. *2 Kings*. FOTL 10. Grand Rapids, MI: Eerdmans, 1991. Form-critical and theological insight with literary sensitivity.

Miscall, Peter D. "Elijah, Ahab, and Jehu: A Prophecy Fulfilled." *Prooftexts* 9 (1989): 73–83. Creative study in the fulfillment of the prophetic word.

Moberly, R. W. L. *Old Testament Theology: Reading the Hebrew Bible as Christian Scripture*. Grand Rapids, MI: Baker, 2013. Collection of essays on the venture of biblical theology.

Mobley, Gregory. "1 and 2 Kings." In *Theological Bible Commentary*, ed. Gail R. O'Day and David L. Petersen. Louisville,

KY: Westminster John Knox Press, 2009. Useful contribution that is part of a work devoted to succinct theological readings.

Nelson, Richard D. *First and Second Kings. Interpretation*. Atlanta, GA: John Knox Press, 1987. Incisive and practical commentary with a host of New Testament interfaces.

Provan, Iain W. *1 and 2 Kings. NIBC 7*. Peabody, MA: Hendrickson, 1995. Compact and illuminating treatment of the text.

Rad, Gerhard von. *Old Testament Theology*, trans. D. M. G. Stalker, 2 vols. New York: Harper & Row, 1962–65. Classic of the field that has retained its currency.

Schulte, Hannelis. "The End of the Omride Dynasty: Social-Ethical Observations on the Subject of Power and Violence." Trans. Carl S. Ehrlich. *Semeia* 66 (1994): 133–48. Raises several pertinent questions for contemporary interpreters.

Seow, Choon Leong. "1 & 2 Kings." In *The New Interpreter's Bible*, vol. 3. Nashville, TN: Abingdon, 1999. Valuable and erudite commentary that can be used profitably by homileticians.

Sweeney, Marvin A. *I & II Kings. OTL*. Louisville, KY: Westminster John Knox Press, 2007. Full-length commentary with insightful discussions of critical issues.

Walsh, Jerome T. *1 Kings. Berit Olam*. Collegeville, MN: Liturgical Press, 1996. Excellent literary reading that raises a host of fascinating matters.

Wray Beal, Lissa. *1 & 2 Kings. AOTC*. Downers Grove, IL: IVP, 2014. A recent commentary of benefit to anyone in a teaching context.

Yee, Gale A. "1, 2 Kings." In *The Fortress Commentary on Bible: The Old Testament and Apocrypha*, ed. Gale A. Yee, Matthew Coomber and Hugh Page, 401–37. Minneapolis, MN: Fortress

Press, 2014. Part of a larger work of commentary that features feminist and other approaches to the biblical text.

Zevit, Ziony. "First and Second Kings." In *The Jewish Study Bible*, ed. Adele Berlin and Marc Zvi Brettler, 668–779. New York: Oxford University Press, 2004. Scholarly and perceptive notes from a Jewish perspective.

Author Index

Abadie, Philippe, 200
Ackroyd, Peter R., 223
Adam, Klaus-Peter 45
Adams, Matthew J., 56, 132, 244
Alter, Robert, 26–7, 32, 41, 69, 108, 134, 159, 198, 243
Althann, Robert, 175
Amit, Yairah, 232
Appler, Deborah A., 20, 160
Arius, xviii
Arnold, Bill T., 135, 193
Aucker, W. Brian, 23, 145, 243
Auerbach, Erich, 26
Auld, A. Graeme, 23, 243

Bammel, Ernst, 232
Barr, James, xviii
Barth, Karl, 97
Bartholomew, Craig, 13, 227
Barton, John, 23, 45, 181, 203, 243–4
Beal, Lissa. M. Wray, 3, 18–20, 45, 59, 82, 92, 104, 108, 114, 124, 132, 143, 158, 166, 204, 246
Beal, Timothy, 238
Beale, G. K., 239
Becking, Bob, 191
Beentjes, Pancratius, 234
Ben Zvi, Ehud, 36, 126, 149, 200
Berlin, Adele, 247
Berner, Christoph, 61
Birch, Bruce C., 110, 116
Birdsong, Shelley L., 217
Blomberg, Craig L., 239
Boda, Mark J., 75, 130
Bodner, Keith, 49
Boling, Robert G., 119

Bosworth, David, 97
Bowen, Nancy R., 208
Brettler, Mark Zvi, 247
Brueggemann, Walter, 13, 27, 35, 48–9, 57, 65, 72, 74, 78, 83–4, 95, 110, 141, 148, 156, 159, 164, 174, 178, 183, 186, 209, 217, 238, 244
Burnside, Jonathan, 37

Camp, Claudia, 208, 238
Carson, D. A., 239
Chapman, Stephen B., 39, 244
Chan, Michael J., 224
Chun, S. Min, 88
Cogan, Mordechai, 61, 115
Collins, John J., 201
Coggins, Richard, 98, 128
Cohn, Robert L., 132, 152, 158, 172, 196, 207, 211, 216, 221, 244
Conti, Marco, 244
Coogan, Michael D., 12
Coomber, Matthew, 246
Corley, Jeremy, 234
Cross, Frank Moore, 22, 45
Culpepper, R. Alan, 241
Curtis, Adrian, 35

Darr, Katheryn Pfisterer, 188
Davies, John A., 63, 79
Day, John, 129, 208, 234
Dell, Katharine, 235
Dever, William G., 56
DeVries, Simon J., 87
Dietrich, Walter, 45, 59, 65, 68, 134, 147, 157, 196, 204, 244
Dozeman, Thomas B., 61, 118

AUTHOR INDEX

Dubovský, Peter, 176
Dunn, J. D. G., 185
Dutcher-Walls, Patricia, 165

Edelman, Diana, 126, 149
Edwards, Jonathan, xvii
Ehrlich, Carl S., 246
Evans, Paul S., 185, 200
Everhart, Janet S., 160

Fewell, Danna Nolan, 245
Finlay, Timothy D., 139
Fishbane, Michael, 227
Freedman, David Noel, 10, 219
Fretheim, Terence E., 4, 40, 58, 66, 83, 86, 103, 108, 110–11, 127, 132, 135, 165, 171, 182, 199, 201, 211, 217, 244
Fritz, Volkmar, 116
Frye, Northrop, 119

Garsiel, Moshe, 129
Gehman, H. S., 3, 70, 116
Gillmayr-Bucher, Susanne, 76
Gilmour, Rachelle, 133, 172
Goldingay, John, 39, 244
Grabbe, Lester L., 106
Gragg, Douglas L., 207
Graham, M. Patrick, 200, 207
Granowski, Jan Jaynes, 244
Gray, John, 54
Green, Joel B., 239
Greenwood, Kyle, 135
Grol, Harm van, 234
Gunn, David M., 27

Hallo, William W., 12
Halpern, Baruch, 56, 132, 244
Harvey, John E., 223
Hays, Christopher B., 137
Hays, Daniel J., 60, 64, 68, 75, 81–2
Hays, Richard B., 53
Heckl, Raik, 235
Henry, Matthew, 106
Hens-Piazza, Gina, 169, 196, 198, 221, 245
Heskett, Randall, 223
Hess, Richard S., 135, 231
Hom, Mary K. Y. H., 199
Horbury, William, 232
Horst, Pieter W. van der, 191
Hutton, Rod R., 105

Irwin, Brian, 223

Janzen, David, 211, 222, 245
Jarick, John, 234
Jeon, Yong Ho, 83
Jones, Gwilym H., 28
Jonker, Louis C., 233

Keck, Leander E., 14
Keener, Craig S., 239
Kelly, Brian E., 230
Klein, Ralph W., 200
Kloppenborg, John S., 240
Knoppers, Gary N., 21, 104, 200, 232
Konkel, August H., 94
Kratz, Reinhard G., 102
Kynes, Will, 235

Lamb, David T., 159
Landy, Francis, 36, 126
Leithart, Peter J., 35, 79, 83, 87, 99, 106, 110, 112, 123, 129, 161, 163, 165, 173, 177, 181, 190, 194, 218, 245
Lemaire, André, 56, 132, 244
Lemche, Niels Peter, 106
Lesley, Michael, 179
Leuchter, Mark, 45, 89
Levenson, Jon, 66, 245
Levin, Christoph, 36
Lieu, Judith M., 13, 244
Lim, Timothy H., 23, 243
Linafelt, Tod, 238
Linville, James R., 183, 245
Long, Burke O., 134–5, 161, 163, 196, 213, 245
Long, Jesse C., 100
Long, V. Philips, 106

Macchi, Jean-Daniel, 24
Machinist, Peter 176, 185
MacIntyre, Alasdair, xviii
Mann, Thomas W., 20
Marsden, George, xvii
McCarter, P. Kyle, 32
McKenzie, Steven L., 13, 23, 32, 200
McConville, J. Gordon, 21, 104
Meadowcroft, Tim, 227
Melugin, Roy F., 188
Meyers, Carol, 219
Michael, Matthew, 59–60
Middlemas, Jill, 75
Miller, Patrick D., 208

AUTHOR INDEX

Miscall, Peter D., 159, 245
Moberly, R. W. L., 29, 195, 245
Mobley, Gregory, 2–3, 5, 16, 18, 86, 134, 147, 175, 245
Moore, Michael S., 107, 160
Monroe, Lauren A. S., 211
Montgomery, J. A., 3, 70, 116
Muddiman, John, 45, 244
Mueller, E. Aydeet, 167
Murray, Donald F., 222

Na'aman, Nadav, 232
Nelson, Richard D., 28, 38–9, 46, 62, 66, 73, 77, 102–3, 109, 114, 121, 132, 149, 152–3, 169, 180, 187, 202, 246
Newsom, Carol A., 208
Noth, Martin, 21–4, 181–2, 222

O'Day, Gail R., 2, 230, 245

Page, Hugh, 246
Paris, Christopher T., 92
Peterson, Brian Neil, 22
Petersen, David L., 2, 110, 230, 245
Pritchard, James B., 12
Provan, Iain, 43, 50, 56, 71, 75, 83, 96, 112, 144, 165, 171, 179, 186, 202, 217, 221, 231, 237, 246
Pury, Albert de, 24

Rad, Gerhard von, 22, 104, 222, 246
Reinhartz, Adele, 139
Rezetko, Robert, 23, 243
Richter, Sandra, 193
Ricouer, Paul, 12
Ringe, Sharon H., 208
Rogerson, John W., 13, 185, 244
Römer, Thomas, 22, 24, 61, 229
Rost, Leonhard, 27
Rowe, C. Kavin, 53
Rudman, Dominic, 187

Satterthwaite, Philip, 231
Schearing, Linda S., 101
Schipper, Jeremy, 45, 80, 101, 121, 200, 222
Schmid, Konrad, 61
Schoors, Anton, 179
Schulte, Hannelis, 246

Schweitzer, Steven J., 234
Seow, Choon Leong, 2, 14, 16, 37, 43, 61, 65, 67–8, 77, 111, 122, 127, 132, 153, 166, 194, 213, 246
Smith, Abraham, 236
Smith-Christopher, Daniel, xix
Spieckermann, Hermann, 102
Spina, Frank Anthony, 8
Stavrakopoulou, Francesca, 205
Steiner, George, 2
Strawn, Brent A., 118, 207–8
Sweeney, Marvin A., 30, 39, 41, 54, 70, 82, 112, 116, 154, 162, 172, 181, 188, 201, 205, 213, 244, 246

Thomas, Heath A., 227
Toews, Wesley I., 94
Tomes, Roger, 185
Toorn, Karel van der, 191
Tull, Patricia K., 229–30

Uehlinger, Christoph, 191

Vanhoozer, Kevin J., 7, 12, 230
Verheyden, Joseph, 240

Walls, Neal H., 107
Walsh, Jerome T., 30, 42, 49, 58, 61, 68, 83, 96, 111, 124, 149, 246
Weaver, John B., 207
Weems, Renita J., 208
Weitzman, Steven, 31, 41–2, 54–5, 63, 76
Wenham, Gordon J., 231
Westbrook, Raymond R., 137
Wolff, Hans Walter, 22, 222
Wieppert, Helga, 104
Wiesel, Elie, 219
Wiggins, Steve A., 107
Williams, Tyler F., 200
Williams, Rowan, xviii
Williamson, H. G. M., 75, 193, 208, 232
Wilson, Ian Douglas, 225
Wiseman, Donald J., 158, 162, 202, 217

Yee, Gale A., 246
Younger, K. Lawson, Jr., 12

Zevit, Ziony, 247

Scripture Index

OLD TESTAMENT

Genesis
2:1-2 68
2:13 36
5:24 131
11:28 10
11:31 10
12 21, 220
15:7 214
15:18 62
18:17 125
19:1 149
19:11 148
22 233
22:2 11
22:17-18 233
27 35
35:22 29
43:30 59
49:3-4 29
50:20 223
50:24-25 224

Exodus
1 61
1:11 88
2 165
2:1-10 165
4:21 127
9:8-12 194
9:12 127
9:14-16 189
10:1 127
10:20 127
10:27 127
11:10 127
14:8 127
14:9 132
14:16 145
14:17 132
14:18 132
14:23 132
14:26 132
14:28 132
15:1 78
15:25 133
16:8 111
21:12-14 37
22:28 123
25:16 166
25:21 166
27:2 37
29:12 37
30:10 37
31:18 166
32 94
32:15 166
33:21-23 118
34:12 197
34:29 166
40 69
40:20 166

Leviticus
4:7 37
11:15 111
13-14 142
13 194
14 240
25:23 123
26:21-22 182

Numbers
  21:4-9 184
  32:13 204
Deuteronomy
  2:30 127
  5:33 204
  6:5 83
  7:1-6 54
  7:2 197
  9:5 182
  11:10 123
  11:22 83
  12:31 178–9
  17 5, 81
  17:14-20 77
  17:16-17 62, 75
  17:16 78, 104, 132
  17:17 82, 213
  20:1 132
  20:16-18 121
  20:19-20 137
  21:15 149
  21:19 149
  22:24 149
  24:5 101
  24:16 172
  25:7 149
  28-30 70
  28 20
  28:1 21
  28:27 194
  28:49-57 217
  28:53-57 148
  28:63 21
  29 210
  32:24 182
Joshua
  1:1-9 40
  3-8 131
  4:5 145
  5:10-11 212
  6-7 108
  6 36, 121
  6:26 108
  7:25 114
  19:18 28
  19:44 101
  24 210
Judges
  2:14 142
  3:8 142

4 116
4:2 142
4:7 116
4:11-12 162
5:21 116
6:25 94
9 91
9:7-20 172
9:23-24 92
9:26-41 119
14:8-9 97
16:2-3 149
16:21-22 218
21:25 57
1 Samuel
  1-4 87
  2:1-10 30
  2:13 49
  2:25 203
  2:27-36 31, 46, 202
  2:29 49
  4-6 229
  8 220
  8:1-18 77
  8:14 123
  10:1 157
  10:5 136
  14:20 137
  15:26 230
  15:27-28 85
  15:28 89
  16 26
  20:29 42
  25:42-44 82
  28:4 28
  28:6 58
2 Samuel
  3:2-5 82
  3:3 54
  3:6-7 44
  3:27 47
  5:11 63
  5:13 82
  6:6-8 205
  7 33, 64
  7:12-16 40
  7:12-13 28
  7:13 33
  7:14 178
  7:15-16 230
  7:18-29 90

SCRIPTURE INDEX

9 222
9:7 42
11-12 92
11 34
12 33
12:5-6 80
12:6 45
12:8 44
12:11 44, 82
12:15-23 211
12:24-25 31
12:24 83
12:25 33, 50
15:1 30
15:10 158
15:30-31 84
16:5-13 41
16:21-22 44
17:14 92
17:17-21 36
17:17-20 90
17:27 42
18:16 36
19:16-23 41
19:23 48
19:41-43 28
20:1 92
20:10 47
20:22 36
20:24 61
24:1 127
1 Kings
  1-2 28, 51
  1 25, 27, 29, 32, 35, 38, 129
  1:4 28
  1:5-6 30
  1:7 41
  1:9 28
  1:10 32
  1:11 33
  1:15 34
  1:36 45
  1:43-48 37
  1:47 28
  1:51-53 37
  2 4, 25–6, 50
  2:2-9 39
  2:2-4 39
  2:3-4 230
  2:4 40, 70, 85

2:5-9 41
2:12 50
2:13-25 44
2:19 44
2:22 46
2:23-24 44
2:27 46
2:28-35 47
2:42 49
2:46 50
3-10 5, 52
3 5, 56–8, 63, 74
3:1-3 56
3:1 53
3:2-3 55
3:2 56
3:3 56, 83
3:4-15 57
3:7 134
3:9 78–9
3:10 57
3:11-14 73
3:13 75
3:15 57
3:16-28 59
4 62, 71
4:1-19 60
4:1-6 60
4:4 46
4:7-19 61, 88
4:11 48
4:15 48
4:20-28 62
4:29-34 62
4:34 76
4:47 42
5 63, 65
5:4 86, 208
5:7 77
5:13 62
6-7 65, 68
6:1 5, 11, 66, 232
6:11-13 58, 67, 72
7:1 64
7:2 64
7:8 54, 68
7:13 64
7:51 68
8 5, 69, 72, 74
8:12-13 71
8:15-21 69

1 Kings (cont.)
8:15-16 73
8:20 73
8:22 95
8:23-53 70
8:25-26 70
8:25 85
8:41-43 73
8:46-53 226
8:46 192
8:61 80, 83
8:62-66 71
8:65 173
9 74
9:1-9 72, 79
9:2-9 58
9:3 72-3
9:4-5 72, 85
9:6-9 73, 192
9:7 231
9:10-28 74
9:11-14 89
9:15 76, 88, 159
9:16 54
9:19 88, 159
9:20 78
9:22 62
9:24 54
9:26-28 75
10 76, 197, 81
10:5 42
10:8-9 78
10:9 76
10:14-29 77
10:14-15 77
10:21 46, 64
10:28-29 77
11-16 6, 81, 103
11-12 56
11 86, 99
11:1-13 81
11:1-2 83
11:1 82
11:4 56, 80
11:5-8 83
11:7-8 56
11:9 85
11:11-13 85, 91
11:11 88, 95
11:12 153
11:14-25 86

11:14 65
11:23-25 78
11:23 65
11:25 86
11:26 87
11:29-30 88
11:33 89
11:36 154, 231
11:37-39 89
11:41-43 90
12 6, 59, 65, 90, 92, 109
12:1-7 62
12:8 134
12:15 6, 92
12:16 92, 233
12:19-20 93
12:25 94
12:26-27 90, 94
12:28 233
13 10, 95-6, 122, 182, 206
13:1-10 95
13:2 205, 209
13:3 98
13:7 99
13:11-34 97
13:32 97, 107
13:33-34 98
13:33 103
14-15 7
14 98
14:6-16 99
14:9 103
14:15 99, 103, 192
14:17-20 99
14:21 93, 100, 134
14:22-24 100
14:25-26 86
14:25 93
14:30 93
14:31 100
15:4 154, 231
15:9 100
15:18 168
15:25-32 101
15:27 104-5
16 7
16:2 102
16:9-22 204
16:9 119
16:11 50
16:22 106

SCRIPTURE INDEX

16:24 98, 107, 123
16:31-33 19
16:34 108
17 19, 113
17:1 115, 110
17:2-6 111
17:7-16 111
17:9-16 138
17:12 114, 141
17:13-14 114
17:13 112
17:17-24 112
17:18 114
17:19-24 129
17:24 140
18 17, 113, 116, 187
18:1-6 141
18:2-16 113
18:4 111
18:9-14 17, 114
18:9 114
18:10 114
18:13 117
18:15 114
18:17-40 115
18:17 151
18:18 114
18:19-20 114
18:19 42
18:21 114
18:24 115
18:36-37 115
18:36 137
18:44 140
19 117, 131
19:3-10 239
19:13-18 238
19:15 153
19:16 155
19:19 130
19:19-21 118, 131
20 8, 78, 119, 122, 182
20:13-22 120
20:13 121
20:20-21 120
20:22 121
20:23-34 120
20:30 127
20:31-34 121
20:31-32 124
20:35-43 120–1

20:36 97
20:39-42 80
20:41 122
20:42 122
21 122, 125
21:17-24 158
21:20-29 158
21:25-26 124
21:28 228
21:29 152
22 78, 125, 136, 154
22:6 116
22:13 122
22:19-23 127
22:27 208
22:30 136
22:32-33 128
22:34-35 122
22:38 20
22:43 56
22:48-49 128
22:49 128
22:50 130
22:52-53 129

2 Kings
1 129, 153
1:1 129, 135
1:3-4 129
1:17 130
2 117, 131
2:13 133
2:19-22 133
2:23 162
2:23-25 133
3-9 131
3 102, 129, 135, 154–5
3:4-27 135
3:10 136–7, 141
3:13 138
3:16-19 136
3:19 137
3:20-23 137
3:27 137, 203
4 138, 140
4:1-7 138
4:8-17 138
4:18-37 139
4:20 140
4:27 144
4:28 140
4:29-31 143

2 Kings (cont.)
4:37 140
4:38-41 140
4:38 141
4:42-44 141
4:44 141
5 8, 78, 142, 152
5:3 142
5:5-6 146
5:15 142, 146
5:19-27 143
5:25 197
6-8 145
6 144, 217
6:7 145
6:8-14 145
6:9-10 146
6:12 146
6:13-23 146
6:15 148
6:16 197
6:17 133, 189
6:18 147, 150
6:21 148, 151
6:24-29 186
6:24 148
6:26-29 150
6:30 151
6:30-31 188
6:31 148, 151
6:33 149
7 78
7:1 149
7:2 149
7:3-20 150
7:5 150
7:6 78
7:10-12 152
7:10 150
8-9 118
8:1-6 151–2
8:5-6 152
8:7-15 12, 153
8:12 153
8:16-24 154
8:18 125
8:19-22 155
8:19 154, 231
8:25-29 155
9-19 8, 156
9-11 18

9-10 75
9 8, 18, 138, 154
9:1-10 145
9:1 157
9:22 159–60
9:25-26 158
9:26 123
9:27-28 159
9:30-37 160
9:36 20
9:37 158
10:1-16 161
10:11 50
10:14 134
10:17-28 162
10:22 163
10:27 135
10:29-36 163
10:30 86, 163
11 9, 155, 162, 164
11:1 164
11:18 204
11:20 204
12 168, 205
12:2 167
12:3 56
12:4 168
12:18 169
12:20-21 168
12:20 205
13-16 9
13 169
13:1-9 169
13:10-25 170
13:20-21 171
13:21 195
13:23 171
14 172
14:4 56
14:19 172
14:23-29 173
14:26-27 173–4
14:27 174
15-16 12, 177
15 174
15:1-7 174
15:4 56
15:16 175
15:22 176
15:25 176
15:32-38 177

/ SCRIPTURE INDEX 257

15:35 56
15:37 177
16 178
16:3 137, 179
16:7 178
16:7-8 198
16:10 228
16:15 179
17-20 200
17 93, 180, 183, 192, 214
17:1-6 180
17:4 222
17:7-23 181
17:19 182
17:24-41 182
17:25-26 97
17:29-32 210
18-19 155, 193
18 9, 15–16
18:4 56, 200
18:5-8 15
18:5 184, 189, 196
18:9-12 184
18:14 214
18:21 184
18:23 186
18:24 184
18:13-16 15
18:15-16 188, 195
18:17 185
18:19-25 185
18:25 186
18:28-35 186
18:36 187
19 188, 193
19:1-2 207
19:2-4 188
19:6-7 188, 196
19:7 191
19:8 188
19:14-19 15
19:15 191
19:19 191, 196
19:20 189
19:21-34 189
19:35 190
19:36-37 190
20-25 9
20 191, 193, 196
20:1-11 193
20:6 194
20:7 194
20:8-11 194
20:12-21 16
20:12-19 195
20:14 197
20:19 206
20:20 199
21 155, 201, 205
21:1-18 200
21:3-9 56
21:6 137
21:7 201–2
21:8 202
21:11-15 201
21:13 201
21:14 231
21:15 201
21:16 201
21:19-26 203
21:24 213
22 205, 207, 220
22:8 206
22:9-10 207
22:13 209
22:16-17 209
22:18-20 209
23 211–12
23:2 208
23:4-20 210
23:10 203
23:13 84
23:16-18 210
23:21-23 212
23:27 212
23:29-30 212
23:33 213, 218
23:34 216
23:36-24:7 214
24:1 181
24:2-4 214
24:2 10
24:12-17 221
24:15 190
24:17-25:7 235
24:18-25:2 216
24:19 237
24:20 216–17
25 2, 10, 21, 40, 125, 155, 181, 183, 229, 231, 237
25:3 217

2 Kings (cont.)
  25:4 10
  25:5 192, 217
  25:16-17 219
  25:21 216–17
  25:22-26 220, 235
  25:27-30 47, 222, 225, 232
  25:29 10, 42
1 Chronicles
  2:55 162
2 Chronicles
  3:1 11, 232
  18:1 125
  21:18-19 155
  22:11 165
  24 168
  26:16-20 174
  32:3-4 199
  32:30 199
  32:30 36
  33:12-16 200
  36 233
  36:22 232
Ezra
  3:12-13 233
Job
  39:19-25 78
Psalms
  2 147, 234
  2:7 178
  2:9 202
  78:40 116
  83:9 116
  89:20 178
  89:26 178
  97:9 151
  113:5 151
  132:12 166
  147:10 78
Ecclesiastes
  12:6 202
Isaiah
  2:2-4 143
  5:1-7 123
  5:28 176
  6:10 127
  7 177
  10:5 186
  10:20-21 148
  23 64
  31:1 132
  34:11 202
  39:1 195
  40 147
  42:1 125
  43:16-21 224
  45:7 127
  51:9-10 224
  52:7-12 224
  55:3 155
  61:1-3 150
Jeremiah
  2:7-13 19
  4:10 127
  7 218
  7:12-14 88
  12:10 123
  19:11 202
  22:28-30 238
  23:3 148
  23:5-6 238
  23:5 125
  26:4-6 88
  26:20-23 235
  28:4 238
  29:26 158
  33:14-18 155
  35:1-16 162
  36:22-24 214
  36:23 235
  36:24 124
  37:16-21 217
  38:4-5 236
  38:10 236
  38:14-27 217
  38:14-28 236
  40-42 235
  51:34 202
Lamentations
  2:8 202
Ezekiel
  26-28 64
  35:10-15 87
  37:1-14 171
  43:20 37
Daniel
  2:21 50
  4:25 50
Hosea
  1:4-5 159
  1:5 19
  7:6-7 175
  7:16 175
  9:1-2 126

SCRIPTURE INDEX

9:7 158
11:8 59
Amos
3:14 37
5:10 149
5:15 148–9
7:9 175
7:11 175
9:7 179, 224
9:11 155
Obadiah
11-14 87
Micah
2:12 148
7:15 224
Haggai
2:3 233
Zechariah
13:4 130
Malachi
4:5 132

NEW TESTAMENT

Matthew
1:1-22 238
2:13-18 165
2:15-16 166
6:24-33 78
11:2-3 239
11:3-4 117
12:24 129
12:42 76
17:3 132
26:53 147
Mark
3:22 129
6:14-29 236

9:4 132
12:42 141
Luke
3:23-38 238
4:25-26 111
4:25-27 239
7:18-19 117
9:30 132
11:14-20 129
11:31 76
12:13-21 78
22:39-48 85
John
6:13 141
Romans
1:3 155
3:21-31 194
4:2-4 194
6:12 73
7:15-23 58
8:37-39 132
9:18 127
11:1-5 238
13:17 39
Galatians
2:1-10 194
5:6 73
Ephesians
4:30 116
6:10-17 132
2 Thessalonians
2:11 127
Hebrews
2:4 148
1 Peter
2:13-14 39
Revelation
16-19 238
16:16 238
22:16 155

THE CANCER-FIGHTING RECIPE BOOK

Discover Nutritious and Delicious Recipes, Loaded with Anti-Oxidants That Can Help You Be Cancer-Free!

Table of Contents

INTRODUCTION 4

1. Pineapple Blueberry Smoothie 5
2. Lemony Spinach Soup 7
3. Cooling Cucumber Avocado Soup 9
4. Baby Bok Choy with Yam and Ginger 11
5. Lemon Berry Detox Juice 14
6. Chicken Bone Broth Soup 16
7. Green Beans with Brazil Nuts and Basil 18
8. Chicken Breasts with Curried Stuffing 20
9. Herbed and Spiced Yogurt 23
10. Blueberry and Citrus Breakfast Parfait 25
11. Spiced Baked Fish 27
12. Turkey Chili 30
13. Lemon Roasted Asparagus 32
14. Green Tea Ginger Lemonade 34
15. Avocado Coconut Soup 36
16. Greek Tempeh-Stuffed Peppers 38
17. Quinoa Porridge with Walnut Cream 41
18. Salmon Lentil Stuffed Tomatoes with Curry Sauce 44
19. Multigrain Bread 47
20. Roasted Kale 50
21. Parsnip Curry.. 52

22. Tuna Salad with White Bean Dressing 55
23. Snow Peas with Shallots 58
24. Chickpea Pitas with Tahini Dressing 60
25. Lemony Apple Fennel Salad 63
26. Zucchini Stir-Fry 65
27. Grilled Greens and Eggplant 67
28. Ginger and Lemon Drink 70
29. Chicken Soup with Zoodles 72
30. Turmeric Glazed Parsnips 74

CONCLUSION **76**

INTRODUCTION

Looking for delicious and nutritious recipes that can help prevent cancer and keep you healthy? If so, look no further than this recipe book! Filled with 30 nutritious and not to mention, delicious recipes, each of them has healthy ingredients that pump your body with antioxidants and nutrients.

There are recipes for all sorts of occasion and so there's no reason not to try them all! Plus, each recipe is easy and comes with step-by-step instructions. So, choose a recipe and let's begin!

1. Pineapple Blueberry Smoothie

Along with whole grain quinoa flakes, tangy coconut water, healthy fat from almonds and the protein in the egg whites, this drink is a complete nutritional and delicious package.

Makes: 2 servings

Prep: 5 mins

Cook: -

Ingredients:

- 2 cups coconut water
- 1 cup pineapple chunks
- 1/3 cup quinoa flakes
- 1/2 cup pasteurized egg whites
- 1/4 cup unsalted raw or roasted almonds
- 1 tsp. vanilla extract or 1/2 tsp. almond extract
- 1/4 tsp. ground cloves
- 1 cup frozen blueberries

Directions:

Place all of the shown ingredients in a blender container and blend until smooth, about 30 seconds.

Divide and serve.

2. Lemony Spinach Soup

Tangy and tart lemon brings out the flavors of baby spinach in this super easy soup. This soup is creamy and clean- the perfect go-to for spring.

Makes: 2 servings

Prep: 5 mins

Cook: -

Ingredients:

- Pepper
- 4 cups baby spinach
- 1 tbsp. lemon zest
- 1 clove minced garlic
- 3 tbsp. lemon juice
- 2 cups nut milk
- 1 chopped scallion
- 3 tbsp. white miso
- Diced avocado, for garnish

Directions:

Blend all ingredients on high until smooth.

Garnish with avocado and serve.

3. Cooling Cucumber Avocado Soup

Avocados - full of good fats and vitamins. They're fun to work with, and delicious.

Makes: 6 servings

Prep: 15 mins + cooling time

Cook: -

Ingredients:

- 2 cups water
- 2 ripe avocados, pitted and peeled
- 1 tbsp. finely chopped fresh cilantro

- 2 lb. English cucumbers, seeded, peeled, & cut into chunks
- ¼ tsp. maple syrup
- 3 tbsp. freshly squeezed lime juice
- Salt
- 1 tbsp. finely chopped fresh mint
- Pinch of cayenne

Directions:

Pour just one cup of water into a blender, & then add the avocados, cucumbers, lime juice, maple syrup, ¼ tsp. of salt, & the cayenne. Blend till smooth, & then gradually adding more water until you reach the desired consistency. Taste & adjust the amount of salt.

Chill for at least two hrs., then stir in the mint & cilantro and serve.

4. Baby Bok Choy with Yam and Ginger

Bok choy is a great vegetable, but tends to be bitter. But that is completely solved here by it being paired with sweet potatoes!

Makes: 12 servings

Prep: 15 mins

Cook: 5 mins

Ingredients:

- 8 heads baby bok choy
- 4 scallions, white part, sliced
- 1/4 cup minced fresh ginger
- 1/4 cup light sesame oil
- 2 cups peeled & finely diced Garnet sweet potato or yam
- Sea salt
- 2 tsp. maple syrup
- 2 tbsp. tamari
- 2 tbsp. freshly squeezed lime juice
- 1/2 tsp. toasted sesame oil (optional)

Directions:

Trim the bases from the bok choy & discard. Trim the leaves from the stems & cut both crosswise into bite-size pieces.

Heat the oil in a pan over med heat, then add the scallions & ginger and sauté for 30 seconds. Add the sweet potato and a pinch of salt and sauté for an additional minute. Add the bok choy stems, tamari, and maple syrup and sauté for 2 minutes more. Add the bok choy leaves, 1/2 tsp. of salt, lime juice, & the toasted sesame oil. Cook for about 2 mins, then taste.

Serve immediately.

5. Lemon Berry Detox Juice

This juice packs a real punch in nutrition and is loaded with vital vitamins, minerals and antioxidants.

Makes: 2 servings

Prep: 10 mins

Cook: -

Ingredients:

- 2 medium green apples, chopped
- 1 handful fresh raspberries
- 1 handful fresh strawberries
- ½ lemon, peeled

Directions:

Press the apples and lemon through your juicer, along with the raspberries and strawberries.

Juice and enjoy!

6. Chicken Bone Broth Soup

Healthy, chicken and veggie broth soup recipe.

Makes: 10-12 servings

Prep: 10 mins

Cook: 8 hrs. 30 mins

Ingredients:

- 2–3 pounds of bony chicken parts (wings, necks, etc.)
- 4 quarts cool, filtered water

- 2 tbsp. apple cider vinegar
- 3 carrots, peeled
- 2 medium onions, chopped
- 3 celery stalks chopped
- ¼ cup chopped parsley

Directions:

Place the pieces in a pot with water, vinegar, and all vegetables except parsley. Let it sit for 30 minutes. Over medium flame, bring to a vigorous boil. Skim off any scum that rises to the top; reduce heat and cover. Simmer for a minimum of 8 hours. For more flavorful stock, simmer longer. Add the parsley for the final 15–30 minutes.

As the soup cools, use a slotted spoon to remove any large chicken and vegetable pieces. Strain out the remaining pieces through a metal colander and pour the broth into one large bowl or several small glass bowls. Chill in your refrigerator, skimming off any fat that congeals at the top.

7. Green Beans with Brazil Nuts and Basil

Green beans are a popular vegetable. This dish is dairy free and delicious. Plus, it's topped with Brazil nuts because they're an amazing source of the mineral selenium, which some research suggests lessens chemotherapy's toxic effects on healthy hair, kidney, and GI tract cells.

Makes: 12 servings

Prep: 15 mins

Cook: 10 mins

Ingredients:

- Freshly squeezed lemon juice
- 2 pound green beans, trimmed
- 1/4 cup olive oil
- 1/4 cup finely chopped fresh basil
- Sea salt
- 1/4 cup chopped shallot
- Freshly ground pepper
- 1/4 cup finely ground Brazil nuts or walnuts
- ½ tsp. lemon zest

Directions:

Bring a good amount of water (about 16 cups) to a boil. Add 1/2 tsp. of salt & the green beans & cook until tender-crisp, 6-8 mins. Drain & then run them under cold water.

Heat the 1/2 cup olive oil in a pan over med heat, & then add the shallot & a pinch of salt & sauté for about 1 minute. Add in the beans, add 1/2 tsp. of salt, & cook, until heated through, about 2 mins. Remove & add several grinds of pepper, a splash of the lemon juice, & the nuts. Toss with the basil & lemon zest before serving.

8. Chicken Breasts with Curried Stuffing

If you love curry powder, this is the recipe for you! Add curry powder to the yogurt topping as well for even more flavor.

Makes: 4 servings

Prep: 10 mins

Cook: 35 mins

Ingredients:

- 1 tbsp. butter
- ¼ cup sliced green onions
- 2 tsp. curry powder
- ½ cup fresh bread crumbs
- ½ cup shredded carrot
- 3 tbsp. dried currants
- 1 tbsp. Chicken Stock
- 4 (4-ounce) boneless, skinless chicken breasts
- ¼ tsp. salt
- 1/8 tsp. black pepper
- ½ tsp. paprika
- 2 tbsp. orange marmalade
- 1/3 cup plain yogurt
- 2 tsp. arrowroot

Directions:

Preheat oven to 350°F.

In a pan, melt butter over med heat. Add carrot, green onions, and curry powder, and cook, stirring, until tender, about 5 mins. Remove & stir in the bread crumbs, currants, and broth.

Place 1 chicken breast half with the boned-side up, between the 2 sheets of plastic wrap. Pound lightly. Repeat with the rest of chicken.

Sprinkle chicken with salt and pepper. Place ¼ from the stuffing mixture on each piece of chicken. Fold chicken over the filling and secure using a toothpick. Place chicken in an 8" square baking dish with 2" sides. Sprinkle with the paprika and cover with foil.

In a small bowl, combine yogurt, arrowroot, and marmalade; spread over chicken.

Bake until chicken is tender and the juices run clear when a piece is pierced, about 25–35 minutes.

9. Herbed and Spiced Yogurt

Real yogurt is a wonderful international culinary staple that is light, delicious and nutritious.

Makes: 2 cups

Prep: 20 mins plus chilling time

Cook: -

Ingredients:

- ⅓ cup finely chopped & loosely packed fresh flat-leaf parsley

- 1 tbsp. extra-virgin olive oil
- 1 tsp. maple syrup
- 1 tsp. freshly squeezed lemon juice
- ¼ tsp. sea salt
- ⅓ cup finely chopped & loosely packed fresh cilantro
- ¼ tsp. ground cumin
- ⅛ tsp. ground cinnamon
- ⅓ cup finely chopped & loosely packed fresh mint leaves
- 2 cups organic plain yogurt

Directions:

Stir all of the shown ingredients together until thoroughly combined.

Cover tightly & chill for 15 mins before serving.

10. Blueberry and Citrus Breakfast Parfait

Parfaits are a simple yet visually pleasing breakfast option. Best of all, you can pack them full of your favorite fruits. Here we've added tangy citrus and antioxidant-loaded blueberries to a crunchy walnut, flax and wheat germ mix. Top it with some yogurt and you will definitely be starting your day off right!

Makes: 4 servings

Prep: 15 mins

Cook: -

Ingredients:

- 3 cups (710 ml) plain nonfat all-natural Greek yogurt or strained plain soy yogurt
- 1 Tbsp. (15 ml) pure maple syrup
- ½ tsp. (2.5 ml) pure vanilla extract
- ½ cup (120 ml) walnuts, chopped
- 2 Tbsp. (30 ml) wheat germ
- 2 Tbsp. (30 ml) cracked flaxseed
- 1 red grapefruit, peeled and cut into small slices
- 1 minneola, peeled and cut into small slices
- 1 cup (240 ml) fresh blueberries

Directions:

Stir together the yogurt, maple syrup and vanilla.

In four parfait glasses, pour in some of the yogurt mixture. Then sprinkle in some of the walnuts, wheat germ and flaxseeds, and then add some of the grapefruit, minneola and blueberries.

Repeat until all of the remaining ingredients are used.

11. Spiced Baked Fish

Moist whole fish is covered with a spiced onion mixture giving you a delicious and cook dinner option that the family will love!

Makes: 4 servings

Prep: 5 mins

Cook: 30 mins

Ingredients:

- 2 lb. whole fish, scaled and cleaned
- 2 onions, sliced
- 4 cloves garlic, crushed
- 1 cup fresh parsley, chopped
- 1 cup fresh cilantro, chopped
- 1 tbsp. coriander powder
- ¼ - ½ tsp. chili powder
- 3 tbsp. lemon juice
- 3 tbsp. oil
- Salt and pepper
- Chopped parsley and lemon wedges for garnish

Directions:

Preheat oven to 450°F.

Heat oil in a pan. Add the fish and fry for 2 minutes on each side to crisp up the skin. Remove and place in a baking pan.

Add the onions to the pan & cook till soft.

Add in the rest of the ingredients and cook for a few more minutes.

Spread this onion mixture onto the fish and inside it.

Add 1 cup of water to the baking pan and bake in the oven for 20 minutes or until fish has cooked through.

Serve sprinkled with fresh parsley and lemon wedges.

12. Turkey Chili

Turkey plus beans make this chili a protein powerhouse!

Makes: 6 servings

Prep: 5 mins

Cook: 3 hrs.

Ingredients:

- 1 pound ground turkey
- 1 cup onions, chopped
- ½ cup green pepper, chopped

- 2 tsp. garlic, finely chopped
- 2 (28-ounce) cans crushed canned tomatoes
- 1 cup canned black beans, drained
- 1 cup canned red kidney beans, drained
- 3 tbsp. chili powder
- 1 tbsp. ground cumin
- 1 tsp. crushed red pepper
- Dash Tabasco

Directions:

Brown the turkey in nonstick pot over med-high heat. Drain any fat.

Add in the chopped onion, garlic and green pepper. Cook for about 5 minutes.

Add remaining ingredients; bring to a slow boil.

Reduce heat, cover, & let simmer at least 2–3 hrs. before serving.

13. Lemon Roasted Asparagus

This lemony roasted asparagus with parmesan and garlic is the perfect recipe for a quick side dish.

Makes: 8 servings

Prep: 10 mins

Cook: 10 mins

Ingredients:

- 2 lb. fresh asparagus, trimmed
- ¼ cup olive oil
- 4 cloves garlic, minced
- 4 tbsp. Parmesan, grated
- 2 lemons, thinly sliced
- 4 tbsp. freshly squeezed lemon juice
- 1 tsp. sea salt
- ½ tsp. ground black pepper

Directions:

Preheat oven to 400°F. Prepare a baking sheet with baking paper.

Add all of the ingredients onto the baking sheet and toss to evenly coat. Place in the oven for about 10-15 minutes or until the asparagus is roasted.

Serve.

14. Green Tea Ginger Lemonade

Green tea is great for you, with many of its compounds linked to potential anticancer benefits.

Makes: 4 cups

Prep: 3 mins

Cook: 25 mins plus chilling time

Ingredients:

- 4 cups water
- 2 green tea bags
- 1 tbsp. lemon juice

- 4 (½-inch) slices fresh ginger
- 2 tsp. honey

Directions:

Bring the water & ginger to boil in a pan, & then lower, cover, & simmer for ten mins. Remove & add in the tea bags, & steep for 10 minutes.

Remove the tea bags & ginger, and then stir in the lemon juice and honey. Chill for 1 hr. before serving over ice.

15. Avocado Coconut Soup

Avocado lends this soup a creamy texture, while coconut milk gives it a fresh and tropical flavor.

Makes: 4 servings

Prep: 2 hrs. + 5 mins

Cook: -

Ingredients:

- 1 1/2 cups coconut milk
- 1 1/2 cups water
- 2 ripe large avocados

- 1/4 cup packed fresh basil
- Juice of 1 lime
- 1 jalapeño chili pepper, seeded and minced
- 1/4 tsp. sea salt
- 1/4 tsp. of freshly ground pepper, preferably white
- Grated zest of 1 lime

Directions:

Place all of the shown ingredients except the lime zest in a blender or food processor container and blend until smooth. If the mixture is too thick, simply blend in more coconut milk or water.

Pour the mixture into a container with a tight-fitting lid and refrigerate for at least 2 hours.

Garnish with lime zest when serving.

16. Greek Tempeh-Stuffed Peppers

Stuffed peppers full of veggies and spice.

Makes: 4 servings

Prep: 20 mins

Cook: 55 mins

Ingredients:

- 8 oz. (225 g) tempeh
- 1 Tbsp. (15 ml) extra virgin olive oil

- 1 onion, finely chopped
- 2 large cloves garlic, minced
- 1/8 tsp. (0.625 ml) red pepper flakes
- ¼ tsp. (1.25 ml) ground allspice
- ¼ tsp. (1.25 ml) ground cinnamon
- ½ tsp. (2.5 ml) paprika
- Pinch freshly grated nutmeg
- 1 baby zucchini, diced
- 1 x 15-oz (440 ml) BPA-free can no-salt-added diced tomatoes, drained and liquid reserved
- ¼ cup pitted kalamata olives, chopped
- 1 cup cooked brown rice
- 2 Tbsp. chopped fresh parsley
- 1 Tbsp. chopped fresh oregano
- Salt & freshly ground black pepper, to taste
- 4 large bell peppers (red, orange, yellow or green)
- 4 tsp. (20 ml) grated Parmigiano Reggiano cheese or nutritional yeast

Directions:

Preheat oven to 400°F (200°C).

Finely grate tempeh or pulse in a food processor into little crumbles.

Heat olive oil in a large nonstick skillet on medium. Add onion & cook until soft and translucent. Add tempeh and garlic and cook, stirring occasionally, until tempeh starts to brown, about 3 minutes. Stir in spices. Add zucchini & cook until it starts to soften. Stir in tomatoes, olives, rice, parsley and oregano, and season with salt and black pepper.

Slice tops off peppers and remove all ribs and seeds. Cut a very thin slice from the base to help the pepper stand upright.

Place peppers in a baking dish & spoon tempeh mixture into peppers. Pour reserved tomato liquid plus ¼ cup (60 ml) water into the dish to surround peppers. Cover dish and bake for about 45 minutes. Remove cover, sprinkle the top of each pepper with 1 tsp. (5 ml) cheese or nutritional yeast and continue baking until cheese is golden, about 10 minutes. Remove from oven and carefully transfer stuffed peppers to serving plates.

17. Quinoa Porridge with Walnut Cream

Protein is really important for staying strong during and after treatment, and quinoa is an excellent vegetable protein source. If you're a fan of oatmeal, millet, or buckwheat, you'll find that the slightly nutty, somewhat crunchy taste and texture of quinoa is right in your wheelhouse.

Makes: 6 servings

Prep: 10 mins

Cook: 20 mins

Ingredients:

Walnut cream

- 1 cup walnuts
- 1 cup water
- 1 tsp. maple syrup
- 1 tsp. freshly squeezed lemon juice
- ½ tsp. sea salt

Quinoa

- 1 cup quinoa
- 2 cups water
- ¼ tsp. sea salt
- ⅛ tsp. ground nutmeg or freshly grated nutmeg
- ½ tsp. of ground ginger
- 1 tbsp. maple syrup
- 2 tbsp. freshly squeezed orange juice
- 1 tsp. ground cinnamon
- 1½ to 2 cups fresh blueberries, blackberries, raspberries
- ¾ cup toasted coarsely chopped walnuts

Directions:

To make the walnut cream, place the walnuts in a bowl, put water to cover, and let stand overnight.

Preheat the oven to 350°F. Drain the walnuts well & spread on a baking pan. Toast for 8-10 mins or until they're lightly browned and aromatic, then cool completely.

Put the toasted walnuts, the lemon juice, 1 cup water, maple syrup, and salt in a blender. Blend on high speed until creamy & smooth, 1 to 2 mins. Move the cream to a bowl or jar.

For quinoa, rinse it in a strainer and drain it well. In a medium pan, bring the salt, quinoa, and water to boil over high. Lower to low, & then cover & simmer for about 15 minutes. Move aside off the heat to cool for a few minutes, then fluff with fork.

When you are ready to serve, stir ½ cup of the prepared walnut cream and the cinnamon, ginger, maple syrup, nutmeg, and orange juice into the cooked quinoa. Serve in bowls, & top with a spoonful of the walnut cream, some blueberries, & a sprinkling of toasted walnuts.

18. Salmon Lentil Stuffed Tomatoes with Curry Sauce

Salmon and green lentils are stuffed into fresh beefsteak tomatoes for a wholesome and delicious meal.

Makes: 4 servings

Prep: 10 mins

Cook: -

Ingredients:

- 1 cup canned green lentils, rinsed and drained

- 1 (6-ounce) can salmon, drained or 1 (6-ounce) salmon pouch
- 1 celery stalk, thinly sliced
- 2 red radishes, diced
- 2 tbsp. capers (optional)
- Juice of 1/2 lemon plus 1 additional tsp. fresh lemon juice, divided
- 1 clove garlic, minced
- 2 tbsp. chopped fresh dill
- 1–2 tsp. Dijon mustard
- 1 tsp. fennel seeds (optional)
- 1/4 tsp. sea salt
- 1/4 tsp. freshly ground black pepper
- 2 tbsp. extra virgin olive oil
- 1/2 cup plain, low-fat yogurt
- 1 tsp. curry powder
- 4 large beefsteak tomatoes

Directions:

In a bowl, combine together the lentils, salmon, celery, radish and capers if using.

In a small bowl, whisk together the juice of 1/2 lemon, garlic, dill, mustard, fennel seeds if using, salt and pepper. Whisk in the olive oil. Add the olive oil mixture to the salmon and lentil mixture and combine gently. In a small bowl, stir together the yogurt, curry powder and remaining 1 tsp. lemon juice.

Slice 1/4" off the tops of the tomatoes and guide a small knife around the interior. Scoop out the innards of each tomato. Fill the tomatoes with the salmon and lentil mixture and top with curry yogurt sauce.

Serve.

19. Multigrain Bread

Whole-wheat flour, rolled oats, sunflower seeds, and millet are the grains in this hearty loaf. The fiber comes from whole wheat, millet, oats, and sunflower seeds. They all add some protein, too.

Makes: 8 servings

Prep: 3 hrs.

Cook: 40 mins

Ingredients:

- 1 (¼-ounce) packet yeast
- 3 tbsp. sugar
- 1 1/3 cups warm water
- 3 tbsp. soft butter
- 1 tsp. salt
- ¼ tsp. baking powder
- 1½ cups all-purpose flour
- 1½ cups whole-wheat flour
- ½ cup rolled oats
- ¼ cup sunflower seeds
- 2 tbsp. uncooked millet

Directions:

Combine ½ tsp. sugar, yeast, & 1/3 cup water in a bowl. Sit for 6 mins.

In a bowl, combine remaining butter, water, salt, sugar and baking powder.

Mix in the flour, followed by the yeast mixture, with an electric mixer.

Add the whole-wheat flour, rolled oats, sunflower seeds, and millet. Knead for 10 mins.

Take dough back into an oiled bowl and put in a warm place. Coat and let rise for two hrs., until doubled in bulk.

Punch dough, & then shape it into a loaf, and place it in an oily loaf pan. Cover & rise in for 1 1/2 hr., until dilated size.

Set oven to 350°F. Bare bread, and bake for about 40 minutes.

20. Roasted Kale

Kale is packed full of cancer-fighting phytonutrients.

Makes: 2 servings

Prep: 10 mins

Cook: 15 mins

Ingredients:

- 6 cups kale
- 1 tbsp. olive oil
- 1 tsp. garlic powder
- 1 tsp. sea salt

Directions:

Preheat oven to 375°F.

Wash & trim kale by pulling leaves off the tough stems or running a sharp knife down the length of the stem.

Place leaves in a medium-size bowl; toss with olive oil and garlic powder.

Roast for 5 minutes; turn kale over and roast another 7–10 minutes, until kale turns brown and becomes paper thin and brittle.

Remove from oven and sprinkle with salt. Serve immediately.

21. Parsnip Curry

Related to carrots, parsnips are even more fibrous and have a stronger flavor. They are a winter vegetable that contains a huge amount of vitamin A.

Makes: 4 servings

Prep: 5 mins

Cook: 30 mins

Ingredients:

- 3 tbsp. canola oil
- 2 minced cloves garlic
- 1 tbsp. grated ginger root
- 1 tsp. minced fresh red chili pepper
- 6" lemongrass stalk, thinly sliced
- 1 cup diced onion
- 1/3 cup tomato paste
- 1½ cups coconut milk
- ½ cup Chicken Stock
- 2 pounds parsnips, peeled and cubed
- 3 tbsp. light soy sauce
- 1 tsp. grated lime zest
- 3 tbsp. fresh lime juice
- 2 tbsp. chopped cilantro
- 4 cups steamed jasmine rice

Directions:

In large pot, heat the oil on medium. Add the garlic, ginger, red chili pepper, lemongrass, and onion and sauté for 10 minutes.

Add the tomato paste; stir well.

Add the coconut milk, chicken stock, and parsnips. Bring to a boil, then reduce and simmer for about 15 minutes, until the parsnips are tender.

Add soy sauce, lime zest, lime juice, and cilantro. Stir and remove from heat.

Pour curry into soup tureen or large serving bowl. Put the steamed jasmine rice on a serving platter and serve it with the curry.

22. Tuna Salad with White Bean Dressing

Influenced by Mediterranean flavors, this salad is a beautiful display of rainbow colors on your plate.

Makes: 4 servings

Prep: 10 mins

Cook: -

Ingredients:

For the salad:

- 6 cups leafy vegetables, such as lettuce, spinach and radicchio
- 1 large red or orange bell pepper, thinly sliced
- 1 cup halved cherry tomatoes
- 1 large avocado, thinly sliced
- 2 cans albacore tuna, drained
- 1/3 cup pitted & sliced Kalamata olives
- 2 tbsp. capers

For the dressing:

- 1 cup canned white navy beans, rinsed and drained
- 1/2 cup plain yogurt
- 1 cup packed flat-leaf parsley
- 1/4 tsp. freshly ground black pepper
- 2 tbsp. tahini
- 1 tsp. Dijon mustard
- Juice of 1/2 lemon
- 2 cloves garlic, finely chopped
- 1/4 tsp. sea salt

Directions:

For salad: In a bowl, combine together the greens, bell pepper, cherry tomatoes and avocado.

Break the tuna meat into chunks with a fork. Divide among plates, and top with the tuna chunks, olives and capers.

For the dressing: Place all dressing ingredients in a blender or food processor container and blend until smooth. Taste and adjust seasonings as needed. Drizzle over the salad.

23. Snow Peas with Shallots

Snow peas are completely edible, pod and all. You can usually find them fully prepped in the produce aisle.

Makes: 4 servings

Prep: 10 mins

Cook: 5 mins

Ingredients:

- 1 pound snow peas
- 2 tbsp. olive oil
- 4 shallots, minced

- ½ pound cremini mushrooms, sliced
- 2 tbsp. sherry vinegar
- 1 tsp. fresh lemon juice

Directions:

Trim off ends of snow peas and pull strings, if necessary.

In large saucepan, heat olive oil over medium heat. Add shallots, snow peas, and mushrooms; stir-fry for 3–5 minutes or until vegetables are crisp-tender.

Stir in vinegar and lemon juice, then remove from heat and serve immediately.

24. Chickpea Pitas with Tahini Dressing

These chickpea pitas are an amazing lunch option, especially with the insanely delicious and creamy tahini dressing.

Makes: 4 servings

Prep: 10 mins

Cook: -

Ingredients:

- 1 (14-ounce) can chickpeas, rinsed and drained
- 1 red bell pepper, diced
- 2 Roma (plum) tomatoes, seeds removed and chopped
- 1 small red onion, finely diced
- 1/2 cup cilantro or parsley, chopped
- 4 ounces cubed feta cheese
- 1/2 English cucumber, diced
- 1/3 cup black olives, chopped
- 4 tbsp. raisins
- 2 tbsp. tahini
- 3 tbsp. extra virgin olive oil
- Juice of 1 lemon
- 1/2 tsp. ground cumin
- 2 cloves garlic
- 1/4 tsp. cayenne
- 1/4 tsp. sea salt
- 1 tbsp. water
- 1/4 tsp. black pepper
- 4 (6-inch) whole grain pitas, sliced in half

Directions:

In a bowl, combine together the chickpeas, bell pepper, cucumber, tomato, red onion, cilantro or parsley, feta cheese, olives and raisins.

Place the olive oil, tahini, lemon juice, garlic, cumin, cayenne, salt, black pepper and water in a blender, and blend until smooth. Add the tahini mixture to the chickpea mixture and stir to coat.

To serve, stuff the chickpea mixture into pitas.

25. Lemony Apple Fennel Salad

With its slight licorice flavor and crunchy texture, fennel is wonderful served raw in salads and it tastes even better combined with apples, arugula and zucchini.

Makes: 4 servings

Prep: 10 mins

Cook: -

Ingredients:

For the salad:

- 1 fennel bulb, thinly sliced

- 2 cups packed arugula
- 1/4 cup chopped fresh mint (optional)
- 2 medium apples, thinly sliced
- 1 medium zucchini, shredded (about 1 cup)

For the dressing:

- 3 tbsp. olive oil
- 1 tbsp. honey
- Juice of 1/2 lemon
- 1 tsp. grated lemon zest
- 1 clove garlic, minced
- 1/4 tsp. sea salt
- 1/4 tsp. freshly ground black pepper

Directions:

For salad: In a bowl, combine together the fennel, apple, arugula, zucchini, and mint if using.

For dressing: In a bowl, combine together the olive oil, honey, lemon juice, lemon zest, garlic, salt, & pepper.

Toss and serve.

26. Zucchini Stir-Fry

If you have a garden, you know August and September can mean bumper crops of zucchini and tomatoes. Use the proceeds in this easy side dish recipe.

Makes: 4 servings

Prep: 5 mins

Cook: 12 mins

Ingredients:

- 2 tbsp. olive oil
- 2 cups sliced zucchini

- 1/8 tsp. black pepper
- 2 shallots, minced
- 2 cups grape tomatoes, halved
- ½ tsp. salt
- ½ tsp. dried thyme leaves

Directions:

In wok/large skillet, heat olive oil over med-high heat. Add zucchini and shallots; stir-fry until crisp-tender, about 5–7 minutes.

Add tomatoes, salt, pepper, and thyme; stir-fry until hot and all vegetables are tender, about 3–5 minutes longer. Serve immediately.

27. Grilled Greens and Eggplant

Grilled greens and eggplant with Greek yogurt and turmeric.

Makes: 4 servings

Prep: 15 mins

Cook: 20 mins

Ingredients:

- ¾ tsp. Turmeric, ground
- ½ cup Mint leaves, fresh
- 3 pieces lemon wedges

- Kosher salt
- Black pepper, freshly ground
- 1/4 tsp. Curry powder/garam masala
- 2 pieces Eggplants, medium, sliced across into half-inch-thick rounds
- 8 tbsp. Olive oil, extra virgin, divided
- 2 bunches Kale/Swiss chard
- 3/4 cup Greek yogurt, plain

Directions:

Preheat the grill on medium-high.

Place the 2 pieces of eggplant in a bowl filled with oil (2 tbsp.), turmeric, and pepper and salt to taste. Toss to combine and set aside.

Fill another large bowl with the greens. Add oil (2 tbsp.), pepper, and salt, and toss until the greens are well-coated. Set aside.

Place the eggplant on the hot grill & cook for about five to eight minutes or until tender and nicely charred. Set aside on a plate.

Place the greens on the hot grill and cook for two minutes (make sure to turn them often) or until some spots are a bit charred. Set aside on a cutting board.

Once the greens are cooled, cut off their thick stems and ribs. Tear the leaves into the eggplant bowl. Add oil (2 tbsp.) and mint, then toss until everything is well-combined.

Meanwhile, stir the garam masala and yogurt together in a deep dish. Add pepper and salt to taste. Smear the yogurt mixture on a platter. Arrange the grilled greens and eggplant on top.

Serve topped with lemon wedges and drizzled with extra oil.

28. Ginger and Lemon Drink

A warm, healing ginger lemon drink with turmeric and honey.

Makes: 3 servings

Prep: 30 mins

Cook: 5 mins

Ingredients:

- 1 piece Lemon, organic, sliced
- 1/8 tsp. Turmeric, ground
- 2 ½ cups Water, boiling
- 1 piece Ginger, fresh, 1-inch, peeled, and sliced
- 2 tsp. Honey

Directions:

Pour water into a pot and heat on medium-high. Once boiling, immediately turn off the heat.

Stir in the turmeric, ginger, and lemon.

Let it steep for 1/2 an hour.

Strain before serving.

Enjoy.

29. Chicken Soup with Zoodles

A hearty and comforting chicken zoodle soup with peas and carrots.

Makes: 4 servings

Prep: 5 mins

Cook: 5 mins

Ingredients:

- 5 cups water
- 3 zucchinis, spiralized into noodles
- 2 cups snow peas, sliced diagonally
- 2 green onions, sliced
- 1 large carrot, shredded
- 1 pound chicken breast
- 1 tsp. Asian sesame oil

Directions:

Heat the water in a large saucepan.

Cut the chicken into bite size pieces.

Once the water and the seasoning have boiled, add the zoodles, chicken, carrot, green onions, and snow peas. Cook over high heat for approximately 5 mins.

Take off the heat, add the sesame oil, divide into bowls and then serve.

30. Turmeric Glazed Parsnips

Delicious turmeric glazed parsnips that make for a perfect side.

Makes: 4 servings

Prep: 10 mins

Cook: 45 mins

Ingredients:

- 1 tbsp. Lime juice, freshly squeezed
- 1/4 tsp. Pepper, freshly cracked
- 1/4 tsp. Salt

- 1 tsp. Cinnamon, ground
- 3 pounds parsnips, whole, peeled
- 1 tsp. Turmeric, ground
- 1/2 tsp. Coriander, ground
- 3 pieces Garlic cloves, minced
- Dill/parsley, fresh
- Olive oil, extra virgin

Directions:

Set the oven at 400 degrees Fahrenheit to preheat.

Spread out the parsnips on a greased baking sheet so they form a single layer. Toss with the olive oil (3 tbsp.), minced garlic, salt, pepper, and spices.

Place in the oven to bake for about forty to forty-five minutes or until caramelized and tenderly cooked.

Serve garnished with fresh parsley/dill.

CONCLUSION

Well, there you go! 30 delicious cancer-fighting recipes for you to enjoy. Try out all the recipes and make sure to share these important and nutritious recipes with your friends and family.

Printed in Great Britain
by Amazon

55500747R00047